D1216192

THE ULTIMATE BOOK OF BUSINESS BREAKTHROUGHS

THE ULTIMATE BOOK OF BUSINESS BREAKTHROUGHS

LESSONS FROM THE 20 GREATEST BUSINESS DECISIONS EVER MADE

TOM CANNON

CAPSTONE

Copyright © Tom Cannon 2000

The right of Tom Cannon to be identified as the author of this work has been asserted in accordance with the Copyright, Designs and Patents Act 1988

First published 2000 by
Capstone Publishing Limited
Oxford Centre for Innovation
Mill Street
Oxford OX2 0JX
United Kingdom
http://www.capstone.co.uk

British Library Cataloguing in Publication Data
A CIP catalogue record for this book is available from the British Library

ISBN 1-84112-028-6

Typeset in 11 pt Plantin by
Sparks Computer Solutions Ltd, Oxford
http://www.sparks.co.uk
Printed and bound by
T.J. International Ltd, Padstow, Cornwall

This book is printed on acid-free paper

Substantial discounts on bulk quantities of Capstone books are available to corporations, professional associations and other organisations. For details telephone Capstone Publishing on (+44-1865-798623) or fax (+44-1865-240941).

Dedication

This book is dedicated to two different groups of people. First there are the innovators, entrepreneurs and leaders who create the breakthroughs – a few of whom are listed here. I've met some and other aspects of their person match their remarkable achievements, surprisingly often. Second, I'd include all those people with whom I have worked over the years. I've been lucky in having some outstanding colleagues at ASKE Research, Warwick, Imperial Group, Durham, Stirling, Manchester and most recently at MCI.

Contents

Acknowledgements

T his book emerged originally from conversations with Mark Allin at Capstone. Mark, and Richard his business partner, played an important part in forming the ideas behind this book. No one, however, played a bigger role in the research and development of the material than my research fellow, Fran Constable. She provided the structure and discipline, which made the diverse and, sometimes, diffuse material underpinning the cases come together. An important role was played by Gresham College in London where I held the Mercers' School Chair of Commerce. The college council provided a research grant, which enabled some of the underpinning research to be completed.

The research and writing was carried out in a mixture of traditional and some not so conventional methods. The quantitative research sought the help of many business leaders. Some, like Michael Eisner of The Walt Disney Company, provided valuable support material. This survey was underpinned by extensive analysis of secondary material. The staff of the University of Manchester's John Rylands library and others were invaluable sources of information. Special mention should go, however, to the archivists from the various companies who supplied information and assistance. These include M. Frings of Bayer, Melanie Aspey of the Rothschild Archive, Karen See and Amanda Purvis of Sony, Michele Hiltzik at the Rockefeller Archive, and all the staff of the Co-operative Archive. I was also lucky to have the help of a talented photographer for original work.

The entire team at Capstone were a massive help especially Mark Allin and Catherine Meyrick. As always my wife Fran, son Robin and daughter Rowan provided support and encouragement throughout.

Introduction

ny attempt to identify, let alone rank, the 20 most significant business breakthroughs – ever – is full of risk. There are so many dramatic, exciting and important business breakthroughs that selecting any 20 is open to debate. Those chosen emerged from a mixture of empirical research, analysis of the ways business develops and study of the implications of these breakthroughs for business and economic development. Despite this, there is certain to be disagreement about the breakthroughs and decisions that underpin them. Some people will question why some business breakthroughs are included and others excluded. Others will identify bias and distortion.

There are many reasons for the choices about breakthroughs that are presented. Perhaps the most basic reason for choosing this group is that they emerged from research into the views of contemporary business leaders about the most significant business breakthroughs and the best business decisions. The chief executives of the 200 largest US companies, the 100 largest UK companies, the 100 largest European companies and the 100 largest Asian businesses were surveyed to find out their views.

The evidence

It was decided, however, not to convert these views into a simple ranking. This decision was made partly because the ranking that emerged was very focused on today's businesses and partly because response rates varied so much between the sub-groups. US business leaders, for example, were far more likely to respond than their European or Asian peers. The breakthroughs highlighted by modern business leaders were heavily skewed towards contemporary events with surprisingly little historical perspective. Even CEOs with direct links to a major past breakthrough – for example, leading the company based on that breakthrough – made little reference to earlier decisions. The overwhelming choice among respondents for the most important breakthrough and best decision was Microsoft's acquisition of the rights to MS-DOS or some aspect of the subsequent development of the company.

The survey of CEOs was complemented by reviews of a variety of secondary sources. These ranged from the US Entrepreneurial Hall of Fame through to the extensive literature on business history. This examination of secondary sources provided a framework for extensive discussions with business analysts and historians.

It was relatively easy to identify the top few breakthroughs and decisions from these sources. Edison and Ford emerged from most of these authorities as the 'fathers' of modern industrial society. The research laboratory and mass production have largely shaped twentieth-century business. Their importance lay also in the speed with which their achievements were disseminated. The survival of their enterprises provides a further cue to the substantive nature of their achievements.

Influences

The further down the ranking, the easier it is to ask why this decision or breakthrough and not another. Sometimes the choices were driven by outside factors. There is clearly a bias towards US and UK sources. This is not to deny the achievements of European, Asian, Latin American or African businesses. Often, however, the lack of source material made it hard to build up a full picture of the breakthroughs that created great enterprises. The Brenninkmeyer, Krupp,

Agnelli, Bosch, Defforey, Toyoda, Yoshida, Li Ka-shing and other families or groups guard their privacy, making its hard to piece together the story of their breakthroughs and the underlying decisions or achievements.

The attempt to understand breakthroughs by analysis of the decisions made and the policies pursued lies at the heart of the book. This desire to build a picture of the approaches that were common to these successes and any significant differences made it inevitable that poorly reported or written up breakthroughs were unlikely to be included. This produced a bias towards relatively modern business breakthroughs.

It would be wrong to understate the achievements of the founders of the first trading banks in Italy at the end of the fifteenth century or Josiah Wedgewood, Richard Arkwright or Richard Cobden who created the breakthroughs that shaped the first industrial revolution. Slightly later, the Boston Associates led by Francis Cabot Lowell achieved a double breakthrough in transferring industrial manufacture to North America. Their breakthroughs, along with those of Krupp, Engelhorn, Seimens, Witte, Nobel and others, made industrial enterprise an international phenomenon.

The breakthroughs achieved by the giants of the last century are understated against the giants of this era. Carnegie, Vanderbilt, Astor built enterprises and fortunes that would dwarf anything seen today – notwithstanding Bill Gates. Corporations like Armour and Co., US Rubber and US Steel in the USA, and J&P Coats, Imperial Tobacco, BASF, AEG in Europe achieved breakthroughs that allowed them to dominate industries and markets.

The story of the way Gerard Philips – a clever young Dutch engineer – converted his intention 'to start a lamp factory ... I can produce very homogeneous carbon filaments in large numbers' into Philips & Co of Eindhoven in 1892. His success in turning Philips into Europe's largest producer of lamps by the end of the century and an industrial giant through a mixture of innovative technologies and clever marketing is hard to beat. Unfortunately, relatively little has been written – apart from material sponsored by Philips – about Gerard's achievements.

Some of the breakthroughs included are disputed or face rival claims. Various authorities claim that the world's first major industrial laboratory was created, not by Thomas Edison – the founder of General Electric – but by General Electric's chief engineer Charles P. Steinmetz. Ford's production line was pre-dated some years earlier by a similar system for moving and packing goods on the Liverpool Docks. Most of these parallels are acknowledged in the text but there will always be gaps and omissions when a range of developments such as this is examined.

Rankings

The specific position of each breakthrough can be arbitrary. Each of the breakthroughs has or had massive consequences. Ranking Boeing ahead of Intel or the Moores ahead of the Roddicks is largely a construct to help locate a set of decisions rather than an absolute statement that one or the other 'outranks' the rest. Despite these reservations, it is probably fair to identify the top five with epoch-making breakthroughs that helped either to define the nature of economic activity or to reshape societies.

Defining their eras, and beyond

Rank	Breakthrough
1	The Industrial Research Laboratory, Thomas Edison and General Electric
2	The Moving Assembly Line, Mass Production and Ford
3	Oil refining, Black Gold and John D. Rockefeller
4	Operating Systems, MS-DOS and Microsoft
5	International Finance, the Rothschilds and Mayer Rothschild

The next five are templates for industrial development with lessons beyond their own sectors. These companies and their leaders reshaped the ways people saw their industries, with knock on consequences for other industries.

Models for development

Rank	Breakthrough
6	Passenger Air Transport, the Boeing 747 and Boeing
7	Silicon Chips, Marketing and Intel
8	Pharmaceuticals, Aspirin and Bayer
9	Images, Soft Drinks, Coca Cola and Robert Woodruff
10	Fast Food, Franchising, McDonalds and Ray Kroc

The next group of business breakthroughs established patterns of activity with widespread effects within their markets.

Patterns for futures

Rank	Breakthrough
11	Retail Co-operatives and the Rochdale Pioneers
12	Sports, Leisurewear and Philip Knight
13	Disneyland and Walt Disney
14	Direct Selling, Dell and Michael Dell
15	Entertainment, the Walkman and Sony

The final group within the top twenty established novel ways of doing business or developing markets.

Novel ways

Rank	Breakthrough
16	Gambling, Football Pools and Littlewoods
17	Personal Hygiene, Sensor and Gillette
18	Soaps and Cosmetics, the Roddicks and The Body Shop
19	Books, Paperbacks and Penguin
20	The Movies, James Bond and Cubbi Broccoli

Common themes and lessons

The breakthroughs identified in these cases cover most of the industrial era and a wide variety of companies and industries. The earliest occurred at the start of the industrial era while the most recent are still relatively young companies. Despite the variety, some common themes emerge about the factors which seem to shape their successes. The most successful breakthroughs and the underlying decisions were founded on the application of powerful, core business principles.

Control

In almost every case, success was founded on an understanding of the forces that shape the industry or market in which the business operated. Rockefeller understood that it was vital to get control of the oil refining process especially in the key locations of Cleveland and Pittsburgh. He appreciated that the key to this control lay in size and costs – the larger the plant, the lower the costs.

Rockefeller took massive risks to achieve this control. In his early years, he battled to ensure that his refineries were the biggest and most productive. He needed a flow of raw materials to keep his plants busy, and access to markets to ensure demand, so he skilfully balanced the rivalries among producers, the railway companies and distributors to ensure his dominance. Only when Standard Oil controlled refining and distribution did it move into the ownership of wells or distribution to end-users.

At the other end of the scale Cubby Broccoli arrived at the same conclusion. He would not join a partnership with Harry Salzman that conceded control of the James Bond property to his 'partner'. Gradually, this control was extended until no-one – neither Harry, nor the stars who played Bond – could challenge Cubby's control over the film series. Control does not simply mean ownership. Walt Disney understood better than anyone the value of control over the quality of service in his theme parks. He refused to accept the conventional wisdom that amusement parks needed lots of concessionaires operating in their own ways and paying rents to the park's owners. Everyone involved in Disneyland would work to Walt's script. When his own company, Walt Disney Productions, sought compromises, he said 'no' and put himself and his life's work at risk.

Ray Kroc shared Walt's determination. Even the McDonald brothers were not allowed to move away from Ray's vision. He was happy to buy them out for more than he could afford, to ensure his control over the way McDonald's and his franchise business developed. Control itself is often founded on a clear vision of the product, the market or the future. Allan Lane was determined that his new paperbacks would be 'clean and bright as a new pin, modern enough not to offend the sophisticated buyer, and yet straightforward and unpretentious.' Michael Dell's 'direct model' for selling and distributing computers was rooted in the failure of existing distribution systems to deliver any real benefits for the mark-ups imposed. Dell uses technology to 'sell ... directly, deal ... directly [and] communicate ... directly'.

Many of the most successful breakthroughs use technology to ensure that the company's control is reinforced. Rockefeller initially resisted the use of pipelines to deliver oil from the market to the refinery or from the refinery to the market. Once, however, he realised that he could not stop the development of pipelines, he used pipelines to increase his control and power over the railway companies, his erstwhile allies. Bill Gates probably understands the value of control more than any other modern businessperson. He learned the hard way. Microsoft had little control over the programs developed using the version of the programming language Basic designed by Bill Gates and Paul Allen. The fees were good but there were few long-term returns. The opportunity to control the operating system used in the IBM personal computer was taken. This eventually gave Microsoft control over the operating systems of every producer of personal computers wanting to offer true compatibility.

The companies identified among these breakthroughs are not alone in spotting the importance of control to long-term success. Gad Rausing built Tetra Laval into one of the most profitable packaging companies in the world – first by designing a packaging system, then by investing in and perfecting the production process. Fiat has survived as a major car manufacturer because its managers and the Agelli family are masters at controlling integrated manufacturing systems. In the perfumes industry the Wertheimer family ensure that the quality, name and identify of Chanel is controlled to tight specifications.

The penalties for loss of control are immense. IBM lost control over the operating systems for its own product and took almost a decade to recover. Kodak first lost control over the popular camera industry, then saw its influence on photographic film weaken; now its chemicals business is under pressure. Wang Laboratories virtually created the word processing industry but lost control to smarter companies who recognised the way the market was developing.

Focus

Often, loss of control is linked to lack of focus. Powerful companies stop focusing on their business or the source(s) of their control. In a sense this happened to Henry Ford when he forgot that his original vision was to build cars with 'the best material ... the best men ... the best designs'. General Motors beat Ford to instalment selling, used car trade-ins and, perhaps most importantly, the closed-body car. GM's production of a closed-body car, at a price comparable to the Model T with its open top, transformed the competitive position of both companies. The customer would pay a bit more for the Chevrolet but got comfort and warmth in return. Decades later, the US car industry ignored Henry's belief that 'a man who bought one of our cars was in my opinion entitled to continuous use of that car' and allowed Japanese cars with far higher levels of reliability to break into the market.

Walt Disney never lost his focus on the importance of service quality to the experience of visitors to Disneyland. His focus seldom shifted from the time he lived in the little apartment above the fire station to his final vision for Disney World in Florida. Thomas Edison knew that people were the key to the success of his research laboratories. He focused immense amounts of time and energy in recruiting the best people – at times interviewing virtually all the laboratory's new employees. This focus on quality people provided opportunities for another form of focus. Surrounded by quality people, Edison could focus his attention on the key aspects of the research process. He could be available whenever there was a problem, leaving his colleagues to pursue their work, follow up leads and refine developments.

Almost a century later, the founders of Intel showed some of the same focus on recruiting the best. Andy Grove would write personally to a graduate the firm wanted to recruit if that made the difference. Intel showed other features of the well-focused company. The catch phrase 'Intel delivers' made it clear to everyone – inside and outside the company – that the company was determined to get ahead technologically and stay ahead.

The toughest part of focus is saying no to interesting, potentially profitable opportunities that can take the business away from its core strength. Gillette showed the dangers of lack of focus when it diversified into markets and industries that drained resources, distracted management attention and made the company vulnerable to predators. Anyone reading *Barbarians at the Gate*, Bryan Burrough and John Helyar's account of the decline and fall of RJR Nabisco, will see the costs involved when a fine company with good products loses focus. More recently in Britain, the difficulties facing Marks and Spencer could be linked with a lack of focus as the company's leadership group became involved in projects as diverse as internationalising the business, widening the product line and framing public policy on corporate governance.

It is possible to argue that the UK's century of economic decline is closely linked to the lack of focus in major industries and companies. Just over a hundred years ago, the British steel industry was the largest in the world. Its subsequent decline started with the failure to focus on production and exploit the cost advantages of integrated production. The decline accelerated when the industry became a political football in the years after World War II when nationalisation was followed by de-nationalisation, then re-nationalisation and eventually privatisation. Other giants showed the same reluctance to focus on the issues that determined their success.

In contrast, Mayer Rothschild embedded a sense of focus in the development of the bank from the earliest years. The best prices, the quickest payments and the best returns were wedded to a fundamental commitment to internationalism that drove the bank forward. Family members liked the honours and titles that European politicians showered on them but never let these trinkets distract them from their core business. Ray Kroc made an especially powerful argument for focus in his famous comment that 'nothing in the world can take the place of persistence.' The early years of McDonald's highlighted Kroc's focus on quality, consistency and service. The company's breakthrough into profitability grew out of this focus. The move into property made it easier for franchisees to obtain premises but it gave the franchisor a powerful tool in its efforts to require each restaurant to deliver the same standard of service.

The willingness to say no was vividly illustrated by Boeing's willingness to give up fighter plane production in favour of bombers and transport aircraft. The US Air Force was keen to buy P-26 fighters from Boeing but there were no synergies for other products. Boeing's focus on large aircraft gave it an edge over rivals like Douglas that produced increasing dividends as demand grew for larger payloads in civil and military aircraft. Vastly removed in scale, Akio Morita made the same decision at Sony when he opted for extreme portability in the development of the Walkman. The team at Sony made similar decisions to the people at Boeing when they rejected the temptation to include features like recording and built-in speakers in their new product.

This type of focus requires confidence and courage. The leadership group must be confident that it understands its business so well that it can, if necessary, defy convention. Phil Knight went against the most powerful players in the athletic footwear industry when he changed the shape of sports shoes. Nike focused its efforts on footwear that protected the athlete off the track in training as well as on the track in competition. Nike focused on using technology to deliver constant improvements in performance and protection. Courage is equally important. John Moores stuck with his idea of a football pool even when his partners dropped out. He then focused his efforts on perfecting the business, especially the use of mailing lists and other devices to reach increasing numbers of clients.

Leverage

Control and focus deliver massive dividends when companies use them to increase their leverage in markets. Microsoft's control over the PC operating system encouraged the company to focus on rapid improvements in the capabilities of MS-DOS. By the time IBM was aware of the risks of its dependence on Microsoft, it lacked the knowledge or market power to abandon the relationship. Microsoft, however, used the leverage from its developments of MS-DOS to reach across the PC market to other producers seeking compatibility with IBM. Microsoft set the industry standard and drove through innovations, which consistently increased its leverage of the PC market. The potential threat from graphical systems was spotted and Windows was developed. This increased the company's leverage, which created opportunities for more growth through applications software, new software products and Internet-based developments.

The approach Bill Gates of Microsoft adopted had some similarities to those employed a century earlier by John D. Rockefeller. Standard Oil's investments in refining made it the cheapest and most efficient oil refiner in the world. On occasion, Rockefeller persuaded rivals to sell out to him by the simple expedient of showing them his balance sheet. The production edge produced a financial edge that Standard Oil levered into market dominance. Rockefeller could guarantee the railway companies large and consistent orders – no wonder they offered him massive discounts over rivals. The leverage produced by these discounts enabled Standard Oil to buy up his rivals or put them out of businesses. During the 'Cleveland Massacre', Rockefeller used the threat of the South Improvement Company to persuade most of his rivals in Cleveland to submit to Standard Oil, or merge their operations.

The leverage used in business breakthroughs operates in different ways. The prospect of working for these dynamic companies provides massive leverage in recruitment. Gordon Moore, Robert Noyce and Andy Grove were able to recruit outstanding talent first from Fairchild Semiconductor, then from across the USA, because the business was linked with business breakthroughs based on outstanding decisions. Walt Disney had the leverage to persuade companies like ABC Television to become his partners in developing Disneyland – even if he struggled to persuade his brother.

This type of leverage is especially important in winning financial support for investment, innovation and growth. At McDonald's a stroke of genius by Kroc's alter ego – Harry Sonneborn – led to the development of the company's property portfolio. This portfolio not only produced a reliable source of revenues but it was an asset against which the business could borrow to grow. This has parallels with the way that Thomas Edison used the research laboratory to increase research productivity. This flow of ideas, in turn, persuaded financiers like J.P. Morgan to underwrite Edison's work. The laboratory form also meant that Edison had the time to spend getting potential backers interested in and excited by his products and businesses.

Allan Lane's leverage was the desire of authors to reach the vast audience created by his new paperbacks. John Moores won leverage from his skilful use of the media. Every big win was publicised. The promise of immense wealth from a tiny investment drove up demand while producing even bigger winnings. With The Body Shop leverage comes from the powerful links between the values of the founders, the company and its customer groups. Campaigns bind the customers to business in ways that the simple purchase act cannot replicate.

The Roddicks were employing a form of relationship marketing to increase the leverage of their efforts elsewhere long before the term was coined in the marketing literature. A similar bond exists between Nike and major groups in the athletic community. The company asserts that 'we are athletes' and translates that sense of identification to its product development, marketing and links with sports stars. Even earlier, during World War II, Robert Woodruff of Coca-Cola linked the brand with the American way of life by a promotion that continues to pay off today. By making Coca-Cola available to US service personnel in every theatre of war, at the same price as at their local soda fountain, he established a powerful bond with a generation of Americans. Coca-Cola used leverage to win access to new markets and obtain new production facilities across the world.

Conclusion

If control, focus and leverage are common themes in business breakthroughs, the variety of ways in which they are interpreted is almost unlimited. Giant multi-generation businesses like General Electric and Ford have used them to secure their market position. In *Hidden Champions* Hermann Simon describes how small specialist companies like Tetra, the world's leader in tropical fish food, use their control of a key aspect of their business as a platform for their market development. These firms focus their energies on their business or segment – resisting both the temptation to move out of their area of expertise and the pressure from larger rivals. This focus produces massive benefits when used to lever strong market positions, production or technological advantages, quality people and financial strength.

The similarities between the biggest business breakthroughs do not prevent significant differences between companies and clustering among the businesses. The breakthroughs described here can be split into four sub-groups. One group, consisting of General Electric,

Boeing, Intel, Aspirin and Sony, achieved greatness by focusing on their strengths and mobilising their resources around these strengths. Another sub-set, containing Ford, Rockefeller, Microsoft, Nike and Littlewoods, created whole new industries or ways of conducting business. Grabbing the moment was crucial to the success of Rothschild, Coke, McDonald's, Gillette and the James Bond films. Others, notably Disney, the Rochdale Pioneers with Co-operative Retailing, Dell, The Body Shop and Penguin, were forced to defy convention to win success.

Part I

Focus on Strengths by Mobilising Resources

It has almost become a cliché to say that the most successful businesses know their strengths, understand how to deploy their distinctive capabilities and use these to win competitive advantage. Often this realisation is hard won. Edison came close to a physical breakdown when he tried to combine working as 'company electrician' for Jay Gould's Atlantic and Pacific Telegraph Company with undertaking his own research and raising finance for his inventions. This experience forced him to rethink his approach to work. He knew that his strengths lay in seeking out new ideas, invention and winning support for his ideas. He created the Menlo Park Research facility, at least in part, so that he could concentrate on the aspects of research that allowed him to add real value.

Other people could manage the laboratory as well as him. He was frequently amazed at the technical skills of his collaborators. He could dip into and out of a project but leave the day-to-day work to his colleagues. Edison developed strategies that rewarded them for their efforts. He had no fear of sharing patents even royalties because he appreciated the value of this approach. He gained on his rivals because they were often spreading themselves too thin. Other inventors worked alone or with small teams – Edison Electric Light appreciated that the industrial age needed to industrialise innovation. Edison mobilised the resources to deliver this new way of working.

Boeing came to the same conclusion from a different direction. The early history of the company saw the production of seaplanes, mail planes and small passenger aircraft. There was a willingness to innovate. Boeing produced the first all-metal aircraft, an early entrant in the transatlantic passenger market, but struggled to turn these innovations into market power or profitability. It was the decision by the leadership team to commit the company to the production of large aircraft that transformed its position and profits.

There were immense risks in this choice. Large aircraft – especially before the jet age – were far more expensive to develop and produce than small planes. With almost every major development from the 1930s onwards the team was forced to 'bet the company' to implement this policy. At times the bet was larger that the net assets of the business. The creation of the 747 took this willingness to take risks a stage further when Boeing's partners – Pan Am and Pratt and Whitney – also had to bet their companies to succeed. Boeing accepted the wider implications of focussing on its strengths. This meant investing in its own wind tunnel, building the largest factory in the world, refusing compromise and pushing the boundaries of technology to gain competitive advantage. Boeing rivals were constantly on the back foot as they were forced to compete on territory that gave Boeing built-in advantages.

Intel has achieved the same competitive advantage in its markets by a similar route. From the start its strength lay in a powerful research focus and willingness to push the boundaries of microprocessor technology. It followed several lines of development in the early years when rivals opted for lower cost, narrower options. In a sense, Intel was following Andy Grove's maxim that 'only the paranoid survive' in even these early years. There was genuine fear among the leadership group that in rejecting a potential line of development, the opportunity was left open for a rival.

The research drive was underpinned by a willingness to invest in quality so its early maxim that 'Intel delivers' could be realised. There were no false promises – even when the company was promising more than its rivals. Its distinctive strength lay in an ability to blend two distinct – and in some eyes incompatible – assets. These were, first, a research drive linked to an advanced industrial product and, second, a willingness to assert the strength of the company through brand-based marketing. Even today, this combination is rare. However, it gives Intel a strength in the market that is hard to match.

Bayer showed the same ability to link strong branding with a research focus. Carl Duisberg invested heavily in his research facilities, encouraging people to develop their interests. He gained a quality edge when he separated the approval of new products from their development. This sometimes produced delays but it won credibility in the marketplace. This was extended into the branding of drugs and the close identification between the brand and the company through the distinctive Bayer Cross. The same principles guided Sony. The development of the Walkman established a distinct technological competence that was reinforced by the market perception of Sony's production.

All successful companies need to understand their strengths, assets and distinctive capabilities. Business breakthroughs often grow out of this understanding and the ability to implement policies that convert a distinctive capability into a competitive advantage. From Thomas Edison to Andy Grove, successful business leaders have built their management decisions around the implementation of policies designed to focus on their strengths and mobilising their resources around these assets.

Chapter 1

Inventing the Century

The Menlo Park Research Laboratory

The century of innovation

T|he twentieth century is the century of innovation. For the first time in history, invention – the creation of new goods or services, often based on scientific discoveries – was combined with a drive to introduce these goods and services into markets to generate wealth. Innovation drives almost every market. Recent research indicates that over half the sales in UK and US supermarkets are from goods not on the market five years earlier. The rate of innovation has accelerated as countries and industries have tried to get ahead by adopting new ideas from elsewhere or encouraging local innovation.

Examination, for example, of the time taken for economies to shift from underdeveloped to developed (defined as doubling real income per capita) shows that this has dropped from around 50 years at the start of the last century to around 10 years at the end of this century (see Table 1.1).

A similar picture emerges at the micro level. In the communications industries, for example, it took more than 50 years for film and radio to move from innovative technologies to mature industries but the mobile telephone and the 'open' Internet took only five years to complete this shift. Even in traditional industries, like textiles and clothing, new materials are being developed and, equally important, novel materials are being used in innovative ways to meet customer

Table 1.1 Drop in time taken for economies to shift from underdeveloped to developed.

Country	Time Period (around)	Time Taken (years)
UK	1780–1838	58
US	1840–1887	47
Germany	1845–1890	45
Japan	1885–1919	34
S Korea	1973–1984	11
China	1977–1987	10

needs. Success in innovation largely determines which companies, communities, nations or regions prosper in the global marketplace.

The contrast with the pre-industrial world could hardly be sharper. The Chinese, Egyptians, Greeks – even Romans – largely saw discovery as an end in itself. As recently as the seventeenth and eighteenth century Newton, Faraday and Babbage had a similar world-view. The first industrial revolution changed this, but there remained a loose, informal link between invention and innovation. One man, above all, changed this. It was Thomas Edison who transformed thinking and attitudes about the link between discovery, production and commercialisation. One biography even describes him as the man who invented the century.[1]

Edison, Thomas Alva (1847–1931), was one of the greatest industrial leaders and perhaps the greatest inventor in history. His 1093 US patents include practical electric lighting, the phonograph and improvements to the stock market ticker tapes, telegraph, telephone and films. Although he received very little formal education, his mother taught him to read and instilled a great love of learning and inquiry. Ironically, the inventor and improver of so many devices for transmitting or receiving sound developed serious hearing problems as a young man, and late in life he could only hear people if they shouted directly into his ear.

He was probably the greatest inventor ever, with over 1000 patents to his name accepted by the US patents offices. (See Table 1.2). This put him well ahead of other prolific inventors like Edwin Land (of Polaroid) and Alexander Graham Bell (the telephone).

Technological innovation is, perhaps, the most powerful driving force in modern economics. Industries, economies and markets are dominated by products and services that were unknown a few years, a decade or a century ago. The industrial research laboratory is the source of developments as diverse as the graphical user interface (GUI), the mouse attached to personal computers, and the power generators that produce electricity to light up whole cities. World famous research laboratories like the Bell Laboratories in the USA or the thousands of other similar facilities work because they have industrialised the process of research and development. Instead of the loneliness of the long-distance scientist beloved of Victorian literature, we have teams of experts working together. This approach was the creation of Thomas Edison who used this method to transform not only R&D but the century itself.

Edison's inventiveness was driven by the desire to solve problems and build up enterprises. His first invention was an improved stock ticket system for providing up-to-date information on changes in stock market prices. He was determined to put his inventions into production, often making seemingly unrealistic claims for the speed of development. He was not content to be the researcher working for others. He set up his own companies. One of these evolved into General Electric, still one of the largest companies in the world and voted America's most admired corporation in 1999.

Table 1.2 The most inventive people (measured by registered patents with the US Patents Office).

Person	Patents
Thomas Alva Edison	1093
Edwin Land	823
Jerry Lemelson	532
Alexander Graham Bell	321

A young man of the highest order of mechanical talent

His patents covered some of the most important innovations of the late nineteenth and early twentieth century. Patents included the phonograph, the incandescent (electric) light bulb, the moving picture camera and the dictating machine, besides the means for generating and distributing sufficient electric power to light homes, factories and cities. Remarkably, in an interview in his later life, he did not identify any of these as his greatest innovation. He gave this accolade to his development of the research laboratory. The industrial research laboratory is now such an integral part of modern industrial society that the pre-history, when people like Alexander Graham Bell worked alone or with small teams of assistants, is alien. Edison was the first to industrialise the process of innovation and in doing so changed the nature of industrial society.

Edison was a successful inventor–innovator before he set up his first research laboratory in his offices and workshops in Ward Street, Newark. His first patent had been for a vote recorder. Subsequent work on stock market ticket machines, telegraphy and related work established his reputation as ' a man of genius ... a young man of the highest order of mechanical talent.' By the time he established his workshop in Ward Street at the age of 27, he had combined this renown as an inventor with at least one business start-up and a good reputation as a popular journalist on science and technology. The research laboratory gave him three things that were important to so many of the breakthroughs he achieved. First, it gave him a controlled working environment. Second, it allowed him to focus his efforts on the needs of his business and clients. Third, it provided the leverage of other people developing and working on his projects and with his genius as the spur.

The importance of this control was a constant theme in Edison's writings and comments. He was determined to 'watch the men and give instructions' even if it meant missing meetings with his financial partners or missing meals and neglecting his family. He tightly scheduled the research team's work with instructions to 'try this ... test this ... See if you can get this ... Conclude at 11 am or [test] for 32 continuous hours.' His time in Newark established several other principles to his methodology that guided him in perfecting the research laboratory, and which still influence contemporary research and development. He placed a premium on the quality and commitment of the people he employed. He tried to employ all of his researchers himself. In one two-year period he interviewed over 2000 people and employed only 80 of them.

Brain power

Although qualifications and capability were important, his absolute priority was the ability and will to think independently. He believed that 'the brain can be developed just the same as the muscles can be developed, if one will only take the pains to train the mind to think.' He built up around him a strong team of collaborators many of whom stayed with him for decades. He forced them to work hard but he rewarded them with shares in the patents and the most exciting research environment in the world. He was an avid reader of the research literature. He followed the classic route of the technological gatekeeper[2] in constantly scanning the research and related literature for novel and useful ideas.

Edison was equally determined to avoid stifling his creativity (and that of his team) with the fear of failure. His partners and paymasters were left in no doubt about the risky and exploratory nature of research. Avenues would be followed that turned into blind alleys. Progress would sometimes be rapid but equally often 'the slower the more sure'. Discovery by its very nature was uncertain, so there was no predicting when results would emerge. Everyone soon knew that in Edison's view 'no experiments are useless'. This open and developmental view of research did not ignore commercial pressures. He learned, however, how to focus his work to produce quick results while still supporting his colleagues in their investigations. This balance between commercial development and solid research was as real for Edison's own projects as for work commissioned by outsiders.

Edison also structured his research on the now familiar five-stage selection and development process.

Fig. 1.1 A man of genius. (Source: Ann Ronan Picture Library.)

Early in 1874, he worked with his colleague Charles Batchelor to draw up a list (or base load) of possible products for the Ward Street laboratory. These ranged from ideas for making and working cast iron to the development of a new type of kerosene lamp. Some of these were eliminated quickly while others were selected for further work. Of these, however, a method for electrical reproduction – Edison's electric pen – was developed into a saleable product. Initial market tests showed that there was considerable demand, especially at the price of \$30 with '$33^1/_3$% for our agents.' There were a number of teething problems, notably its size and the lack of suitable power source as Edison tested different approaches. Solving these difficulties led to the creation of the Edison Pen and Press Company and an advertising campaign for the new apparatus when it was launched, which described how it 'excites interest wherever it is exhibited'.

The invention factory

The Ward Street facilities had allowed Edison to establish himself as one of the leading innovators in the new and growing world of telegraphy. He had achieved several noticeable commercial successes. Edison had established useful working relations with some of the most significant financiers of the era, especially Jay Gould, the railway owner, investor and speculator for whom the term 'robber baron' was almost coined.[3] Ward Street provided an environment in which the basic principles behind the successful development of the research laboratory were framed. Edison had created the research team that would accompany him for most of the next 20 years.

Edison had, however, pushed himself too hard. His health deteriorated under the combined pressures of running his business, managing the laboratory, raising finance and working as the 'company electrician' for Gould's Atlantic and Pacific Telegraph Company. He also became involved in a complex scientific controversy around his belief that he had discovered a new form of energy which could even explain some supernatural phenomena. Although, eventually it emerged that he was observing the effects of electromagnetic energy, the controversy further sapped Edison's strength.

The immediate cause of his move to Menlo Park was a dispute with the landlord of his premises in Newark. The move allowed him to design and develop a fully integrated research facility close to his home in a relatively secluded environment. The importance of this development is hard to overestimate. It was a genuine breakthrough, 'a new model that helped to transform American invention [although] in the traditional co-operative shop, neither Edison nor most of his contemporaries were lone inventors ... they were generally independent inventors. The creation of the laboratory itself, however, was made possible by the growing interest of large scale, technology based companies such as Western Union in acquiring greater control over the inventive process by supporting the work of these inventors ... the Laboratory enabled Edison to make invention a more regular and predictable process and [Western Union] was thus willing to provide direct support for it ... [this] helped to demonstrate the value of invention to industry and showed that invention itself could become an industrial process.'[4]

Edison had identified the pinch point in industrial innovation up to the creation of Menlo Park – the inventors themselves. There was far too much dependence on their genius. The inventors were too thinly spread – gathering background material, initiating projects, raising funds, acquiring equipment, managing the experiments, building the equipment and turning the idea into a business. The research laboratory frees the innovator from many of these tasks. The large research-based company provides the core finance. For Edison it was originally Western Union and later Edison Electric Light. The facility was fully equipped to encompass a range of situations. Edison's invention factory had a self-contained library. There was a machine shop, test beds, laboratory tables and a wide range of equipment.

He had built up a strong research team, which had peaked at over 300 people in Newark, and the key people moved to Menlo Park with him. Charles Batchelor, James Adams and John Kruesi (other important collaborators) moved in as neighbours to the Edison household. Menlo Park itself was, according to the *Newark Daily Advertiser*, 'a very wise selection … He [Edison] is not hampered by the noise and confusion of a large city, while he is near enough to reach one in a short time.' The returns from the move were almost immediate, with five new patents registered within six months.

The most important early development was a significant improvement in the telephone technology that Alexander Graham Bell had developed. Edison produced a carbon transmitter that significantly improved the quality and reliability of Bell's invention at a lower price. This success highlighted the value of the research laboratory – the sunk investment. Edison put this at over $40,000. It meant that he could undertake more complex research over a longer time than any rivals. Edison could leave his fellow researchers to follow particular enquiries until they either made headway so that he could make strategic inputs, or reached dead ends.

Mary had a little lamb

The real breakthrough for Edison and the Menlo Park laboratory was the phonograph. The origins of this development lay largely in a futile attempt to develop a superior telephone system to Bell. He was, however, still tied to a mindset that had been developed during his time as a telegraph operator for Western Union. He assumed that telephone messages would be taken and written down by a specialist clerk before getting passed on to the recipient. Edison, therefore, set about designing a recording machine that would save the clerks having to write down these messages.

The development of his phonograph brilliantly illustrated the value of the laboratory method. The first designs were simple sketches of a machine that converted speech to an impression on a tinfoil cylinder. The speech could be replayed by putting a needle on the groove and feeding the sound out. Edison was in control of the original development but he used the laboratory to focus his work on the core development. The sketches were passed to other members of the team – notably John Kruesi – who were excellent mechanics, designers and improvisers. Within weeks they had produced a working model, which astonished Edison by working first time.

The next stages further illustrated the advantages of the research laboratory. Edison could get involved at key stages in the development but leave his colleagues to progress the work while he secured finance, completed the patenting process and publicised the invention. Like so many laboratory developments, it was difficult to create a reliable marketing product quickly out of the experimental machine that had translated 'Mary had a little lamb' so successfully. Edison replaced the hand crank for turning the cylinder with a clockwork drive. A flywheel was introduced to ensure that the machine turned at a constant speed. A funnel was added for additional volume. He eventually replaced tinfoil with wax and the clockwork mechanism with an electric motor before the phonograph could be produced and sold in sufficient volume to produce profits.

Throughout these years of development, the value of the laboratory as a means of ensuring maximum control, enabling Edison to focus on the key issues and eventually gain maximum leverage for his genius, was proved. He could leave Charles Batchelor to concentrate on the best alternative to tinfoil. Another team could work on the best motors. Someone else could concentrate on checking the results for consistency and coherence. Simultaneously, the production facilities were being developed. Much of Edison's own energies were focused on developing designs that were fully modular so that incremental improvements could be introduced over time.

As the development process drew to a close, attention shifted to promoting the product. Two key markets were initially identified: the business market – for dictation – and entertainment. Initially the former seemed the more promising but the latter eventually produced the greater dividends. The research laboratory showed its potential with the development of the phonograph. Research could be sustained over long periods of time. When competition emerged – as with the gramophone – extra resources could be mobilised to get ahead of rivals. The laboratory could also experiment with methods of production. It was, for example, the superior production quality of the phonograph that kept the gramophone at bay for so long.

The light of the future

The phonograph projected Edison into the front rank of his contemporaries. The next major development to emerge from his laboratory confirmed his place in history. The development of the incandescent electric light changed the world. Before its creation, mankind's life and work were largely regulated by daylight. Gas, kerosene, candles, torches and other forms of lighting could push back darkness a little but they were wholly unsuitable for most of the activities that now regularly take place in a darkened world. Edison recognised the potential very early. He said that 'the electric light is the light of the future – and it will be my light.' His early development and subsequent success with electric lighting grew from his increasing confidence in his capabilities and that of his colleagues. His initial inspiration came from a visit to the factory of William Wallace, whose brass and copper foundry had been the home for early development work on carbon arc lighting.

Wallace's factory contained the world's most powerful electro-magnetic generator. It showed that a powerful arc could be created and maintained if sufficient power could be produced. According to contemporary accounts 'Edison was enraptured. He fairly gloated over it ... he ran from the instruments to the lights and from the lights back to the instruments. He sprawled over a table with the simplicity of a child.'

Edison was acting as the laboratory's 'technological gatekeeper'. He had found a machine capable of keeping ten lights working at once. He became convinced that he 'could keep a thousand – aye ten thousand – from one machine.' The work on electricity marked the true transition from the independent inventor to the industrial innovator. He built a team of different talents and diverse expertise. He recruited graduates in science and technologies outside his own and eventually recruited, in Francis Upton, a manager for his research effort.

Upton was a science graduate from Princeton who had studied in Germany. He was skilled in desk research, filling his notebooks with insights from the best contemporary research. He systematically fed these findings into the work of the rest of the team. Upton focused much of his energy on the research process. He was determined to make the team work effectively together. This was increasingly important as the research group expanded to include chemists, metallurgists, physicists, engineers and mathematicians. Behind them all was Edison's restless energy, 'never in a rut because he was never satisfied.'

Teamwork

The complementary nature of the team's skills went beyond their specific areas of expertise. Edison's greatness went far beyond his ability to identify new areas of development. He could persuade hard-bitten financiers like J.P. Morgan to back his ideas while enthusing the press and public about his visions. Alongside him was Charles Batchelor whose patience and persistence was essential to the proper testing of new ideas. John Kruesi seemed able to turn ideas to working models with the mixture of mechanical skills and insight that made him a vital partner to Edison's creative leaps. Francis Upton, in turn, reported, codified and organised the work. The three crucial breakthroughs in the development of incandescent electric lighting and power system showed the power of the research laboratory.

- The most well known was the development of the filament in the lamp. Edison recognised that he needed a filament to carry the charge. This component would, however, need to be small enough for domestic use; capable of carrying a relatively large electrical charge; cheap and long lasting. Preliminary research showed that platinum met some of these tests while experimental work showed that its technical advantages did not compensate for its high costs and low availability. The breakthrough with the U-shaped, carbon-coated spiral filament came from a series of 'very interesting experiments', which allowed Batchelor to try different shapes, base materials and formulations.
- Alongside work on the filament went complementary developments on the bulb itself. Edison had recruited a glassblower to ensure a ready supply of containers. The laboratory was forced to push the boundaries of work on vacuums to create an environment within the bulb for the filament to work.
- Access to the resources of a well-found research laboratory was especially important to the third component in the power system – the generator and distribution system. Initially this meant using technologies developed originally by William Wallace, whose machine had so 'enraptured' in September 1878. A year later, developments had moved so much further ahead that he was abandoning Wallace and developing his own system 'to give the greatest amount of electricity per horsepower.' Despite Wallace's protest that he could 'build one better to your [Edison's] purpose', the resources of Menlo Park were turned towards the development of technologies that could produce sufficient power. There is no contemporary way to estimate the scale of the challenge. New buildings were erected and additional finance raised. By the time, the switch was thrown in New

York's first district for the world's first large-scale, local-area electricity network on the 4 September 1882, Edison's genius and the power of his research techniques was well established.

The advantage of Edison's approach was equally well demonstrated when he competed with rivals to turn research into development.

Initially, he competed neck and neck with another gifted inventor – William Sawyer – in work to perfect the incandescent lamp. Sawyer, however, could never compete with the resources available at Menlo Park. Sawyer's initial capital was $4000 while Edison's well-found laboratory had around $130,000 for its development work. Sawyer had at most a team of four or five assistants, but Edison could turn to specialists to protect his patents while others undertook extensive searches of the literature and large teams could be set the task of developing resistors and batteries, improving switching systems, experimenting with materials.

An unassailable edge

It was the capacity of the Menlo Park facility to push into substantial development work that gave this research approach a massive and almost unassailable edge. Edison's team could work the research and development system through from invention of a technology – the glass bulb with a carbon filament – to the introduction of electric lighting to major cities. 'Edison evolved from an inventor experimenting intensively with a few close associates to a director of a large-scale research laboratory.'[5]

Others now emulated the approach. Alexander Graham Bell based his Volta Laboratory in Washington on the 'celebrated laboratory at Menlo Park.' The Bell Telephone Company recruited a former Menlo Park employee to try to match its success.

Laboratories became increasingly the norm in major companies but none matched the fertility of the original. In two years, between 1881 and 1883, 259 patents were registered. This built on the 59 patents registered in 1880. The fertility of the laboratory stretched the capacity of its facilities, eventually forcing Edison to transfer his operational headquarters to New York and, among other initiatives, start planning another laboratory in West Orange, New Jersey. This laboratory was 10 times the size of the one in Menlo Park.

The new facility used all the lessons that had been learned at Menlo Park. The library contained thousands of journals and books. There was an advanced machine shop plus space for chemical, mechanical and electrical experiments. The extra scale meant that Edison could expand on his belief that a research project achieved its real value when converted to production. Small-scale manufacturing became part of the research and development process. The Edison Electric Light Company was, perhaps, the first true research-based corporation in the world.

The enterprise won the backing of some of the sharpest business leaders in the world as it extended its operations within the USA and across the world. It eventually combined with others to become the General Electric Company in 1892. In analysing industry at the end of the nineteenth century, Chandler concluded that the new research organisations assured 'the continuing dominance of ... pioneering firms'.[6] A century later in 1999, General Electric was ranked at number one in the USA's most admired companies.

The Black Maria

The last great triumph of Edison's research method in the nineteenth century emerged from the new laboratory. In early 1888, he met British-born photographer Edward Muybridge. This meeting prompted Edison to develop a method to capture pictures on film in ways that could make the images move when projected. Within five years, a practical system for capturing images on film (so that they could be played back to customers) was discovered, tested and commercialised. The original projection device was a variation on the peep shows in funfairs where customers put coins in the machine to watch a short film.

Soon after, the first motion picture studio (The Black Maria[7]) was built at West Orange, the first public film display of *The Blacksmith Scene* occured at the Brooklyn Institute of Science and Arts on 9 May 1893. It took some time and a parting of the ways with his initial partner in motion picture developments, W.K. Dickson, for Edison to move the motion picture from the world of peep shows to the 'big' screen. Even here, the advantages of the well-resourced research laboratory backed by corporate resources became evident. The innovative but under-funded work of Francis Jenkins and Thomas Armat on projection was absorbed and became the basis for the Motion Picture Patents Company, which largely controlled the production, distribution and exhibition of motion pictures until 1917, when the US Supreme Court of the United States ruled that the company was an illegal monopoly.

One per cent inspiration

The advantages of Edison's approach to research and development were as evident in his comparative failures as in his triumphs. His work on ore mining consumed resources that would have destroyed a less well resourced programme. The company was able to transfer the lessons learned from trying to process low grade iron ore into high-grade ore, to cement manufacture. In the early 1900s, Edison was operating one of the largest cement plants in the world. His enthusiasm and belief in promoting product use prompted the Orange County laboratory to develop uses of cement that ranged from large-scale construction, such as New York's Yankee Stadium, to concrete furniture.

The flow of inventions, innovations, developments and improvements from Orange County continued for decades. The twin strands of the research laboratory's success lay first in its ability to control the research and development process so that lessons could be accumulated, advanced and tested. Second, talented researchers – notably Edison himself – could then focus their attention on the key issues that reflected their knowledge, expertise and interest. The division of labour could be applied to a new industrial process. This produced massive leverage so that breakthroughs in science, markets, production or finance could be effectively exploited.

Edison's decision to build his first laboratory in Ward Street, to extend its operations at Menlo Park and transform its capabilities at Orange County changed the nature of industry, producing the type of research or science-driven society we know today. Ultimately, the decision to industrialise research and development was the final affirmation of Edison's famous comment that 'genius is one per cent inspiration and ninety nine per cent perspiration.' The research laboratory created an environment in which the research genius could focus and get maximum leverage from their one per cent – if necessary using someone else's perspiration.

Further reading

Baldwin, N. (1994) *Edison; Inventing the Century*, Hyperion, New York.

Davidson, M. (1992) *The Story of Thomas Alva Edison, Inventor: The Wizard of Menlo Park*, Scholastic Paperbacks, New York.

Israel, P. (1998) *Edison: A Life of Invention*, John Wiley, New York.

Pretzer, W. (1989) *Working on Inventing: Thomas A Edison and the Menlo Park Experience*, Henry Ford Museum, Dearborn.

Wettereau, R. (1996) *The Wizard of Menlo Park*, Amereon, New York.

Notes

1   Baldwin, N. (1994) *Edison; Inventing the Century*, Hyperion, New York.

2   Technological gatekeepers are those people in enterprises who scan developments in outside knowledge and open the gates of the organisation to useful developments.

3   Josephson, M. (1934) *Robber Barons*, Harcourt Brace, New York.

4   Israel, P. (1998) *Edison: A Life of Invention*, John Wiley, New York.

5 Israel, P. (1998) *Edison: A Life of Invention*, John Wiley, New York.
6 Chandler, A. (1977) *The Visible Hand: The Managerial Revolution in American Business*, The Belknap Press, Cambridge.
7 So named after the police paddy wagon that it resembled.

Betting the Company

Boeing and the Jumbo Jet

The missed opportunity

M any of the greatest business breakthroughs start in failure. Few of these disappointments produce more dramatic, long-term results than Boeing's failure in 1965 to win the order for the US Air Force's new generation of transport aircraft. This forced Boeing to rethink its future plans, redirect its business efforts and focus more intensively than ever before on commercial aircraft production. This shift in emphasis led directly to negotiations with Pan Am about commercial aircraft. These discussions, in turn, prompted Boeing to convert its plans for a giant US Air Force transport aircraft into the development of the giant passenger aircraft – the C-5 – that became the Boeing 747 or the 'Jumbo' Jet.

Some of the energy that Boeing invested in the new commercial aircraft reflected the company's anger at losing out to Lockheed in the battle to produce the giant C-5 Air Force transport. Boeing was well placed to develop the new transport aircraft. They had been producing planes for the US Air Force since World War I. Over this time they had established a reputation for quality, reliability, manufacturing excellence and low prices that was unrivalled. The strength of their relationship with the government often hampered their relations with commercial carriers. Passenger airlines were often reluctant to use Boeing because they believed they would always come second to the Department of Defence in Boeing's priorities. The C-5 was, in a real sense, a Boeing development. The company had committed itself to developing a reputation for building large aircraft some years earlier. The massive transport was the ultimate expression of this vision.

The idea that the US Air Force should build this plane came initially from Boeing. 'Boeing submitted an unsolicited preliminary proposal for the company's brainchild that persuaded Pentagon officials to sponsor development of such an aircraft'.[1] Boeing was also involved in preparing the budget paper that backed the successful bid to the US Congress for funds to develop the aircraft. Despite this preliminary work, Boeing knew that they would face fierce competition from other leading companies notably Lockheed and Douglas. All three companies invested heavily in their bids for the project. The total volume of paperwork from the three bidders weighed over 35 tons. Boeing's bid filled a transport aircraft. Boeing knew that it was in 'the most strenuous (competition) in aerospace history' but felt confident of ultimate success.

Built where the spruce grows

The roots of this confidence lay deep in the company's history. William Boeing, the company's founder, was a lumberman who seems to have become involved in airframe production largely by accident. Boeing owned and operated an immensely successful lumber business based on the vast timber resources of the US Pacific Northwest. He became an enthusiastic pilot before World War I and, with a friend, started a company (Boeing and Westervelt – or B&W – based on the partners' surnames) and commenced production in 1915. Initially, the company was built around two of William Boeing existing businesses – timber and boat-building. Wood was the main production material and their earliest products were seaplanes that used Boeing boat-building expertise.

The first significant order for the company came from the US Navy which commended the new company for the quality of

Boeing's breakthrough highlights the importance of two recurrent themes in business success. These themes are resilience and risk taking. The company's early years saw a number of setbacks, which it survived largely because its founder, Bill Boeing, was independently wealthy. During the 1920s it achieved some stability because of its contracts with the US Mail but it was forced to give up this business and concentrate on production. Boeing was linked with a series of major innovations, notably the first all metal airliner and the first transatlantic passenger aircraft, but its defence contracts dominated the company. It was, however, the collapse of a bid to the US Defence Department that forced it to convert the designs for a giant transport plane to the 'Jumbo' jet. This setback, sometimes placed at the door of Robert MacNamara – the US Defence Secretary who apparently thought the links between Boeing and the US Air Force were too strong – forced Boeing to seek new markets for its expertise. The success of the 747 and its successors has given Boeing a dominance of the commercial aircraft industry that continues to today.

its products and its low prices. The company's promotional line that it 'built where the spruce grows' was paying dividends in low raw material costs and skilled labour.

The post World War I years were tough for Boeing, but a mixture of William Boeing's willingness to bankroll the company and the firm's core strengths were major assets. By the end of the 1920s, the company was well established with a significant production arm, important contracts with the US Mail and significant links with United Airlines, through the United Aircraft and Transport Company (UATC). UATC was formed into a Trust that pulled together these various interests.

The 1930s saw growing evidence of the key strengths that became synonymous with Boeing's success:

1   The willingness to lead technologically to get an edge in markets – in 1933 the company produced the first all-metal airliner.
2   The powerful links with the US military that produced a series of very successful collaborations especially in bombers.
3   The commitment to size which meant that the firm concentrated on larger two-, four- and eventually eight-engined planes.
4   The willingness to 'bet the company' on major developments.

Some of these decisions were forced on the company by outside circumstances.

Betting the company

Technological innovation became increasingly important as Boeing was forced to sever its links with the US Mail, United Airlines and the engine producer Pratt & Whitney. United Aircraft and Transport Company was forcibly broken up by the US Congress following a public outcry about the power of Trusts. United Airlines, Boeing and Pratt & Whitney were made into separate and independent companies. This created short-term difficulties for the cash starved manufacturer but in the medium to long term, it produced focus and control.

The dangers of the close links with a specific airline were vividly illustrated in the relative failure of the Boeing 247, the world's first all-metal passenger aircraft. This was designed in close collaboration with United Airlines. Unfortunately for Boeing this meant that it failed to meet the needs of United's major rivals – notably TWA. These rivals turned to Donald Douglas's company, which produced the larger, technologically superior DC-3. The Douglas aircraft went on to vastly outsell Boeing's rival plane.

The link with the military paid massive dividends as the world geared up for war in the late 1930s. The cornerstone of these developments for Boeing was the B-17 bomber known as the 'Flying

Fortress.' The nature of this aircraft and its ultimate success grew out of the third key decision by Boeing's top management – to commit the company to large aircraft. The B-17 was far larger and better armed than any rival aircraft, hence its nickname. The link between military and civilian craft became well established at Boeing over the next thirty years. Development work on military aircraft reduced the development costs of civilian planes. Pan Am, for example, purchased a number of Atlantic Clippers from Boeing for the first scheduled passenger service to Europe in the late 1930s. The design of the Clippers was largely based on an experimental aircraft that Boeing were developing for the US military.

It was, however, the willingness to 'bet the company' that marked out many of these developments, and highlighted Boeing's willingness to take large risks for major returns within an overall strategy. The B-17 project came at a difficult time for Boeing. Major revenue sources had disappeared. William Boeing, for example, was largely driven from the company after the anti-trust pressure, which led to the break-up of United Aircraft and Transport Company. The Depression was in full force. The project itself was far larger than any development that the company had ever undertaken. The costs were only slightly smaller than the value of the company itself. Despite this, the company was so confident in both its strategy and capability that it risked its future on the project.

This willingness to risk everything, if the strategy and the capabilities are right, lies at the heart of most of the breakthroughs that pushed Boeing forward.[2] The risks were tangible and sometimes outside the company's control. The initial order for four-engined bombers, for example, was lost because the bomber crew piloting the test plane made a mistake on take off. This mistake led to the crash that cost the crew their lives and Boeing an order for 350 aircraft. The company was saved from bankruptcy by a small order for test aircraft from an Air Force that recognised that its errors had deprived them of a far superior aircraft. Boeing turned to Pan Am for business in a way that would establish a precedent for the 747.

Investing for the future

The focus on larger aircraft and the investment in innovation was central to this ability to switch from one customer to others. Boeing's technological and production skills were rooted in the long-established policy of recruiting outstanding engineers from universities. It started with William Boeing, continued throughout the firm's history, and gave the company control over its most important asset – technology. The policy was reinforced by a consistent strategy of investing for the future.[3]

This meant that, as early as 1919, the company built one of the largest production facilities in the world. Later, Boeing was the first US airframe producer to develop its own wind tunnel. Eventually, the production facility for the 747 would be not only the largest factory in the world but according to *The Guinness Book of Records*, the largest fully enclosed space in the world. Control of these resources provided a competitive edge that grew increasingly important as aircraft production became increasingly complex.

The entry of the USA into World War II transformed Boeing's prospects. The B-17 was the major long-range bomber used by the US Air Force in Europe during hostilities. The even larger, B-24 Liberator and B-29 Superfortress played an equally significant role in the Pacific war. The war earned Boeing large profits but locked it into the defence industry with even greater strength. The years immediately after the war were lean, as Boeing's reputation as a military contractor made commercial airlines reluctant to give the producer large orders.

Interestingly, the next breakthrough came courtesy of the trust that existed between Boeing and the military. The company was given access to information on jet engine developments. These came initially from the collaborations between the US Air Force and Britain's Royal Air Force. Later, Boeing were among the first companies to be given data on the German ME262 jet fighter.

The value of this latter piece of information was increased when Boeing saw the wind tunnel tests on the German plane. It became clear that the basic configuration of aircraft would need to be changed fundamentally to exploit the advantages of the new jet engines. The change was that the aircraft's wing would need to be swept back – at an angle of 45 degrees from the fuselage – instead of sticking straight out. Boeing was the first US airframe manufacturer to realise the significance of this change. Awareness was heightened by results that were emerging from its own wind tunnel experiments on airframe construction.

Boeing, alone among the major US aircraft producers, built and operated its own wind tunnel. Douglas, Lockheed and other companies generally used wind tunnels owned by public agencies like universities. Not only did Boeing operate its own wind tunnel but had it built to a higher specification – capable of dealing with greater speeds – than those managed by Universities. This decision to invest in plant, capable of dealing with eventualities far beyond those currently required, was a further example of Boeing's wish to control outcomes, and the company's focus on the future. Boeing had the additional advantage of operating near the newly constructed Grand Coolee Dam. The dam produced low price electricity which made the higher specifications of the wind tunnel more economical.

Control over its own wind tunnel and access to German jet fighter technology gave Boeing the platform on which to build two of its most important large aircraft. These were the B-47 and B-52 bombers. Although the B-52 achieved almost legendary status in bomber technology, the B-47 was probably more important to Boeing. Control over superior airframe technology gave Boeing extra focus and leverage. The company's major rivals persevered with traditional designs for bombers i.e. with wings sticking straight out from the fuselage. Jet engines performed so much worse with this technology that the same companies stuck with propeller or turbo-prop[4] technologies. The combination of these effects gave Boeing a double advantage – an earlier move to jet engines and a far more efficient design for the airframe. Boeing eventually built over 2000 B-47s, at a cost of over $6 billion. The success of the B-47 led directly to the US government giving Boeing the contract to build the next generation of bombers – the B-52.

Betting the company's tax dollars

The combination of these programmes reinforced Boeing's position at the forefront of the key technologies needed to construct large, jet-engined aircraft. They controlled the test facilities, much of the expertise, and had more experience than any of their rivals. They used this control to focus on the next stage of the company's evolution from predominantly a defence contractor, to the dominant manufacturer of aircraft in the world. The development of the Boeing 707 was the key stage in this transition.

Commercial aircraft were not new to Boeing. There were long established relationships with United Airlines, Pan Am and TWA. Aircraft like the Atlantic Clipper held significant places in the development of long distance, commercial air travel. Like these earlier developments, the Boeing 707 linked defence dollars for research and development to lever projects for the commercial market. The core technology for the Boeing 707 was based on a jet tanker that Boeing was developing for the US Air Force.

There was, however, an early setback for Boeing in this attempt to link the two developments. The Air Force decided to place the order for the new tanker with Lockheed. Boeing were faced with a crucial decision about the commercial jet's development. The risks were immense. Prototype development would be about $15 million or a quarter of the company's net worth (about $500 million at current prices). The scale of the development would prevent Boeing from undertaking any other significant developments – all the company's eggs were in this basket. The major commercial customers were already involved in a major reinvestment programme based on existing propeller-driven aircraft. No civil aviation authority had yet certified a jet airliner as safe for commercial passenger flight. The aircraft could not come into service for many years – by which time demand could change completely. There was always the risk that well-established commercial producers would steel a march.

Against this were three key counter-balancing forces. First, success would give the company a leading – perhaps dominant – position in the commercial sector. Second, defence work was drying up with no major new programmes in prospect. Third, some of the costs could be offset against a tax law that was introduced during the Korean War. This 'excess profits tax' was designed to prevent defence companies making excess profits out of their government work. It meant that a company's profits in the years immediately after the Korean War would be compared with those in the years immediately before the war. Those with much higher profits would pay an 'excess profits tax,' that in Boeing's case was 82 cents in the dollar. Spending money on Research and Development cut profits, so that the tax was reduced. In effect, $12 million of the projected $15 million investment would come out of a reduced tax bill.

Wary customers

Despite the risks, Boeing committed itself to betting the company and its excess tax dollars on the development of the Boeing 707. Some of the gains from this willingness to take risks and focus their efforts on the new technologies came very quickly. The Air Force was so impressed by the prototype for the new aircraft that they cancelled the Lockheed order and transferred the contract to Boeing. Simultaneously, they agreed to let Boeing amortise some of its costs for developing the commercial craft against work on the defence contract.

In contrast, the commercial airline operators remained wary of Boeing. The proposed aircraft came close to meeting their specifications but fell short in key areas especially range and payload. The Douglas Company, with a far better track record in commercial aircraft, proposed to develop a commercial jet with greater range, more passengers, greater comfort and at a lower price. The price was matched quickly but competing on the other features required a major redesign. Again it was Boeing's control over the technology and ability to focus its efforts quickly on the problem that allowed the company to turn the situation around. The newly formatted 707-120 went into service with Pan Am in 1958, initiating the first jet transport service between the USA and Europe. It was over a year before the rival Douglas DC-8 made its first commercial flight. Boeing had used its control and focus to lever itself into a position to challenge its rival for dominance in the commercial sector. The costs were vast. Total development expenditure was almost $200 million ($2 billion at current prices) by 1957. This was made up of $16 million for the prototype, $100 million for production, $45 million in capital and equipment, $25 million for testing and over $5 million for promotion.

This massive expenditure plus the high production costs meant that it took almost a decade for Boeing to recover its costs and make a profit on its investment in the Boeing 707. After this, profits grew rapidly. The returns took three forms. There was the sale of over 700 commercial aircraft. Alongside this, the defence department purchased large numbers of the jet tanker that underpinned the development. Later, the US Air Force's AWACS (Airborne Warning And Control System) was built around the Boeing 707. Perhaps more important for Boeing's long term competitiveness, was the fact that Douglas's dominant position in the commercial aircraft position was undermined as it fought to keep up with Boeing.

One of Douglas's Vice Presidents commented that the battle to compete 'almost broke the company, but not quite.' The next few years saw Boeing bite deeply into Douglas' share of the commercial market. In the mid 1960s, Boeing's market share of commercial aircraft sales approached 40 per cent while Douglas' fell below 30 per cent for the first time in thirty years. Douglas was desperate for a breakthrough while Boeing grew in strength as military and commercial sales of first the 707, then the 727 and eventually the 737 grew.

Another failure

Douglas' opportunity seemed to arrive when the link between defence and commercial aircraft was broken at a key moment in the development of the military transport and commercial passenger market. Boeing was working with the US Department of Defence to build a giant new transport aircraft called the C-5. This aircraft would use new engine technologies to transform the movement of goods and materials by air. The development offered Boeing the chance to repeat the formula that had worked so well with the Boeing 707 – develop an aircraft for the military and use this work to underwrite development of a new passenger aircraft. The company's plans started unravelling when the order for the C-5 went to Lockheed not Boeing.

This posed immediate problems for Boeing, as it had already enthused an old ally Juan Trippe, the boss of Pan Am, with its plans for a new, giant aircraft that would transform the economics of passenger air transport by carrying far more passengers than any other aircraft. Boeing had undertaken initial research among airlines to gauge demand for aircraft carrying 250, 300 or 350 passengers. The largest of these had won the greatest support. Pan Am was especially keen to push the limits even further. Trippe wanted an aircraft that would carry more than 400 passengers.

It was not just the failure of the C-5 bid that forced Boeing to be radical in its proposals to Pan Am. It was forced into this position by the disadvantages of its existing 'big' plane when faced with the competition – the Douglas DC-8. Boeing's 707 and the DC-8 were the main rivals for larger, long-haul traffic. The advantages to the operators in larger planes were immense. Operating costs were lower. Bigger planes reduced airport costs and congestion. Together, these savings led to lower fares, more custom and higher profits.

Douglas had an initial advantage in the battle to build a bigger plane. This edge lay in the relative ease with which the DC-8 could be stretched to accommodate another seventy seats. Stretching meant 'chopping' the fuselage in half and inserting a new section with the extra seating. There were some technical problems with this on the DC-8 but they were solved with relative ease. This was not possible with the 707. Boeing's configuration meant that the tail of the reconfigured plane would hit the runway on every take off. Even if this was safe, it was hard to see passengers travelling in an aircraft with this feature. Boeing were forced into a complete rethink to stay in the market for big jets.

Even if it takes the entire company

Boeing's initial problem lay in the risk posed by the scale of the development needed to meet Pan Am's needs. This sense of risk was sharpened by the enforced break with the company's traditional approach to linking military and civil aircraft. For the first time, Boeing was stepping into the unknown without a major defence contract to underpin the project. The company's leadership had to decide whether to bet the company once again. This time, however, they were on their own, with only their commercial partners – especially Pan Am and their suppliers, notably Pratt and Whitney – alongside them.

The risk was increased by fears that initiatives in supersonic air travel would overtake their work. Top management at Boeing and Pan Am had to chose between the two technological developments that had driven progress in air transport – the search for speed versus the demand for volume. There were powerful arguments in favour of both lines of development. Key stages in Boeing's earlier history had seen the same dilemma, notably the creation of the 247 and the Atlantic Clipper. Then, Boeing had opted (with Pan Am) for the newer technology, speed and luxury. Each time, Douglas had scooped the market by going for numbers. The decision, this time, was made easier by Boeing's earlier decision to commit its expertise and technological resources to large-scale aircraft. Boeing decided to defer investment in supersonic air transport and commit itself to the 400 seater project.[5]

All three companies were at risk. The early estimates at Boeing placed its development costs in the region of $500 million (almost $5 billion at current costs). In its annual report, the company acknowledged that 'the costs and overall financial risks of the program and the demands on facilities, engineering and management are substantially greater than for any of the company's previous commercial programmes.' For Boeing, this project was the ultimate test of the twin strands of its long-term policy – going for size and reducing its dependence on defence projects. It is a clear illustration of the company's confidence in both its strategy and its capability that it was willing, once again, to bet the company. This determination was symbolised by William Allen – Boeing's CEO and architect of the strategy – who commented that, 'if the Boeing Company says we'll build it, we will build it, even if it takes the entire company.'

The risk for Pan Am was equally great. The initial order was for 25 aircraft at $18,767,000 each or over $500 million with extras (over $4 billion at today's prices). This order was greater than Pan Am's total revenues for its best ever year of operations. Pratt and Whitney faced similar risks in developing engines that would drive the new giant. The initial projections for the costs of developing the engines were over $250 million but these more than doubled as the specifications for the engines became greater and the technology became more demanding.[6]

Not surprisingly, the development placed relations between the three companies at risk. Sometimes the tensions grew from within the project. Pan Am was worried about the increased weight of the aircraft and any reductions in capacity. This forced Boeing to seek improvements in engine technologies that placed further pressures on Pratt and Whitney. Other pressures came from rivals. Douglas persuaded airlines like American Airlines that aircraft of this size were not needed. A mid-sized plane – bigger than the 707 but smaller than the Boeing giant – won supporters in the media and industry. Despite these pressures Boeing stuck with its strategy. Boeing knew its market; it was in control, focused and now ready to gain the maximum leverage from its decisions. It was also proceeding with the new project at a speed that was unrivalled in past projects.

Glitches were common. Some were small – like problems with the evacuation procedure – and solved relatively easily. Others were massive, like the need to redesign the nose of the plane. None significantly delayed the project. The project was driven forward by the willingness to innovate and the determination to let nothing stand in the way of success. Fifty years of building up the company's technological competence came together, so that the largest factory in the world could be built, advanced technologies incorporated and new forms of partnership development created without distracting the firm from its sense of purpose. Two and a half years after the Boeing board of directors approved the project, the first, finished

747 emerged from the giant factory that was built for it. The logos of the twenty-six airlines that had ordered the aircraft were on display and their orders for 200 aircraft guaranteed its success.

Boeing had achieved several breakthroughs simultaneously. The company had transformed the nature of passenger air travel. The Boeing 747, or Jumbo Jet, changed the economics of long distance travel initiating a world of mass international travel. All the company's traditional rivals for commercial passenger aircraft were overtaken. Douglas and Lockheed's entrants into the market were marginalised and their commercial business base collapsed. The new aircraft achieved levels of stability and safety that surprised even its makers. 'Despite the airplane's elephantine size, designers had given it such superb handling characteristics that … the 747 proved, amazingly, to be the easiest jetliner to land.'[7]

The breakthroughs were rooted in decisions taken at key stages in the firm's history. Some were fundamental decisions about policy. The decision to go for size and become pre-eminent in producing large aircraft was crucial. It was not easy. It meant, for example, abandoning valuable contracts for smaller aircraft, like the P-26 fighter. Other decisions permeated the firm's operations. There was the commitment to talent, especially that of engineers. There was a willingness to overcome time constraints. The most extreme example was the B-52 bomber project, when Boeing staff were asked to come up with designs over a weekend. Ultimately the decision to 'bet the company' to achieve a breakthrough symbolised both the underlying strength of Boeing and the decisiveness of its leadership.

The rollout in September 1968 did not end the problems. Boeing's anger with Pratt and Whitney grew as the new engines did not perform to specification. Pratt and Whitney despaired at Boeing's demands. Pan Am was furious at both companies because of further delays and variations in specifications. Lawsuits were threatened or taken out between all three 'partners' as costs grew and each company saw the risks increase and the danger of losses grow. At one point Boeing, for example, estimated that the total development costs exceeded the market value of the company. The introduction of the airline coincided with a downturn in passenger volumes so that it took until the late 1970s for nominal break-even to occur.

By the 1980s, however, the 747 or Jumbo was dominating Boeing's profits as much as it dominated the world's long-distance air routes. The size of the aircraft plus its ability to carry freight as well as people transformed the economics of air transport. Even the downside of the 747 experience had its positive effects. Boeing learned that inadequate pre-planning, skimping on early development, led to huge cost overruns. The company also realised the limits of its in-house capabilities. Partnerships became more important. Boeing found that control over the process of development was as important as control over the technologies of development. Boeing now focuses as closely on these processes as on the specifics of a project. This gives the company increased leverage as it concentrates on its core business while building wider arrays of partnerships.

Further reading

Boeing Company (1994) *A Brief History of the Boeing Company*, The Boeing Company, Seattle.

Irving, C. (1993) *Wide-Body: The Triumph of the 747*, William Morrow & Company, New York.

Kuter, L.S. (1973) *The Great Gamble: The Boeing 747*, University of Alabama Press, Alabama University.

Rodgers, E. (1996) *Flying High*, The Atlantic Monthly Press, New York.

Notes

1   Rodgers, E. (1996) *Flying High*, The Atlantic Monthly Press, New York.

2   Serling, R.J. (1992) *Legend and Legacy: The Story of Boeing and its People*, St. Martin's Press, New York.

3 Boeing Company (1994) *A Brief History of the Boeing Company*, The Boeing Company, Seattle, WA.
4 Turbo-props are engines that combine some of the features of jet and propeller driven engines.
5 Irving, C. (1993) *Wide-Body: The Triumph of the 747*, William Morrow & Company, New York.
6 Kuter, L.S. (1973) *The Great Gamble: The Boeing 747*, University of Alabama Press, Alabama University.
7 Rodgers, E. (1996) *Flying High*, The Atlantic Monthly Press, New York.

Earning Bucketfuls by Selling Sand

Inside Intel

Real revolutionaries

N ot many company leaders have a 'natural' law named after them. Few companies have two leaders, each with a 'law' named after them. Intel is one of those companies. The first is sometimes described as the 'first law of computing' or Moore's Law – after Gordon Moore, one of the founders of Intel. This law states that the number of transistors on a chip will double every 12–18 months. In fact this observation, that seemed wildly optimistic at the time, is an understatement. An estimate in Forbes magazine indicated that you can 'double something every eighteen months for thirty years and it increases by a factor of over a million to one. Moore was close: today's four-megabit chip is four million times more powerful than its predecessor, the transistor.' Moore had an advantage in making this prediction in that no company has done more to make it come true than Intel.

Moore had a major ally in turning this vision into a reality in Andy Grove, the first Director of Operations at Intel. Grove set up and implemented the management and operations systems that converted Intel from an interesting and innovative producer, first of integrated circuits and then of microprocessors. His move from Director of Operations to Chief Executive reflected the company's shift from a development 'hothouse' to a research, production and marketing company that dominates the world markets in integrated circuits, including microprocessors, flash memory chips and chip sets. Grove's Law, that 'only the paranoid survive' reflects an approach to total business development that is increasingly important today. We face an environment in which even businesses based on research into advanced technologies, like Intel, are forced to think through and manage their operations, from the point of access to research and development, through to the end-user market.

The best talent

Grove's management methods were as much concerned with recruiting the best research talent as promoting the *Intel Inside* message to teenagers buying personal computers on which to play games. One story about Grove recounts how he was told that one especially bright candidate had received dozens of jobs offers and was not likely to take up Intel's offer 'Tell you what I'll do,' said Grove (to his head of personnel), ' if this guy's such a star, you write him a letter from me saying why he ought to come, and I'll sign it.'

Three days later the letter had been signed and mailed out – and the young graduate, astounded to receive a letter from the guy who had just been on the cover of a business magazine, called to say that if the company were that keen for him to join, then Intel was the place he wanted to work.'[1]

This approach did not mean that Grove saw people management or getting the best out of people as a soft option. Grove was tough, demanding, and sometimes as paranoid as his book indicates. At one point he was so angry about poor timekeeping that he made every employee arriving after 8 am sign in as late – even if they'd been working until the early hours. He was author of Intel's famous Scrooge memo that reminded staff that although Christmas Day was a holiday Christmas Eve was not, so employees could not leave early. The apparent contradiction in working very hard to recruit the most talented and then forcing the pace of their work was resolved by Grove's determination to get the best (employees) and get the best out of them.

Intel has grown to symbolise the type of knowledge-based company that many commentators expect to dominate industry in the future. Intel was created by a group of researchers, scientists and engineers who were frustrated by the failure of their then employer, Fairchild Semi-Conductor, to realise the potential of the new information industries. The company pioneered the development of the silicon chip, and developed new ways of producing them in volume at ever reducing prices. Scientific and production advances went alongside innovations in marketing and organisation structure, that allowed the company first to beat their rivals to market, then combine massive expenditure on research and development with reducing prices, and finally create consumer demand for their product initially through the *Intel Delivers* message and now through the *Intel Inside* proposition. This combination of technological expertise and marketing skill allowed Intel to create the business breakthrough that many others are struggling to match even today.

Build a better mousetrap

The same total management approach gradually emerged in the company's approach to customer relations. Initially, the Intel approach could be summarised in the old maxim: 'build a better mousetrap, and the world will beat a path to your door.' Intel was driven by a strong technological imperative. The founders, Gordon Moore and Robert Noyce, formed Intel because they were frustrated by the reluctance of their previous employers at Fairchild Semiconductor to invest in research, development and innovation. Their first recruits were people like Andy Grove who believed strongly in the value of engineering and the power of technological change.

Their products were generally either so far ahead of the competition or superior in other ways that customers generally did 'beat a path to their door.' From the start, continuous change was part of the company's philosophy. While most companies tried to consolidate around a change, Intel was in a state of constant change, even turmoil. Moore was convinced very early on that their innovations would change the world. In the 1960s he commented that 'we are really the revolutionaries in the world today – not the kids with the long hair and beards.' This attitude pre-dated the continuous-improvement, organic-change types of management style which dominate much current management thinking.

When their chips were not technologically more advanced, they were typically more reliable, produced before their rivals or more competitively priced. The decision to introduce the catch phrase *Intel Delivers* symbolised this determination to get ahead technologically and stay ahead. Bob Noyce developed and tested the first integrated chip. Intel was the first company to perfect the 'silicon gate' technology that was fundamental to the development of microprocessor technology using silicon chips. Intel also created the production technology that first drove wastage rates down, and then cut production and end-user costs. A series of chips, typically numbered in a series starting like 1101, 4004 or 8080, pushed up microprocessing power in line with (Gordon) Moore's Law.

The first major challenge to this dominance occurred at a crucial period in the evolution of the computer industry. These were the years between 1976 and 1980, when personal computers emerged to challenge the dominance of mainframe computers, and brought computing power into the office and home.

Operation crush

Intel, however, faced a novel challenge to its dominance of microprocessor technology when Motorola introduced first the 6800 and, then, the 68000 chips that were 'better designed, faster, cheaper *and* easier to use.' Intel's traditional method of addressing a technological threat had been to invest more resources and try to leapfrog the rival technology. The breakthrough that transformed Intel from an important but secondary player in the computer industry to a dominant force lay in a fundamental shift in strategy.

Intel decided to shift from being a technology driven company, to a market *and* technology driven company. Customer needs, the desire to meet client needs – rather than sell products – became central to the company's strategies. Perhaps more importantly, Intel decided to sell through its immediate clients to their customers and, eventually, end-users. This was a radical departure for a research-based company that might be expected to assume that the end-users of the products containing its technology had neither the interest nor the knowledge to understand its products.

The challenge from Motorola forced Intel to stretch its definition of the products it produced and sold. This shifted attention from the immediate product – the chip – to the range of benefits that Intel delivered. These extended from its reputation as an innovator, through its product range and the support it could deliver, to a strong brand image. These ideas emerged from a major review of the company's operations that was eventually code-named 'Project Crush.' This in turn led to a view of marketing in technologies, that is now associated with firms as diverse as Intel itself, Microsoft, ABB, Nike, General Electric, Hoechst and Mitsubishi. This view is contained in the phrase, 'we don't beat the opposition, we crush it.' This total marketing or total system approach drove Motorola from a position of almost matching Intel for market share in the late 1970s to less than 15 per cent of the market in 1980.

This success for Intel occurred at a crucial time in the evolution of computing. During 1980, IBM was facing major difficulties in developing its first personal or desktop computers. The computer giant was struggling to develop a computer that met its price requirements while still delivering a basic computing capacity. Machines that used the latest technology were too expensive for the retail market that IBM wished to build, while older technologies were too far behind rival machines to be acceptable. Intel's decision to widen its range and offer a full service solved IBM's problems. The microprocessor company was able to offer IBM a modified version of its main chip – the 8086. This new variant was the 8088. This chip became the microprocessor that was used not only in the first IBM microprocessor but in most of the IBM clones that flooded on to the market. Intel supplied over 80 per cent of the chips used in the half million PCs that were sold over the next two years.

The shift to a total marketing approach was further vindicated as the company faced up to consumer demand for increased processing power to meet the needs of new applications. These applications ranged from novel business products like word processing and spreadsheets, through educational applications and research tools, to games. Well established equipment manufacturers like IBM could not dictate the pace of development as the barriers to entry were so low that newly formed companies could emerge to threaten their market position in months rather than years. Companies like Compaq won market share because they could offer superior technology at lower prices. End-users wanted the applications and the applications needed computing power. Intel knew that control of the technology was crucial to its long term growth.

Stretching the market

New personal computers emerged, like the IBM AT (Advanced Technology), based on faster chips. The AT used an 80286 with far more computing power than its predecessor. The next generation of IBM machines, the PS/2, used the 386 chip (the 80 prefix gradually disappeared). By the time of the PS/2, however, IBM's market power had diminished to such a degree that its product introductions no longer shaped the development of the market. The launch of the 386 chip marked a series of other, major developments in the total marketing approach that produced the breakthrough that transformed Intel.

The chip was far more powerful that its predecessor 286 chip – 'a zillion per cent better' according to one Intel ad. Intel started talking directly to end-users, persuading them to demand the 386 from PC suppliers. Up until then, the major PC manufacturers had forced Intel to share its secrets with rival companies – that could act as second sources of supply – in case there were any problems with Intel's output. In theory, second sources reassured customers that any production problems at Intel would not hit their own output. In practice, second sources were often used to force Intel's prices down. Consumer 'pull' was seen as crucial to freeing Intel from the need to accommodate second sources. Customers would demand the Intel chip, and computer companies would be obliged to supply it.

The Red Cross Campaign

The Red Cross campaign produced two major benefits to Intel. First, it reinforced the importance of the move from a 286 to a 386 chip. This was important as many computer companies still held stock of 286 chips that could delay the penetration of the new chip. Alongside this, the 386 was Intel's property and the company identified itself in the eyes of end-users with the latest technology. The campaign was a complete success, so much so that 'by December, you couldn't find a single retail ad in which the 386SX [the chip's full name] was not displayed with its price.'

These successes drove company sales up from less than $3000 when it was formed in 1968, to over $600 million in 1978; it reached almost $3 billion by 1988 with $1.1 billion coming from the 386. The increased market power produced by a focus on customer needs, increased Intel's leverage over the rest of the market. This was reinforced with the twin launch of the Pentium chip, with its vastly increased power over the 486, and the *Intel Inside* promotional campaign. In 1998, total sales reached $26.273 billion, which placed Intel comfortably in the fifty largest corporations in the USA. However, profits of $6.068 billion positioned Intel as the sixth most profitable US company. No other company in the top fifty showed such a positive and large difference between its turnover rank (40) and its profits. A year earlier, profits had been even higher, making it the fourth most profitable corporation in the world. Intel's technological, production and marketing decisions had achieved a massive breakthrough for a company whose foundations are truly built on sand.

Further reading

Grove, A. (1996) *Only the Paranoid Survive*, Doubleday & Co., New York.
Jackson, J. (1997) *Inside Intel*, HarperCollins, London.
Yu, A. (1998) *Creating the Digital Future*, Simon and Schuster, New York.

Notes

1   Jackson, J. (1997) *Inside Intel*, HarperCollins, London.

Chapter 4

The Usual Berliner Bragging

The Development and Success of Asprin

Background

P ain has been part of the human experience for as long as people have existed. The search for pain relief, or cures for pain, can be dated as far back as records exist. There is even evidence that herbal medicines were used for treating pain throughout pre-history. The oldest known written record of drug use is a clay tablet made around 2000 BC, listing about a dozen drug prescriptions.

The ancient Egyptians, Greeks and Roman had well established pharmacopoeia and complementary systems of medical expertise. An Egyptian scroll from about 1550 BC names more than 800 prescriptions containing about 700 drugs; some, at least, were used for pain relief. The world's first hospital was built in China during 2 AD. Around the same time, the Romans opened the first pharmacy. Treatments for pain were developed by the Greeks and Romans who used opium for pain relief.

Alongside herbal medicines, the ancients used other more intrusive and radical treatments for pain relief. Trepanning – skull surgery involving the drilling of a hole into the skull – was used extensively: 'from the megalith builders of ancient Europe to the Incas of Peru.'[1] An important purpose of these operations was the treatment of 'incurable headaches (that) ... were another common complaint that ancient surgeons believed could be cured by "relieving the pressure" on the brain.'

The modern study of medicine, pain relief and the use of drugs, can be dated to the 1500s and 1600s when doctors and scientists made systematic studies in pharmacology (the study of drugs). The first pharmacopoeia was the Nuremberg Pharmacopoeia. It was published in Germany in 1542. This work provided the foundations for the rapid progress in pharmacology during and after the eighteenth century. Edward Jenner's development of the smallpox vaccine in 1796, the isolation of morphine and quinine between 1805 and 1815, and the development and use of anaesthetics in the 1840s created a wave of interest in the use of drugs to tackle illness and relieve symptoms. The first modern national pharmacopoeias were published initially in the USA (1820), later in Britain (1864), and followed this century by the European Pharmacopoeia and the International Pharmacopoeia.

The last quarter of the nineteenth century saw a rapid expansion in the search for drugs and drug treatments, as the chemical and pharmaceutical industries grew into maturity. Inventions or discoveries – as diverse as DDT and synthetic detergents – emerged from the first laboratories with clear and specific industrial or economic goals. In Germany in particular, the combination of a economic growth, a strong scientific base and Bismarck's initiatives to support industrial growth, created a powerful platform for the development of science-based industries like chemicals and pharmaceuticals.

During the last quarter of the nineteenth century, German companies like BASF, Bayer and Hoechst had established 'production facilities, created the worldwide marketing networks, and recruited the managerial organisation necessary to acquire the first mover advantages that permitted them to dominate and share world markets.'[2] Their success was driven by an ability to mobilise scientific expertise to serve the goals of the enterprise, and industrialise research and development to solve specific problems. Initially, they were especially effective at taking an established product, for example a dye, and developing systems for driving down prices by improved production methods. Between 1869 and 1886, for example, the price of red alizarin, a new synthetic dye, was cut from 270 marks per kilo to 9 marks per kilo. Gradually, these skills were adapted to the development of new proprietary products and their production.

In March 1999, Bayer celebrated the 100th anniversary of Aspirin® entering into the trademark register of the Imperial Patent Office in Berlin. A few months later in 1900 the American patent authorities awarded Dr Felix Hoffmann a patent for his discovery of the synthesis of ASA – acetylsalicylic acid. Aspirin was the first laboratory-designed non-steroidal anti-inflammatory agent which became available for industrial mass production in a chemically pure and stable form. Although first sold as a powder, it is the Aspirin tablet that emerged as one of the first and, according to *The Guinness Book of Records*, the most successful retail, branded drug in history. Its longevity as a treatment for headaches and other pains is now matched by increasing awareness of its value in treating other ailments.

Aspirin's success highlights the value of both the research process that produced the product, and the skillful branding and marketing that means that it is sold under the Bayer brand in over eighty countries, and even joined Neil Armstrong on the first trip to the moon. In theory, he could have walked to the moon on a carpet of Aspirins as, if the current annual output of the active substance acetylsalicylic acid produced by Bayer and other companies was pressed into 500-milligram tablets, the 100 billion resulting tablets would make a path that would easily stretch from the earth to the moon and back.

A lucky accident

Coal tar played an especially important part in the early development of the chemicals industries. Coal tar is a residual product left over when coal is heated to a high temperature in a vacuum to produce an inflammable gas. Initially, this residue was treated as a waste, but in 1856 William Perkin found that a dye could be derived from coal tar. This was the first synthetic aniline dye. It produced a brilliant mauve colour which was lightfast, and resistant to washing. The new dye was a popular and fashion sensation, with

Queen Victoria wearing a mauve dress to open the International Exhibition of 1862, and early postage stamps being dyed mauve.

The chemicals industry grew rapidly as new dyes, uses and products emerged. The bridge with the pharmaceutical occurred when two research scientists accidentally treated a patient with a coal tar derivative, acetanilid, that successfully reduced his fever. The new product, branded as Antifebrin, quickly won acceptance and encouraged several chemicals companies to move into the development of drugs to treat pain and fever.

Among the pioneers of this shift was Farbenfabriken Bayer. The company's chief scientist, Carl Duisberg, spotted both the opportunity of this new area of work and the potential inherent in another waste product from dye making. The company's existing manufacturing processes produced large quantities of par-nitrophenol as a waste by-product. Par-nitrophenol was very similar in chemical composition and properties to acetanilid. The efforts of Bayer's research team soon bore fruit and a new product branded as Phenacetin was produced.

'Duisberg's accomplishment was revolutionary. For the first time, a drug had been conceived, developed, tested and marketed, all by a private company.'[3] Phenacetin linked Bayer's interests in chemicals and pharmaceuticals, highlighted the value of sustained research and development, opened up world markets and highlighted the value of strong branding. For Duisberg, Phenacetin's success also highlighted the value of control over the production and research processes, and the intellectual and market property rights of a pharmaceutical brand.

In 1891, Duisberg expanded and divided Bayer's research operations. In Leverkusen, the production and development of dyes and related chemicals was concentrated. This provided the opportunity to establish a dedicated pharmaceutical research unit in the company's existing facilities in Elberfeld. Duisberg was preoccupied with finding the best and most efficient ways to produce the company's growing range of popular and new products. He wanted to 'unite (all intermediate products) ... for the sake of quality control, simplification of preparation and cost production.' The integration of research and production was central to Duisberg's vision of the best way to combine effective innovation and successful production. He wanted to ensure that 'works chemists can at any time get into direct communication with the works engineers.' Control here was to be the key to Bayer's success.

The new division

The expansion and development of Bayer was focused initially on new dyes, a widening array of related chemicals, and the ability Duisberg showed in combining innovation with price cuts. Growth in pharmaceutical products was much more opportunistic. The success of Phenacetin showed the potential gains. Much of the early work of the new laboratory concentrated on the development of alternatives to Phenacetin but with fewer negative side effects. Alongside this, the company undertook work on the development of sedatives. This eventually led to the production of Sulfonal. This, in turn was replaced by another sedative, Trional and eventually led to the creation of a barbituate, Vernal. Much of this early work followed two distinct paths. First, there was the process that had produced Phenacetin. This built on work that was emerging across the chemicals industry on the properties of new materials and discoveries.

Alongside this, within the laboratory, there was systematic examination of both the properties of traditional natural products and the wider research literature for new compounds. As part of this work, Felix Hoffman, a researcher at Elberfeld, came across the work of Charles Frederic Gerhardt who had synthesised acetylsalicylic acid (ASA) out of traditional materials for pain relief.

Willow bark

For centuries the bark of willows had been used to relieve pain and fever. Willow bark works because it contains a chemical that is converted by the body to a salicylate. Acetylsalicylic acid works by blocking the formation of certain prostaglandins (hormone-like chemicals found throughout the body). Although prostaglandins are generally beneficial, when a person's physical condition is impaired they can be produced in excess quantities. These quantities produce pain, and other potentially harmful effects.

There are many stories about the early development of Aspirin. Some of these tales emphasise the role of Hoffman. It is claimed that he 'discovered' ASA when searching for a treatment for his father's chronic rheumatism. Other stories highlight the problems Hoffman faced in persuading the director of the Bayer testing service to clear the drug for general use. The director was especially dismissive of Hoffman's claims describing them as 'the usual Berliner bragging.'

There is even the legend that the director's reluctance was linked to his support for an alternative painkiller. This latter product got its common name from the general feeling of well-being it produced. Its users felt so heroic after treatment, that the company named the drug Heroin. Repeat sales of this alternative to ASA were so good that Bayer was reluctant to prescribe an alternative. Despite this, ASA won the support of other champions in the company. Gradually, they won support for clinical trials. These were so successful that the new product, with its distinctive brand name Aspirin, was launched in January 1899.

Caruso's endorsement

The success of Aspirin built on the business approach that Duisberg had created. The systematic organisation and clear focus of Bayer's research laboratories had identified a solution to a widespread problem. Even the delays were, in a sense, a tribute to Duisberg's methods. He had insisted in separating the testing of new drugs from their development. The director of the testing laboratory, Heinrich Dreser, had the power to block the introduction of ASA because Duisberg set up the organisation to place this power in his hands. This division of control reassured potential customers that Bayer could be trusted.

Once the product reached the market, other aspects of Duisberg's approach to management bore fruit and provided added leverage. The use of the trade name, Aspirin, rather than the scientific name, acetyl-salicylic acid, gave Bayer control over the product's development and exploitation. The product's remarkable technical qualities mean that besides relieving pain from headaches and arthritis, and reducing fever from infections, it also reduces inflammation and can prevent heart attacks, and some strokes, by interfering with blood clotting.

The immediate success was, however, as a painkiller. Headaches, in particular, were seen in the late 19th and early 20th centuries as part of 'the curse of modern living.' Aspirin was the first reliable treatment with minimal side effects for these aches and pains. The mass market for the new treatment was driven by celebrity endorsements. Enrico Caruso, the singer, demanded that impresarios provided him with Aspirin at every performance, while Kafka claimed that only Aspirin made bearable the pain of being.

The use of the brand name gave Bayer a platform to protect its market position and expand its sales overseas. The company focused its efforts on protecting and developing 'the most used and beloved medicine we manufacture.' Growth in German sales was soon followed by expansion into other European countries and, in the early years of the century, the USA. By the start of the First World War, Aspirin was probably the most heavily used drug in the world. Bayer focused its promotional efforts on its trademark, Aspirin.

In the USA and the United Kingdom, trademark protection laws made it relatively easy to build a near monopoly around Aspirin. However, many rival companies claimed, with perfect legitimacy, that the basic product, ASA or acetylsalicylic acid, could not be reserved by Bayer as it had been developed by others, much earlier than Bayer. In the UK, an attempt to protect its 'rights' led Bayer into a costly and unsuccessful court action. Even in the USA where its court action was successful, the costs of enforcement were so high that the gains were minimal.

Duisberg, instead, used the company's highly efficient production processes, in conjunction with its increasingly sophisticated marketing efforts, to build a powerful brand identity around the Aspirin trademark. A powerful link was made with the Bayer corporate logo in a series of steps that infuriated the medical profession in

Fig. 4.1 First switched on in 1933, the Bayer Cross towered over the Leverkusen headquarters of the German Bayer company until it was dismantled at the beginning of the Second World War. Some 236 feet in diameter, it was the biggest lighted sign in the world – a huge electric aspirin tablet. (Source: Bayer AG/Bayer-Archiv.)

the USA. The emphasis in the company's advertising was to reassure customers that ' "The Bayer Cross" on every package and on every tablet of Genuine Aspirin protect you against all counterfeits and substitutes.'

This link between the company name – that of the product and the brand symbol – was the first attempt in the pharmaceutical industry to gain maximum leverage to promote a product to end-users rather than doctors or pharmacists. The success of this promotion meant that by 1909, Aspirin was easily the most successful painkiller, or ethical drug in the world. During that year, Aspirin accounted for around 70 per cent of Bayer's US sales and dominated US sales of painkillers. From its base in Germany, it exported to most of Europe and parts of Asia. Its operations in the USA gave it a platform to build up its business in Latin America.

A cash cow

World War I was a major setback to Bayer. It lost most of its business in the allied countries, and in the immediate aftermath of the war was forced to sell its rights to Aspirin and the Bayer name to Sterling Products in the USA, UK, Canada, the British Empire and Latin America. The inter-war years saw demand for Aspirin grow across the world. None of the major new drugs developed in the 1920s or 1930s – insulin, penicillin, amphetamines, sulfa drugs, synthetic tranquillisers – matched either its universal appeal or its relatively small number of negative side effects.

Within Germany, Bayer was involved in the massive restructuring of the chemicals and pharmaceutical industries that led to the creation of the reviled and infamous I.G. Farben Group of Companies. Aspirin was a cash cow for both I.G. Farben and Sterling Products. One estimate suggests that Aspirin or Aspirin based products, produced over 25 per cent of I.G. Farben's profits during the 1930s (around $75 m) and over 50 per cent of Sterling's profits during the same period (around $20m). World War II caused another crisis in Bayer's sales of Aspirin. By this time, however, a host of Aspirin based alternatives were available across the world.

Decline and recovery

The post World War II era saw the market for branded medicines, especially those based on Aspirin, become dominated by mass advertising. New brands like Bufferin, Aspro and Anacin, emerged to challenge Bayer and its US partner Sterling. The market shares of the established producers slumped under pressure from the newcomers, but the core strength of the brand, allied to the continuing value of the product, saw Bayer through the difficulties of the 1940s and 1950s. The competitive battle centred on the claims of rival producers: about how quickly their formulations worked, their relative strength and their side effects.

The same period saw the emergence of a range of non-Aspirin based analgesics such as paracetamol and codeine. By the end of 1986, Bayer's share of the Aspirin market in the USA had dropped below 6 per cent and its share of European markets (excluding Germany) was down below 25 per cent of a market which faced more rivals than ever before. Within two years, however, the situation was reversed as the links between aspirin and the prevention of heart attacks and some forms of strokes emerged. At the same time, Bayer rebuilt its international interests, especially in the USA. Aspirin is once again the most heavily used drug in the world – perhaps the only mass-market scientific product from the nineteenth century holding that position.

Further reading

Leighton, I. (1949) *The Aspirin Years*, Simon and Schuster, New York.
Mann, C.C. and Plummer, M.L. (1991) *The Aspirin Wars*, Alfred A. Knopf, New York.

Notes

1   James, P. and Thorpe, N. (1995) *Ancient Inventions*, Michael O'Mara Books, London.
2   Chandler, A. Jnr (1990) *Scale and Scope: The Dynamics of Industrial Capitalism*, Harvard University Press, Cambridge, MA.
3   Mann, C.C. and Plummer, M.L. (1991) *The Asprin Wars*, Alfred A. Knopf, New York.

Chapter 5

'This is an Order: The Name is Walkman'

Creating an International Icon out of the Sony Walkman

Made in Japan

The story of the Sony Walkman shows how a major business breakthrough can be achieved by creative management, almost in spite of their own prior beliefs and assumptions. At almost every stage in its development, the company was forced to rethink decisions and reverse actions. In part, this reflected the distinctive challenges facing a Japanese company striving to win success in international consumer markets. The Walkman also confounded many assumptions about the ways consumer markets operate. In establishing the Walkman as a global success story, Sony showed that some of the best decisions emerge from being open-minded and refusing to be trapped into established thinking.

The choice of name illustrates this willingness to learn and adapt. Akio Morita, Sony's Chairman at the time of the launch, admitted that 'I never really liked the name Walkman ... (I wanted our marketing team) to change the name to something like Walking Stereo, or anything a bit more grammatical.' He was, however, forced into agreeing to use the name in Japan by being told that all the advertising materials were already prepared. The cost of change would be too high. Morita found allies for his views in Sony America and Sony UK. Neither of these major overseas partner companies wanted to use such an ungrammatical name. In the USA, the name chosen was Sound About, and in Britain Stow Away won the day.

The name is Walkman

The appeal of these names to the firm's advertising and marketing teams was not shared by consumers. Further confusion was added when tourists imported the Japanese products bearing the name Walkman. The poor appeal of the US and UK brand names contrasted sharply with the product's early success in Japan, (even at the relatively high price of ¥33,000 (£100). Morita disliked the name but was an enthusiast for the product so he intervened directly.

'I called up Sony America and Sony UK and said, "This is an order: the name is Walkman!" Now I'm told it is a great name.'[1]

The name is so closely associated with the product that it's now the generic name given to all such products – regardless of their maker.

The early development of the Walkman grew out of the determination of Akio Morita, and Sony's founder Masura Ibuka, to move out of the ghetto into which many Japanese goods were placed in the international market. They knew that their products were improving rapidly in quality and appeal. They were fed up with printing 'Made in Japan' as small as possible to avoid customer hostility and rejection. Sony needed a powerful new brand to free the business from these image problems.

The company was also determined to break free of the limitations imposed by the complex and multi-layered Japanese distribution system in which, 'there are primary, secondary, and even tertiary wholesalers dealing with some goods before they reach the retailer, layer after layer of middlemen in between the maker and the ultimate user of the product. This distribution system has some social value – it provides plenty of jobs – but it is costly and inefficient.'[2]

The new product Morita was chasing had to free them from these constraints, deliver a breakthrough into new markets and give them control over these markets. The decision was made to respond to an apparent market need, by building on two of the firm's existing strengths. These were, an ability to use 'magnetised tape to convey aural and visual recording', and outstanding marketing. Both strengths came together in the Walkman. In coming together, they created additional and increasingly powerful competencies in miniaturisation

The Sony Walkman was developed to solve a particular problem but eventually became a template for Sony's later success and an international icon. The specific problem that Akio Morita, Sony's Chief Executive, spotted was the desire of people to have access to music while they were moving about. Sony's solution was to develop a product that focussed on portability even if it meant abandoning features of the product such as the ability to record and speakers that were, until then, synonymous with tape players. This product innovation was backed by a commitment to powerful branding and international promotion that freed Sony from the dominance of retailers by creating customer pull for the brand. This emphasis of simple, innovative, miniaturised products backed by strong branding and consumer promotion has characterised Sony's domestic and international success ever since.

and design, backed by innovative technology. Sony decided to break out of the limitations imposed by their existing marketplaces by 'leading the public with new products rather than asking them what they want.'

No obvious market need

The Walkman met no obvious market need, but reflected Morita's sensitivity to burgeoning customer expectations for mobility and access to music. In outlining the origins of the Walkman, Morita describes how his daughter's desire for music in her room, his observation of 'people with big tape recorders and radios perched on their shoulders' in New York, even Tokyo, made him sensitive to the opportunity. This made him very receptive when one of his colleagues came to him with a portable stereo tape recorders and a pair of our standard size headphones, complaining about their size and weight. His colleague said, 'I like to listen to music, but I don't want to disturb others. I can't sit there by my stereo all day. This is my solution – I take the music with me. But it's too heavy.'

Morita's decision was to use the search for extreme portability to draw together the company's strengths in innovative technology, design and marketing, to create a wholly new product. The move into a novel product would give Sony control of the market – at least initially – while allowing the firm to reach the end consumer directly. There was resistance inside and outside the firm to overcome. Innovation was not new for Sony.

Masura Ibuka had ensured that the firm was committed to innovation from the start. He was one of the first people to spot the opportunities created by the development of transistors. The principles which Ibuka drew up when he founded the company emphasised highly advanced technologies, commercial products based on research, ideal factory conditions and a dynamic approach to markets. Although the economic resurrection of Japan was integral, Tokyo Telecommunications (the predecessor company to Sony) was determined to achieve this in partnership with the USA.

Morita moved to the USA in 1957, establishing his family there by 1963. This shift in location allowed him to wed increasing control of the research, development and production process with a powerful focus on meeting customer needs. He understood both his companies core competencies and the ways that markets were changing. An integral element of the marketing breakthrough that he achieved through the Walkman was the creation of a new distinct competence, and added leverage by linking three existing competencies. These competencies were:

1 technological innovation linked to very high quality standards,
2 a focus on the use of magnetic tape to convey aural recordings, and
3 skills in packing increasing technological capability into smaller products.

The Walkman took all three to their technological limits and produced a fourth – miniaturisation of well designed products for consumer markets.

Fig. 5.1 The Sony Walkman. (Source: Sony.)

Overcoming resistance

This combination of strengths allowed the team working on the
Walkman to overcome internal and external resistance. Morita's
market knowledge prompted him to reject suggestions that they retain the facility to record – it would mean a bulkier product. Miniaturisation was the company's core strength, portability was a vital
product attribute; once these principles were accepted the decision
not to have a record facility on the Walkman was easy. It was equally
easy to decide to leave out the integral loudspeaker, and use headphones to project the sound. The clear focus behind the product
made these decisions simple – even where they went against conventional wisdom.

It is worth summarising the radical nature of Sony's decision.
They were taking tape recorders that could not record and had no
internal means of projecting sound. It was not surprising that the
initial reaction from the company's marketing staff was lukewarm.
They though distributors would not want to handle the product,
customers would not understand it, and the promotional costs

would be too high. In practice, consumer pull was so strong that high levels of demand allowed the firm to get enormous leverage over distributors, and promotional costs were kept low because of the value of word-of-mouth promotion. Sales were higher than expected because Morita's original assumption, that people would share their Walkmans, was confounded by people's desire for personal sounds.

The success of the Walkman went beyond the sales of a specific product. The Walkman, in its various guises, has sold almost 50 million units for Sony alone. The real effect of the Walkman on Sony lies in the effect across the firm. Miniaturisation with style and marketing flair, is a combination of competitive advantages that is hard for rivals to match. 'Core competencies are the collective learning of the organisation, especially how to co-ordinate diverse production skills and integrate multiple streams of technologies ... Among Sony's competencies is miniaturisation. To bring miniaturisation to its products, Sony must ensure that technologists, engineers and marketers have a shared understanding of customer needs and of technological capabilities.'[3] The Walkman was the catalyst that converted the company's potential to bring these elements together into tangible reality in the global marketplace.

Ibuka disliked everything derivative

The basic decisions were technical – take out the record facility, eliminate the integral speaker – but the key to these decisions lay in Morita's decision to focus his attentions on the changing nature of market needs. His move to the USA shocked many of his contemporaries, but this lay at the heart of his decision to make Sony a market-driven company. These decisions were rooted in earlier decisions by the company's founder – Masura Ibuka – to avoid derivative products and emphasise innovation, when much of Japanese industry was preoccupied with copying other people's products. 'Ibuka disliked everything derivative ... this brought about a revolution in the Japanese component industry.'[4]

The Walkman was introduced in 1979. The technical problems had been solved and the sound was extremely good for a small machine. Teenagers were the initial target market in Japan but it soon emerged that somewhat older, more affluent consumers were the first to take up the product. Initial sales exceeded expectations but the firm pressed on with the US launch under the Soundabout name. This was quickly withdrawn and replaced with 'Walkman.' Sony's technological capability and market knowledge led to control and the ability to focus on the core capabilities of the company. Importantly, Sony appreciated the dynamic nature of competencies and capabilities.

New, especially powerful sources of competitive advantage, were created by linking established strengths into a new advantage – miniaturisation with marketing and design. Focusing on this new source of competitive advantage led Sony to adopt new brand-building policies to maximise the leverage from these core strengths. Sony came to replace Tokyo Communications Company as the business name. Sony also became the logo which links Playstations, Video, Camcorders and, of course, new generations of Walkman. In annual sales, Sony struggles to stay in the top fifty Japanese companies but its image and reputation are assets to the whole of Japanese industry.

Further reading

Fukuyama, F. (1995) *Trust: The Social Virtues and the Creation of Prosperity*, Hamish Hamilton, London.

Lessem, R. (1987) *The Global Business*, Prentice Hall International, London.

Lyons, N. (1976) *The Sony Vision*, Wiley, London.

Morita, A., with Reingold, E.M. and Shimomura, M. (1990) *Made in Japan: Akio Morita and Sony*, Fontana, London.

Notes

1 Morita, A., with Reingold, E.M. and Shimomura, M. (1990) *Made in Japan: Akio Morita and Sony*, Fontana, London.
2 Morita, *ibid.*
3 Pralahad, C.K. and Hamel, G. 'The Core Competencies of the Corporation', *Harvard Business Review*, May–June 1990.
4 Lyons, N. (1976) *The Sony Vision*, Wiley, London.

Part II

A Whole New Industry or Way of Doing Things

F or some companies, their business breakthrough required the creation of a whole new industry or way of conducting business. Henry Ford created the mass-produced automobile. Before him, cars were luxury products individually designed around the needs of a particular person. After him, the car was a product for the multitude. Phil Knight achieved a similar breakthrough by taking specialist running shoes away from the track and putting them on the feet of people who wanted style, innovation and, sometimes, fitness.

In creating new industries, these entrepreneurs were often forced to find new ways of conducting business. Henry Ford could not reach a mass market with the production methods that had dominated the nineteenth century. His vision of the best materials and the simplest design for the multitude could only be delivered if Ford transformed the mass production of complex products. Earlier mass-produced products were largely homogeneous items that could be produced in volume, like textiles, or relatively simple products like guns. The car was a complex product that would be used by non-specialists. Mass-producing vehicles called for a revolution in design, engineering and manufacture. Integrated production, novel machine tools and the moving assembly line came together to achieve this transformation.

Standard Oil needed a similar shift in ways of work to create its new industry and way of doing things. Rockefeller shared Ford's attention to detail. He knew that his large and complex organisation would not survive without new ways of working. The rationalisation of the refineries in Cleveland and elsewhere was only part of the picture. His giant enterprise could easily collapse under the scale of its operations. It thrived because Standard Oil pioneered new forms of management. The managerial revolution of the last hundred years has its roots in Standard Oil's ways of working. Standard Oil's use of professional managers, the investment in their training, the emphasis on expertise rather that family or social connection marked the shift from proprietor capitalism to managerial capitalism.

Just as Standard Oil helped to create a new way of managing at the end of the last century, Microsoft is pioneering new ways of managing at the end this century. Microsoft has led a revolution in the use of information and knowledge to gain competitive advantage. The development of MS-DOS as the operating system for personal computers created a global industry standard. Without this standard, it is hard to imagine information technology along its current lines. Before the partnership between IBM and Microsoft there were large numbers of incompatible, conflicting and inaccessible operating systems. The rapid expansion of the market, the large number of applications, the Internet would not be possible with this variety of systems. Microsoft can claim to have created the global market in personal computing.

It calls for a mixture of technical expertise, risk taking and marketing insight to achieve this type of breakthrough. John Moores showed all these in the development of Littlewoods pools. Littlewoods adapted the ideas of John Barnard, the inventor of the first pool, but John Moores created the pools industry. In part, he succeeded because he combined a number of developments in a new unity. These separate elements included the pool itself, mailing lists, the capability of the Post Office to handle documents. These were underpinned by a creative approach to marketing, which allowed his name to be inseparable from the new industry he created.

Chapter 6

Moving Assembly

Henry Ford and the Age of Mass Production

History is bunk

No business leader and no business breakthrough has generated more stories, legends, myths, theories, or had a greater impact on either the popular imagination or academic literature, than Henry Ford and his moving assembly line. This is not really surprising. The twentieth century could reasonably be described as the century of the automobile; and Henry Ford created the mass-produced car. Fordism is the term generally used by academics to define the type of industrial system that has dominated the century.

Henry Ford (1863–1947), was the son of a farmer in rural Michigan (USA) who created then built the Ford Motor Company to the point at which it dominated the US car industry. The company then dominated the US car industry from the turn of the century until the late 1920s through a combination of low prices, volume production and product reliability. Ford's dominance was challenged then overtaken by the US General Motors Corporation (GM). Henry Ford retired from active involvement in the company in the early 1940s but continued the wide range of philanthropic pursuits that had started forty years earlier.

The automobile industry is vast. The latest Fortune 500 (1999) listing of the largest corporations in the USA, ranks General Motors first and Ford second, while two other firms – Exxon and General

Electric – with strong links with the automobile sector, appear in the top five. Elsewhere in the world the pattern is repeated, especially in the biggest and strongest economies. In Japan, Mitsui, Mitsubishi and Toyota (all with strong links to car production) are in the top ten largest companies. The two largest corporations in Germany are Daimler-Benz and Volkswagen. France includes Renault and Peugeot in its top ten, with oil companies like Elf Aquitaine and Total joining them. Italy's largest firm is Fiat, while even Britain's largest company BP has strong links with the motor vehicle industry.

The size of the industry is only part of the picture. Few other industries have captured the imagination as much as cars. Within a few years of the start of the century, and only ten years after the introduction of the Model T Ford in 1908, Tarkington Booth was using the development of the automobile industry as a metaphor for the change from the society and economy of the nineteenth century to modern industrial economy. Booth's *The Magnificent Ambersons* traces the fall of the Amberson family – representing old wealth – and the rise of the Morgans, led by Eugene Morgan, a car producer. Orson Welles' film of the book is just one of many movies that place the automobile at the centre of the plot. As each new communication medium has emerged over the century, it has found a place for the automobile – from TV programmes reviewing cars to computer games simulating driving.

Getting the car to the multitude

Henry Ford would probably have little patience with this romantic view of the automobile. He saw the car primarily as a means of getting from A to B. His oft-quoted approach that 'you can have any colour, so long as its is black' reflected this view – that cars were commodities, and the main determinant of which car to buy was price. Ford had little doubt that his aim was 'to get the car to the multitude' and that this breakthrough required far lower prices and a revolution in production methods. His ambition was clear. He wanted 'to construct and market an automobile, specially designed for everyday wear and

The Ford Motor Company has emerged at the end of the 1990s, once again, as the largest car producer in the USA. In 1998, Ford sold 4.37 million vehicles in the USA and almost 2.5 million elsewhere. Since its formation in 1903, the company has sold over 270 million vehicles worldwide. The foundation of this success was Henry Ford's determination to produce a simple, well designed and engineered car 'so low in price that no man making a good salary will be unable to own one'. Ford rethought the entire production process of automobiles to create in the Tin Lizzie, or Model T, the vehicle to turn this vision into reality. Eventually, the Model T sold so many cars that it has only been outsold by two other vehicles in history, despite the vastly increased levels of car use and production over the sixty years since the Model T ceased production. Ford's personal stamp on the business was so great that it is, perhaps, no coincidence that it once again tops the car sales league table when his grandson, Henry Ford III, is company chairman. Even the company's greatest rivals – from General Motors in the US to the Japanese car giants – have adopted and adapted many of Ford's ideas and principles, even when his successors at Ford ignored them.

tear – business, professional and family use ... a machine which will be admired by man, woman, and child for its compactness, its simplicity, its safety, its all-round convenience, and – last but not least – its exceedingly reasonable price, which places it within the reach of many thousands who could not think of paying the comparatively fabulous prices asked for most machines.'

This vision could not be delivered by the production systems that dominated car manufacture when Henry Ford started making cars in the 1890s and the early years of this century. Most cars were made by hand. In 1899, there were thirty manufacturers in the USA producing around 2500 cars – or less than thirty cars each. Henry Ford's first car was built over several months in a garden shed next to his house. The shed's doorway was, however, too small for the new automobile so Ford had to break down the wall to liberate his new vehicle. This experience probably taught him his first important lesson in car production – never let your production facilities limit your product capabilities. Later he was to build the largest factories in the world, first at Highland Park and then at River Rouge.

By the time River Rouge was in full production, it included all the elements needed for the large-scale production of cars. The plant incorporated a steel mill, glass factory and the automobile assembly line. It was the first fully integrated factory system, with iron ore and coal arriving at the docks on the Great Lakes to be converted into the high tensile steel needed for car springs, axles and car bodies, and eventually the cars themselves. In effect, coal and iron ore went in one end and cars came out the other. By 1930 there were over 80,000 men on the pay roll and the factory had cost $269 million dollars to build.

Twenty five years earlier, Ford employed 125 people to produce 1700 vehicles a year. This was not his first move into car production. Besides making cars for his own use (and subsequent sale), Ford had already helped to set up the Detroit Automobile Company. When that failed, he moved on to the Henry Ford Company (after a brief excursion to racing cars), which survived only four months before he left the company that bore his name. Soon after, he started Ford & Malcomson and its subsidiary, the Ford Motor Company. His partnership with Alex Y. Malcomson lasted several years, until it collapsed with a row between the two principals over the future direction of car production.

Initially, Ford and Malcomson shared the view of the five hundred or more other automobile producers that started in the USA around the turn of the century. Most saw cars as essentially a luxury item, made 'to order and to get the largest possible price for each car.'[1] The company did very well at this. Its first car, the Model A, cost $554 to produce, and sold for $750. By the end of the first year, it had made 1695 vehicles and earned profits of $98,851 (over $3 million at current prices). Ford, however, was not content. He disliked the constant modifications and product changes with the models B, C and F on the stocks. He jibbed at the idea of a new grand luxury touring car, the Model K, which would sell for $1375.[2]

Growing by leaps and bounds

Henry Ford's determination to move in the opposite direction, and produce the cheaper, lower profit margin Model N, provoked a rupture with Malcomson. In November 1905, the Ford Manufacturing Company was incorporated, and less than a year later Henry Ford bought out Malcomston's stock in the Ford Motor Company. He was in full control and determined 'that it will grow by leaps and bounds.' Ford had already decided what kind of car he wanted to build in order to break out from the confines of small scale, bespoke manufacture. In 1907 his prospectus said: 'It [the car] will be large enough for the family, but small enough for the individual to run and take care of. It will be constructed of the best material, by the best men to be hired, after the simplest designs that modern engineering can devise. But it will be so low in price that no man making a good salary will be unable to own one.'

Few business people have been so clear about their vision, and so determined (and successful) in realising their aspiration. The story of Henry Ford's breakthrough can almost be structured in terms of this prospectus. His first substantial problem was fitting the body with the engine that he wanted to use.

Ford realised very early that reliability was an important consideration for the vast market of middle to lower income buyers that he wanted to reach. They could not afford to have their cars off the road or out of action for days while mechanics tinkered and repaired the vehicle. This might be part of the fun for the first generation of users but his potential customers wanted a workhorse that would go on forever. Henry Ford was determined that 'a man who bought one of our cars was in my opinion entitled to continuous use of that car.'[3] His initial success was in the use of the rugged four-cylinder engine in the Model N. This engine was reliable but still struggled to cope with the weight of a car made with conventional steels.

Henry Ford decided to tackle this problem head-on with a search for much lighter steels with good tensile strength. This would give body strength without weight. Ford's search led the company to a French-made vanadium alloy with a tensile strength three times that of the best US steels i.e. 170,000 lbs of tensile strength versus 60,000 lbs. Once the body weight was reduced, several additional developments could be incorporated into the car. The first was an engine, redesigned to improve further its reliability. This was achieved by moving to a single caste engine block, which contained all four cylinders instead of bolting the cylinders together. Second, a new transmission system was introduced and finally the electrics were developed.

These improvements in the car's configuration were not, of themselves, enough to deliver his vision, but he was using 'the best material' and his designs were probably the simplest 'that modern engineering can devise.' In his factory on Piquette Avenue, Ford was experimenting with the approach to production that would underpin his business breakthrough. He had long made no secret of his irritation with the traditional way of making cars based on individual models with wide variations in specifications. In 1907, he decided to drop all other models under production in favour of the Model N. The results were dramatic. Output soared to over 8,000 vehicles and profits broke through the $1 million barrier. Despite this success, Ford was already working in a room with 'a good lock for the door (and) ... a door in big enough to run a car in and out' on the next stage in his breakthrough.

In this development he showed many of the key characteristics of the outstanding entrepreneur. He could immerse himself in detail while still keeping his eye on the big picture. The early magnitos did not work. He tinkered until he discovered not only that the problem was poor insulation but, with the help of several large maple syrup boiling kettles, found a way to produce better insulation. He 'walked the talk' by involving himself fully with the team, tackling the problem with no barriers of status, position or wealth. Ford also showed that distinctive ability to think long – envisaging a mass market for cars – and act short; building a car that the mass market could afford.

Tin Lizzie

The car that turned Henry Ford's vision into reality was the Model T. It achieved almost instant success, with demand far outstripping supply despite a sixty per cent increase in factory output. The Model T's success was based on a simple but radical decision. Henry Ford decided to reverse engineer his new car. This meant that he started with the production process and built the car for ease, speed and reliability of production. Until then, the car was designed around the customer's personal specifications and the production process was then fitted around the car. This is inevitable in bespoke cars – why should buyers worry about the way the way vehicles were made, provided they fit their specifications and the agreed price.

This shift to large-scale production transformed the car market by creating the pattern of 'push and pull' that still dominates the vehicle industry. The 'push' of production – large numbers of cars coming out of the production line – forces car companies to stimulate demand, arrive at clever methods of finance and develop incentives like trade-ins. The efforts to stimulate demand or 'pull' from the market, when successful, produce pressure on the factory to increase and improve output. More output 'push' demands more market 'pull' and a better understanding of market needs – and so on. While Ford was devising methods of improving productivity, he was also introducing a range of promotional ploys such as the Ford rodeos in which cowboys in Model Ts tried to rope calves.

Highland Park

Output increased at the Piquette Avenue factory but not enough to keep up with demand. Within two years of starting production of the Model T in 1908, Ford moved production into a new purpose built factory in Highland Park. Initially, there was no significant change in production methods with teams of workers working on the car from start to finish. This method, however, still failed to keep up with demand, which was soaring ahead of supply – despite doubling output every year. Output increased from just under 1600 cars in 1906, to 78,440 in 1912.

Ford's manufacturing breakthrough – that changed the nature of industry – was based on three principles. The first was his decision to standardise the product so that each car was the same 'just like one pin is like another pin when it comes from the pin factory, or one match is like another match when it comes from the match factory.' His second decision was to standardise the components used in manufacture, thereby reducing the amount of technical skill required by workers. These two actions allowed productivity to increase but output was still restricted by the requirement for a team of workers to work together on a single vehicle.

The symbol of modern mass production

The real breakthrough occurred when Ford introduced the moving assembly line. Alfred D. Chandler Jr, the leading business historian, describes the scale of the change:

> 'The moving assembly line was first tried in assembling the flywheel magnito, then other parts of the engine, next the engine itself, and finally in October 1913, in assembling the chassis and completed car. The innovation – the moving assembly line – was an immediate success. The speed of throughput soared. Labour time expended in making a Model T dropped from 12 hours and 8 minutes to 2 hours and 35 minutes per car. By the spring of 1914 the Highland Park plant was turning out 1000 cars a day and the average labour time per car dropped to 1 hour and 33 minutes. The moving assembly line quickly became the best-known symbol of modern mass production.'

The introduction of the moving assembly line saw output double immediately, from just under 80,000 vehicles to almost 160,000. Equally striking was the impact on productivity. Increased output had, in the past, required almost equivalent increases in the size of the labour force. The introduction of the moving assembly line vastly increased output but the number of workers actually dropped. Output continued to increase so that in 1914 Ford produced 250,000 Model Ts with largely the same size workforce as had been needed for much smaller production levels.

At the same time the company initiated a series of price cuts that reflected the reductions in production costs. The 'Tin Lizzie' cost over $800 when it was introduced in 1908 but the price soon dropped below $700 getting down to $575 by 1912 and around $450 at the start of 1914. The reductions in price coincided with a boom in the US economy that saw wages increase significantly. This meant that when the Model T was introduced in 1908, its price was slightly less than the average male annual wage. By 1914 the combination of higher wages and lower prices meant that the price was more like a third of average annual wages.

The impact went beyond improvements in productivity and reductions in prices. John D. Rockefeller described Highland Park as 'the industrial miracle of the age.' While the social reformer Edward S. Filene said that 'mass production is … production for the masses … (and is) based upon the clear understanding that increased production requires increased buying, and that the greatest total profits can be obtained only if the masses can and do enjoy a higher and ever higher standard of living.' Not everyone was as enthusiastic. A worker's wife wrote to Henry Ford that 'the chain system that you have is a slave driver.' One worker commented that 'a man checks in his brain and his freedom at the door when he goes to work at Ford's.'

Save ten steps a day

Henry Ford claimed that the inspiration for his innovation came 'in a general way from the overhead trolly that Chicago packers use in dressing beef.' He had noticed how butchers in the stockyards pushed the carcass from one to the other cutting off certain pieces as it moved along. This reduced the amount of time butchers were obliged to spend moving from one position to the next. 'Save ten steps a day for each of 12,000 employees, and you will have saved fifty miles of wasted motion and misspent energy.' Henry Ford's energy went into saving his workers engaging in unproductive tasks 'there is no lifting or trucking ... no workman has anything to do with lifting or trucking.' The impact on output was dramatic. Ten years earlier Ford needed 300 men to produce 658 cars in a factory covering 1.4 acres. In 1914, 13,000 workers produced 260,720 cars – up from slightly more than 2 cars per man-year to more than twenty. No other car producer came close. Across the rest of the US vehicles industry 66,350 workers made 286,770 cars – only slightly better production rates than Ford was achieving a decade earlier.

Ford was now in control of a production process that seemed to confirm his view that 'everything can always be done better than it is being done.' He focused his considerable energies in doing just that. The 'endless chain driven belt' was introduced at Highland Park at the start of 1914. Shortly after, the system was reconfigured to be 'man high' so that belts and parts moved at waist high. Operations could be repeated without workers needing to stoop or bend. Process innovations (improvements in the ways of making cars) continued apace. New machine tools built increasingly standardised parts. Dedicated machines were developed which performed a single purpose. A Ford drill press, for example, simultaneously drilled forty-five holes in an engine block from various angles. Gravity slides were introduced that speeded the movement of components so that nothing was delayed because of a lack of parts.

The decision to focus on production efficiency did not distract Ford from the need to continually stimulate demand and ensure that dealer networks existed to elicit the maximum demand for his output. Ford imposed strict targets on its dealers. One dealer describes the change this produced. 'When I first took the agency I was my own boss like any other business man, selling as many cars as I could and buying more when I needed them ... Then one day a representative of the (Ford) Company came to see me ... and said ten cars a month was not enough for a dealer like me to sell. It seems that the company had done a survey of my territory and decided that the sales possibilities were much greater. Benson (the Ford representative) said that my quota had been fixed at twenty cars a month, and from then on that number would be shipped to me ... I told Benson where to get off at ... Benson was pretty hard boiled ... Either I could buy twenty cars a month or the company would find another dealer.'[4]

The twin pressures of price reductions and increased prosperity drove up US demand for cars. In 1916 the Model T's price was cut to $360 while total output exceeded 500,000 vehicles – roughly half the total US production – and profits doubled from $30 million to $60 million. By then, however, new challenges were emerging to test Henry Ford's ability to sustain his breakthrough. The first was technical. The problems with the Highland Park complex were becoming apparent. A multi-story building was not the optimum configuration for flow product. A larger flat site was necessary to minimise unproductive activities like transporting goods to upper levels, or shifting products from floor to floor. Besides this, a newly designed facility could gain maximum production leverage from the new scale of operations. The plant could consume the output of a steel mill or glassworks, so why not have these as integral parts of the factory. A new plant to incorporate these ideas was under development before the Highland Park plant reached maximum production.

The weight of a tack

The other difficulty faced by Ford did not lend itself to such an engineered solution. The new production methods were deeply unpopular with workers. One man working on seat upholstery described the problem. 'The weight of a tack in the hands of an upholsterer is insignificant, but if you have to drive eight tacks in every Ford cushion that goes past your station within a certain time, and you know that if you fail to do it you are going to tie up the entire platform, and you continue to do this for four years, you are going to break

under the strain.'[5] Ford had achieved the breakthrough in car production described in his 1907 vision statement but his workers hated
their job and labour turnover rates were increasing even faster that
output. In 1913, to retain 100 people on the payroll, Ford had to
recruit 963 workers.

His solution lay in an initiative in social engineering. At the
beginning of 1914, he announced a new minimum wage of $5 a
day. This was an unheard of amount for an unskilled manual worker
and transformed, once again, the economics of the industry. The
immediate response was a vast surge in demand for work at the
company as thousands queued for work. This pool of new labour
enabled Ford to introduce two related changes. These were, the
move from a nine-hour to an eight-hour day and the introduction
of a third shift. The factory could now work around the clock in
three eight-hour shifts instead of the two nine-hour shifts followed
by a close down. The immediate impact was a surge in popularity
as the $5 a day became seen as 'a blessing – bigger than you know.'

Output surged again with the added advantage for Ford that his
rivals were forced to match his high wage rates but with lower outputs to cover their costs. In 1919 output was over 750,000 vehicles
(out of a total, industry production of 1.7 million vehicles). Despite
the post-war slump in the US economy, car sales continued to be
strong, and reached the magic one million mark in 1922. Ford had
actually broken through the one million vehicle mark several years
before, when sales of trucks were included.

The early 1920s completed Ford's breakthrough from an idi-
osyncratic manufacturer of bespoke vehicles to the dominant producer of the most important manufactured product in the world.
Work on the giant River Rouge plant that would incorporate all his
innovations was well advanced. His great rival, Alfred P. Sloan of
General Motors, summarised the breakthrough. 'There was a period before 1908, which with its expensive cars was entirely that of a
class market; then from the period 1908 to the mid-twenties which
was primarily that of a mass market, *ruled by Ford* (my italics).'[6] At
its peak, the Model T was selling over two million a year, at a price
which bottomed out at $260 in 1925.

The decisions Ford made; to standardise production methods, to concentrate on one model, to use standard components and design the car to be produced, transformed industry. He showed a remarkable ability to think long and act short, such as when he developed first Highland Park then River Rouge. The same insight was shown when he confounded convention by introducing the $5 wage, the inflatable tyre and the closed-in, weatherproof car. The high point, however, was his decision to change the way cars were made and introduce mass production based on the continuously moving assembly line. This breakthrough changed the world. A few years later, his great rival Alfred P. Sloan at General Motors overtook Ford in sales and market power. It is, however, fitting that in the last years of the century Ford is once again the largest manufacturer of cars in the USA – a century Henry Ford helped to create.

Further reading

Batchelor, R. (1995) *Henry Ford, Mass Production and Design*, St Martin's Press, London.

Lacey, R. (1986) *Ford*, Pan Books, London.

Nevins, A. and Hill, F. (1954, 1957, 1963) *Ford*, (3 Volumes), Charles Schribner and Sons, New York.

Wik, R.M. (1972) *Henry Ford and Grass Roots America*, University of Michigan Press, MI.

Notes

1   Ford, Henry (1922) 'What I Learned About Business', from Henry Ford with Samuel Crowther, *My Life and Work*, Doubleday, New York; reprinted in Krass, P. (1997) *The Book of Business Wisdom*, John Wiley and Sons, London.

2   Lacey, R. (1986) *Ford*, Pan Books, London.

3   Ford, Henry (1922) 'What I Learned About Business', *ibid.*

4   American Social History Project (1992) *Who Built America,* Paneon Books, New York.
5   American Social History Project (1992) *ibid.*
6   Sloan, A.P. (1986) *My Years with General Motors,* Penguin, Harmondsworth.

Chapter 7

The Great Octopus

John D. Rockefeller and Standard Oil

A Baptist fundamentalist with a head for figures

J ohn Davison Rockefeller (1839–1937) was probably the richest man in history, with a fortune estimated at around $150 billion at current values. Born in Richford, near Ithaca, New York, he made his fortune in the oil business during the Cleveland oil boom. His Standard Oil Company dominated almost all United States oil production, refining and distribution, and much of the world's oil trade. He saw the oil industry shift from a producer of lighting fuels (kerosene) to the main source of energy during the twentieth century. Standard Oil's control of the oil industry was so great that the US Supreme Court forced the company to dissolve. Rockefeller devoted much of his later life to philanthropy.

During his ascendancy at Standard Oil, John D. Rockefeller's associates, rivals and critics attributed to him superhuman powers as a business builder and manager. Edward T. Bedford, a Standard Oil executive commented that: 'Mr Rockefeller was really a superman. He not only envisaged a new system of business upon grand scale but he also had the patience, the courage and the audacity to put it into effect in the face of almost insuperable difficulties, sticking to his purpose with a tenacity and confidence [that were] simply amazing.'[1] John D. Archibold – a one time critic, then associate and later Rockefeller's successor – said 'Rockefeller always sees a little

further than the rest of us – and then he sees around the corner.'
Vision, audacity, patience, tenacity and confidence, these were some
of the characteristics that led to the creation of first Standard Oil,
then the Standard Oil Trust.

This enterprise – The Great Octopus or The Anaconda –once
controlled almost 90 per cent of the US oil industry and around
three-quarters of the world market. Standard Oil grew out of a series
of decisions made by Rockefeller and his associates in 1872. This
annus mirabilis for Standard Oil illustrates how breakthroughs often
emerge from a set of decisions or actions rather than a single action.
The skill with which the ground was prepared, the audacity of their
execution and the brilliance of the follow-up provide a timeless example for business building. The breakthrough, which established
Standard Oil's dominance of the oil industry for at least half a century, was built on three related decisions.

The first was that the industry in which Standard operated – oil
refining – was in urgent need of consolidation. The second decision
was that attention to detail was the key to success despite the industry's turbulence. The oil industry that Rockefeller entered in 1862 at
the age of 23 seems a strange choice for a Baptist fundamentalist
with a head for figures and a love of order. Third, he used his financial skills to build up a strong asset base, which he refused to dilute.
He preferred to give stock than pay cash. He liked to describe himself as 'just a man of figures (who) learned to have great respect for
figures and facts, no matter how small they were ... I had a passion
for detail which afterwards I was forced to strive to modify.'[2] When
searching for his first full-time job, it is said that his opening line was
'I understand bookkeeping, and I'd like to get work.' In contrast, he
was entering a boom industry, in which natural assets, invention and
enterprise had become a magnet for 'hundreds of thousands of provi-
dent working men, who prefer the profits of petroleum to the small
rates of interest afforded by savings banks'. Congressman and future
President of the United States, James Garfield commented that 'the
(oil) fever has assailed Congress.'

Rockefeller was drawn into the oil industry by a fellow Baptist,
Samuel Andrews, who had developed a system for distilling oil-based

Few companies have ever achieved the type of dominance that Standard Oil exercised in the USA at the turn of this century. Its success was built around a revolution in organisation and management that was orchestrated by John D. Rockefeller. His turbulent early life with a father who was both a bigamist and a 'snake oil' salesman probably made him crave order. Standard Oil's breakthrough was based on the order the company imposed, first on the refinery industry in Cleveland, then on the US oil industry. In the last quarter of the nineteenth century Standard Oil and the Standard Oil Trust controlled over ninety per cent of the US oil refinery output and had a dominant position across the world. Rockefeller spotted that control could be imposed by achieving economies of scale and driving costs down. He linked this to the creation of a new cadre of professional manager who changed the face of industry. Even after Standard Oil was broken up by order of the US government, the successor companies like Exxon continued to grow and prosper because of the systems and structures set up by Rockefeller. Decades later these successor businesses still control over half the US market and have major shares across the world.

kerosene from crude oil. The crude itself came from the booming oil fields of Pennsylvania. The boom was sparked by Colonel Edwin L. Drake's success in drilling for oil in Titusville, Pennsylvania. Drake was acting on behalf of a group of investors who had developed a method of drilling for oil. His success was so great that he was soon overrun by competitors. The timing of Drake's discovery was excellent. The US population was surging ahead. In the cities, in particular, demand for cheap and reliable fuel for lighting soared. The Civil War cut off supplies of the only reliable alternative – the turpentine derivative, camphene.

Tinkers and tailors and the boys who followed the plough

During the 1860s, production boomed as new fields were discovered. Within a year of Drake's breakthrough, there were 50 other wells in the area. A year later, the number had doubled. The pace of exploitation was increased by the system of exploitation known as the 'rule of capture'. This meant that once a discovery was made, rivals could tap the same source by drilling diagonally into the field. There was no incentive to husband or conserve supplies. Production and waste increased while prices soared and collapsed as old sources ran out and new reserves were discovered.

The first refineries opened shortly after. Within three years of Drake's discovery, there were 20 small refineries in the Oil Regions; five in Pittsburgh, and the first refineries were started in Cleveland. During 1860, almost half a million barrels of oil (up from 2000 barrels in 1859) were shipped from western Pennsylvania, at prices that seldom dropped below $10 a barrel. The economics of the industry were transformed again when the Empire Well became the first 'gusher', producing 3000 barrels a day and provoking a collapse in oil prices from $10 a day in January 1861 to 50 cents in June and 10 cents in December. Demand, however, soon caught up and prices were back to $5 a barrel by the end of 1861. The end of the Civil War 'released thousands and thousands of veterans who poured into the oil regions to start their lives again and seek their fortunes.'[3]

Prices would creep up – to as high as $12 a barrel in 1864 – and collapse as new wells or new technologies emerged – down to just over $2 in 1865. Profits followed prices. Rockefeller saw 'tinkers and tailors and the boys who followed the plough' enter the industry and emerge 'disappointed if they did not make one hundred per cent profit in a year – sometimes in six months.'[4] Production, however, continued to surge during the 1860s. Output grew from half a million barrels in 1859 to three million barrels in 1862 and just under 5.5 million in 1871, but the pressure on prices was inexorably down.

Opportunity in every disaster

The two sides of Rockefeller's personality – his desire for order and his belief in 'seeing opportunity in every disaster' – combined to prompt him to find ways to break out of this vicious circle of boom and bust. The crisis of 1870 forced his hand. During that year total refining capacity was three times the amount of oil being pumped and an estimated 90 per cent of refineries were operating in the red. Rockefeller acknowledged that his decision to eliminate the 'ruinous competition' in the industry was made around that time, especially as the purchase of a major rival in 1870 gave him the leverage he needed to act.

He decided to replace competition with co-operation and establish firm control of the refinery sector. He recognised that the key to most business breakthroughs was control of a key process on the route from extraction of a natural resource to the end-user. There is usually some point along the way where a specific opportunity exists – especially in the early years of an industry's development – to consolidate and achieve control. In the oil industry of the late nineteenth century that point existed in the refining process. This was partly because refining offered genuine cost economies of scale in production. The unit costs of production, for example, could be halved by increasing output from 500 barrels a day to 1500 barrels a day. There were no similar opportunities in production or taking the product to market. Rockefeller's bookkeeping, his attention to detail and his determination to squeeze costs combined with his willingness to invest in increased capacity strengthened his position. At the start of his battle for control in 1870 his new company, Standard Oil, was the largest and easily the most profitable refiner in the world.

The Cleveland Massacre

In the battle for the control required for a breakthrough, allies were sought vertically and horizontally. Rockefeller drew his rival refiners into the newly formed South Improvement Company. Virtually every refiner in Cleveland joined the South Improvement Company and in the process ceded its independence to Standard Oil. The offer made to most was very simple. One refiner summed it up as 'if we did not sell out, we would be crushed out.' Another quoted Rockefeller as saying, 'this scheme is bound to work. It means an absolute control by us of the oil business. There is no chance for anyone outside.' The threat, however, was mixed with the promise of secure prices and incomes, and long-term growth and profits. Consolidation and control were so important to the breakthrough that weak companies were given surprisingly generous terms to join the combine. Even rivals conceded that 'some refineries were not making money and they were the first to run for cover and sell out.'[5]

Rockefeller's planning was meticulous. In his own words: ' I had our plan clearly in mind. It was right. I knew it as a matter of conscience … If I had to do it tomorrow, I would do it again in the same way – do it a hundred times.'[6] He also knew that his control had to extend down the distribution system. The railway companies were essential allies. Without their support – especially through rebates – new rivals could emerge, get access to markets and undermine Standard Oil's control. The support of the railway companies added further steel to the invitation to join the South Improvement Company. Frank Rockefeller (John D.'s estranged brother) quoted this side of the promise as: 'If you don't sell your property to us it will become valueless, because we've got the advantage with the railways.'

The basic deal with the railways was very simple. Standard and the South Improvement Company would guarantee the railway companies fixed and large orders for shipping their product. In return there would be massive rebates on the published charges for shipping crude and refined oil: 40–50 per cent off the quoted prices for shipping crude and 25–50 per cent off the prices for shipping refined oil. The most controversial aspect of the deal was the drawbacks the company was promised on the shipments made by rivals. This meant that when rivals shipped oil by the participating railways, the South Improvement Company was paid up to 40 cents for every barrel shipped (around 25 per cent of the shipping costs). The Company agreed to allocate its shipments among the railways to a fixed formula, with the Pennsylvania Railway getting 45 per cent and the Erie and New York Central getting 27.5 per cent each.

There was nothing new about rebates on oil shipments. In 1870, Rockefeller's partner, Henry Flagler, had negotiated a deal with the New York Central Railway that gave Standard Oil a rebate of 35 per cent off the published charges – in return for guaranteed volumes. It was its scale, comprehensive nature and the added twist of the drawback that made the proposals of the South Improvement Company so controversial. Once it was exposed, and before any oil was shipped, the plans leaked. The oilfields exploded in protest against 'the cruellest and most deadly [device against the extinction of competition] yet conceived by any group of American industrialists.' Within weeks the 'great conspiracy' was on the point of collapse especially as the New York refiners, who had been left out of the original arrangements, combined with the independents and the producers to put pressure on the railway companies. By mid-April, the South Improvement Company was dead as the Pennsylvania legislature cancelled its charter, Congress attacked the 'gigantic and daring conspiracy' and the rebates were declared void.

The collapse of the Company merely highlighted the skill with which Rockefeller had placed himself in a win–win situation. The edifice of the South Improvement Company was destroyed but Standard Oil had won control of virtually all of Cleveland's oil refining capacity. The 'Cleveland Massacre' saw him wipe out local rivals and acquire 22 out of 25 rivals in just over a month. He had achieved control of a major refining centre. He had also learned how to use Standard Oil's economic power to force rivals into submission and suppliers into partnership. He used these lessons to provide focus for his company and leverage for his resources in the next stages of his breakthrough. Standard Oil was 'ready to take on the entire oil industry.'[7]

Within weeks of the collapse of the South Improvement Company, Standard Oil executives opened negotiations with major refineries in Pittsburgh to absorb their operations while the railways were under new pressure on rebates. The message combined the familiar with the new. The established message was that by acting together they were stronger than as rivals. The new message was that Standard Oil's Cleveland-based operations were now so large, efficient and well resourced that opposition would be pointless. The thrust of all these efforts was to focus the resources generated by scale and control to build up market power. This market power could then be applied to gain maximum leverage for the company's efforts. This combination of control, focus and leverage creates a virtuous circle that recurs in many business breakthroughs and the best business decisions.

The idea was mine

Preparation is essential. Rockefeller showed this in the ways that he prepared the ground for his breakthrough. His groundwork is shown in the way he built Standard Oil in the days before the breakthroughs of 1872. The quality of his preparation was also shown in the financial muscle he organised to back his efforts. After 1872, he saw the experiences of that year as essential preparation for extending his control beyond Cleveland, across the USA and to the world. In his later life, he was not afraid to say, 'the idea was mine. The idea was persisted in, too, in spite of the opposition of some who became faint hearted at the magnitude of the undertaking, as it constantly assumed larger proportions.'

The building blocks of Standard Oil's success were an attention to detail that became legendary and an ability to see the big picture – especially the links between the components in that big picture. The attention to detail is illustrated by the story told of Rockefeller's encounter with a welder who was spot welding oil tanks. He asked how many welds were used to seal a tank. On being told 50, he asked the welder to try a smaller number, until a seal was made. Eventually, they found that a seal with 49 welds was sufficient – saving only cents on a tank but thousands of dollars across a production run. Rockefeller innovated to save money and to get an advantage. He constantly sought uses for 'waste' products. These contributed to his reputation for probity and his company's strong balance sheet. He never made a loss and at the end of the 1860s managed to pay a dividend of over 100 per cent during one of the century's worst financial bloodbaths.

Standard Oil's strong balance sheet and Rockefeller's reputation meant that neither was short of backers at the start of 1872. This was essential as, in preparation for the battles ahead, Standard Oil extended its capital base from $1 million to $3.5 million. On the day the company's executive committee agreed to reinforce the capital base, it went on to agree the acquisition strategy that would underpin their policies for the rest of the year. They knew that in their struggle for a breakthrough, deep pockets were essential.

Standard Oil made other preparations to secure its position. Several years earlier, William Rockefeller, John's other brother, set up a New York office with a particular role to build up exports. Even earlier, Rockefeller pioneered the use of metal tank cars to replace the dangerous and wasteful wooden barrels used originally by the railways. The company acquired large numbers of these cars, giving it a powerful bargaining counter with the railways. Acquisitions were undertaken with speed and secrecy. Many newly acquired firms retained their name and identify but were firmly controlled from the centre.

Turning the screw

This approach paid massive dividends when the first steps were taken to gain maximum leverage from the control achieved in Cleveland during 1872. The initial targets were the leading refiners in the main competing centres of Pittsburgh/Philadelphia and New York. By late 1874, half the refineries in Pittsburgh/Philadelphia and leading companies in New York were acquired. It is said that one rival was induced to join with the simple expedient of inviting him to inspect the books and then decide whether he wanted to battle on. Increasing control meant that attention could be focussed on those who stood out against Standard Oil's market power. The technique known as 'turning the screw' took two basic forms – friendly and unfriendly. The former meant that an opportunity was presented to merge into the company – often with a good salary, shares and a degree of autonomy. Unfriendly led to sharp hikes in freight charges from shippers, new competitors arriving at your doorstep with vastly reduced prices or quiet advice to traders not to stock. The policies were classic examples of game theory applied before the underlying theory was expounded. Pittsburg, New York, even Oil Creek – the original source of oil and home of The Anaconda's fiercest enemies – were soon dominated by Standard Oil.

The new challenge facing Rockefeller and Standard Oil lay in building on this control, retaining the central focus of the company, building on its core competencies and getting maximum leverage from their power and resources. The immediate difficulty lay in stopping the company from collapsing under the weight of its size and complexity. Confounding the prediction of one rival that 'it [Standard Oil] has no future, the organisation will fall under its own weight' was the immediate challenge.

From its earliest days, Standard Oil placed a massive premium on talent. Some of its most important leaders won their position because they had challenged its power from outside and demonstrated their abilities. John Archibold emerged originally as a powerful opponent of the South Improvement Company. His energy, talent and determination so impressed Rockefeller that Archibold was persuaded to join Standard Oil and eventually succeeded him at the top of the firm. Talent, energy, drive, loyalty and discretion were far more important to success at Standard Oil than social position or influence. This emphasis on people skills recurred in Rockefeller's actions and comments. His view that 'I will pay more for the ability to deal with people than for any other under the sun' highlights the priority he placed on talent.

This collection of talent was welded together in a surprisingly democratic way. Rockefeller managed by consensus, which he explained as '(making) sure that we were right and planned for every contingency before we went ahead.' This delivered three tangible benefits. First, it avoided the stresses between powerful leaders that could destroy the company. Second, it forced them to plan for the unexpected in a new and changing industry. Finally, it allowed Rockefeller to distance himself from the less acceptable actions of his subordinates. The success of this approach led Ralph and Muriel Hidy, the historians of Standard Oil, to conclude that 'his greatest contribution, beyond the concept of the Standard Oil combination itself, was the persuasion of strong men to join the alliance and to work together effectively in its management.' As Standard Oil grew, the underlying approach became more formalised. A committee system emerged which formalised this approach to management and became the bedrock of Standard Oil's system of management.

A pipeline to the sea

Secure in its home base with increasing control over overseas markets, Standard Oil's focus shifted to gaining increased leverage by an even sharper emphasis on getting the best from its assets. It initially involved seeing off a major challenge to its market dominance. In the process, the company undermined the power of its only serious rival for control over market access. The challenge came from the Tidewater PipeLine Company. This was created by a group of independent refiners and producers that sought to break the stranglehold on railway rates that Standard established in 1872. The Tidewater PipeLine Company's aim was to build a pipeline from the oil regions to the sea – effectively eliminating the need to ship by rail. The technical, operational and legal difficulties were immense. No one had ever shipped oil over these distances and Standard Oil was determined to block the pipeline's progress. Despite these obstacles the pipe was built and went into operation in less than a year.

Initially, Rockefeller's response was to challenge and compete with Tidewater. Gradually, however, he sought to win control of its operations. Eventually, Standard Oil won control of the pipeline so that by 1882 it controlled almost 90 per cent of the pipeline trade. In defeating this threat to its control over the refineries, Standard Oil destroyed any threat that the railways might pose to its control over access to markets. Rates were forced down and rebates were increased while the network of pipelines expanded across the USA. The Standard Oil Trust – which consolidated control over the industry – was established as the new pipelines neared completion. Processing costs dropped from 2.5 cents a gallon in 1880 to 0.4 cents a gallon in 1885. Shipping costs dropped equally quickly but profit margins soared. The same years saw control of the Trust move to its new headquarters in New York where Rockefeller established perhaps the first 'extensive managerial hierarchy to co-ordinate, monitor and plan for this global industrial empire.'[8]

The final twist in the sequence of events that flowed from the breakthrough of 1872 seems at first to challenge this view of the enterprise as increasingly dominated by managers and bureaucrats. The Trust's control over processing, distribution and market access left only one major domestic source of threat – the raw material itself. Two fears interacted to prompt concern about supplies. First, there were worries about total stocks. In the early 1880s, Pennsylvania was the only significant source of oil. How would this great company survive if stocks ran out? Second, there were worries about the impact of new discoveries outside the firm's areas of operation. It had shown the ways profits could be won. This might encourage rivals.

The second fear was realised with the discovery of oil in Ohio and Indiana. The oil itself was of poor quality. A major research programme was required to develop a refining process that would produce an acceptable product. The costs of this research could only be justified if Standard owned sufficient leases on the wells themselves to ensure a return. Rockefeller was determined to hold onto the market power and control that had been achieved. He pressed for major investments in the purchase of leases and the research programme. He faced major opposition on the board that went on 'day by day, month by month, year after year.' The impasse was broken when Rockefeller put his fate and that of his fortune at risk with a daring offer. He pledged $3 million of his own money for the investment with the offer 'if it is a success the company can reimburse me. If it is a failure, I will take the loss.' His chastened colleagues capitulated, rejected his offer and agreed to the investment. Soon, the weak link in Standard Oil's chain of control had been eliminated.

Architects of success

The architects of the successes of 1872, especially Rockefeller and Flagler, won immense personal wealth. The Standard Oil Trust grew rapidly until the US Supreme Court broke it up into its 38 subsidiary companies. It was one of the largest corporations in the world, while Rockefeller was the richest person. Many of the successor companies – Exxon Corporation, Mobil Corporation, Chevron Corporation, Amoco Corporation, and Atlantic Richfield Company – still feature in rankings of the world's largest corporations. The combined market capitalisation of these companies is around $500 billion, which is around $100 billion bigger than Microsoft, the contemporary firm with the largest market capitalisation. Rockefeller seems to have made good the promise to Isaac Hewitt, a rival refiner, in 1872 that 'I have ways of making money you know nothing about.'

Further reading

Chernow, R. (1998) *Titan: The Life of John D. Rockefeller, Sr.*, Random House, New York.
Coffey, Ellen G. (1989) *John D. Rockefeller: Empire Builder*, Silver Burdett, New York. (For younger readers.)
Harr, John E. and Johnson, P.J. (1988) *The Rockefeller Century*, Scribner, New York.
Nevins, Allan (1940, reprinted 1976) *John D. Rockefeller: The Heroic Age of American Enterprise* (2 volumes), Kraus, New York.

Notes

1   Chernow, R. (1998) *Titan: The Life of John D. Rockefeller, Sr.*, Random House, New York.
2   Rockefeller, J.D. (1984) *Random Reminiscences of Men and Events*, Sleepy Hollow Press and RAC, Tarrytown, NY.
3   Yergin, D. (1991) *The Prize*, Simon and Schuster, London.

4   Rockefeller Archive Centre, Sleepy Hollow, New York, quoted in Chernow, R. (1998) *Titan: The Life of John D. Rockefeller, Sr.*, Random House, New York.
5   Quoted in Chernow, R. (1998) *Titan: The Life of John D. Rockefeller, Sr.*, Random House, New York.
6   Josephson, M. (1932) *The Robber Barons*, Harvest, New York.
7   Yergin, D. (1991) *The Prize*, Simon and Schuster, London.
8   Chandler, A.D. Jr (1990) *Scale and Scope: the Dynamics of Industrial Capitalism*, Harvard University Press, Cambridge, MA.

Chapter 8

Microsoft

Retaining the Rights to MS-DOS.

A cheesy little operating system

D uring the research for this book it soon became clear that one contemporary business breakthrough stands apart from all others. Virtually all those business leaders expressing opinions about the best business decision put Microsoft's retention of the rights to MS-DOS – the software operating system used in most personal computers – at the top of their list. In a sense, this consensus is almost as surprising as the item itself. After all, MS-DOS seems, at first glance, to be an unlikely item to generate such a weight of opinion. A computer operating system lacks the visibility of McDonalds, the excitement of Disneyland, the scale of a Jumbo jet or the glamour of James Bond. Despite that, Microsoft's retention of the copyright for the operating systems used on IBM's personal computers is a good contender for the best ever business decision.

The tangible returns from the decision are vast. Within months of the launch of the IBM personal computer, Microsoft's turnover soared as it was transformed from a small, specialist producer of programming languages to a strategic partner of one of the most powerful companies in the world. Every personal computer IBM sold became a vehicle for promoting Microsoft. Every time one of IBM's rivals tried to compete by promoting full IBM compatibility, they promoted Microsoft's operating systems. The harder the producers of personal computers tried to compete by promoting the twin messages of compatibility and progress, the stronger Microsoft became.

A virtuous circle

The business breakthrough was based on the ultimate virtuous circle for Microsoft. The starting point was the growth in demand for personal computers, especially as innovative applications like word processing and spreadsheets became increasingly important in business. People could see the benefits of using personal computers. The greatest barriers to increased use lay in fear and novelty. People's fear of the new technology was increased by their unfamiliarity with the new companies like Apple, Commodore and Altair who dominated personal computers and related technologies in the early years. IBM's involvement reassured users while opening the gates for other producers to compete by producing IBM clones – machines that acted in every way like IBM's equipment. IBM made it easy for clones by using standard equipment and systems. The biggest winner among its suppliers was Microsoft. Its operating system was the key to true compatibility.

Ownership of the rights to the operating system put Microsoft at the heart of all upgrades and improvements in the technologies and their uses. An improved microprocessor, for example, created opportunities for new uses. These enhancements could not be achieved without changes in the operating system. This built-in obsolescence fuelled Microsoft's growth as DOS 1.0 was replaced by DOS 1.1, 1.2 and eventually DOS 2.0, 3.0, 4.0, 5.0. In the first five years of the 1980s Microsoft's sales grew from under $10 million to over $100 million. Control over the operating system gave Microsoft an edge as it moved into applications and related developments as 'this cheesy little operating system was supporting Microsoft's fledgling applications business too.'[1]

Sales of the IBM PC and its emulators meant that MS-DOS soon became Microsoft's main source of revenue and the main catalyst for

In the research for this book, the most frequently mentioned business breakthrough was the success of Microsoft in growing to dominate the world software industry. In less than twenty-five years, the company grew from a small, quite specialised software development company to the leading company in its global marketplace. In the process, Microsoft overtook its original partner in the development of the control systems for personal computers – IBM – in market capitalisation. In the process of building up the business, Microsoft established a set of international standards that have allowed computers, operation and software systems to interact and link up. It is hard to imagine either the rapid growth of the digital economy or the mixture of innovation and low prices that stimulated this growth without the standards set by Microsoft. The success of Microsoft means that one of its founders, Bill Gates, became the world's first $100 billion man (others like Rockefeller were probably worth more in real terms).

the company's growth. Their sales increased sixfold in the three years after the 1981 release of IBM PC, with MS-DOS. By the end of the decade, Microsoft was making $200 million per year in revenues from MS-DOS. The massive success of the operating system transformed the computing industry. IBM's failure to change plunged 'Big Blue' into decline while Microsoft's success accelerated. During the 1990s IBM was overtaken in market value by the company that it had done so much to develop.

The phenomenon

The breakthrough achieved by Microsoft is based on a distinctive mixture of personality (of the key players, especially Bill Gates), fundamental change and key decisions. Many accounts of the success of Microsoft focus on one or more of these elements. There is the personality of Bill Gates. He is sometimes portrayed as everything from the ultimate computer 'nerd', with no interests outside the technology, to a latter-day robber baron – ruthlessly competitive and determined to control the future of computing. His coolness and knowledge is legendary. At one of the first meetings with IBM it is said that 'one programmer harassed Gates about some work that Microsoft had done for a Tandy machine, saying that it wasn't up to IBM standards and that Gates had better think again if he planned to try to fob off that kind of shoddy work on IBM. The IBMers, thinking Gates was at a disadvantage, didn't know the half of it: Gates was operating without having slept for more than thirty six hours. But he slowly won the group over by staying cool under fire and by displaying a dazzling range of technical knowledge.'[2]

The scale of the breakthrough is hard to separate from the insight that the people at the top had of the extent of the change in markets and technologies. Prior to the mid-1970s, the computer industry was dominated by large machines which were mainly confined to large corporations and government departments. They were operated by specialist staff. In less than a decade the personal computer changed this. Large numbers of machines used by non-specialists became the norm in homes, offices – even on trains and planes. IBM had become the biggest computer company in the world by building two to three thousand mainframe machines a year. Within the first year after the introduction of the IBM PC, the company had sold a quarter of a million machines, just over a year later the number reached a million, and soon after monthly sales were 200,000 machines.

As the importance of information technology in everyday life continues to grow, Microsoft maintains its position as the most influential player in the computer industry. Over 95% of all new PCs are packaged with a version of Windows, Microsoft's graphical operating system. Bill Gates, the co-founder and public face of the company, has become the richest man in the world, as Microsoft has grown from a two-person partnership formed in 1975 to the behemoth it is today. Microsoft's growth has been so rapid that Gates was a billionaire before his thirty-second birthday.[3] In 1991, Microsoft's Dow Jones stock valuation was higher than that of General Motors. A company formed just twenty-five years ago, in a highly competitive market, is now under investigation by the US Justice Department for taking advantage of its market monopoly. The latest Fortune 500 (1999) places Microsoft at the top of its listing for US Corporations ranked by market value (See Table 8.1).

Microsoft continues to lead the way in software innovation. The latest incarnation of its operating system, Windows 98, integrates the personal home computer with the wider world of the Internet.

Gates seems unwilling to rest on his laurels, pointing out that 'The only big companies that succeed will be those that obsolete their own products before somebody else does.' Microsoft is determined to maintain its premier position in the computer industry. Now targeting the Internet, Microsoft has successfully beaten competition from the previous market leader in Internet 'browser' software and made its own Internet Explorer an integrated part of Windows 98 (the reason for the Justice Department's anti-trust investigation) and the industry standard.

Table 8.1 The top ten corporations in the USA by market value 1998.

Rank	Company	Value $ billion
1	Microsoft	419
2	General Electric	360
3	Wal-Mart Stores	213
4	Merck	199
5	Intel	197
6	Pfitzer	162
7	AT&T	180
8	EXXON	179
9	Coca-Cola	169
10	Cisco Systems	167

The brains of a new machine

The breakthroughs that saw Microsoft emerge as the dominant (or domineering) IT corporation in the world were driven by a mixture of energy, insight, knowledge and determination. At virtually every stage in the company's growth and development, the combination of these features gave Microsoft an edge over larger, technically superior, better resourced – even more innovative – rivals. Microsoft won its battles with these rivals partly because it understood the distinctive architecture of the new industry better than its competitors. The company also appreciated earlier than anyone else, that operating systems were the pinch points of the new industries. The team at Microsoft, then decided to control these pinch points – focusing all their skills on these issues, refusing to be distracted – and eventually gained maximum leverage from their control.

In the beginning there was just Bill Gates and his friend Paul Allen poring 'over the description of a kit computer in *Popular Electronics* magazine. As we read excitedly about the first truly personal computer, Paul and I didn't know exactly how it would be used, but we were sure that it would change us and the world of computing.' In fact, this first machine – the Altair – is now largely forgotten, except in stories about Microsoft and Bill Gates.

In 1974, Intel released the 8080 microchip. Ed Roberts, owner of struggling MITS, a company building calculator kits, decided to use the 8080 as the basis for what he dubbed a 'personal computer'. The 'Altair', as the computer was called, was featured on the cover of Popular Electronics, in its January 1975 issue. At this time, computers were generally large, highly expensive mainframe models. The idea of a 'micro' computer available at an affordable price, was a new one, and the 500,000 subscribers to Popular Electronics, including Paul Allen, were the first to have news of it.

Privilege

It was the combination of Allen and Gates that changed the world of computing. Gates and Allen came from the type of privileged background that was probably necessary to get ahead in the early years of computing. They went to a private school where their parents were so determined to give their children an edge that the Mother's Club paid extra to buy time for pupils on a computer. Gates and Allen were using computers at a time when this type of access was largely confined to university academics, government specialists and large corporations.

The edge produced early dividends when Allen and Gates started their own business in 1975. Although Gates would not be twenty until later that year and Allen was slightly older at twenty-two, both had years of experience working with computers and developing software. They were well placed to respond to the surge in demand for software developers that the new technologies were producing. Their specialist language – BASIC – had many features: simplicity, ease of use and flexibility, that made it ideal for the new generation of computers. Demand for their services grew so rapidly that Gates soon decided to give up his studies at Harvard and concentrate on building the company.

This decision was a classic think long, act short type action. Gates could see the potential of the market, 'a zillion machines all running on his software',[4] and knew that he had to act now, when his competitive edge was greatest, to get into the market. Allen and Gates were quick to spot that the pinch point in the market was not the hardware – the machines or components – but the software – the encoded instructions that converted electronic impulses to useful data and information. MITS, the company behind the Altair, and its founder Ed Roberts were soon working in partnership with Microsoft.

Programming languages, such as PASCAL, FORTRAN, or more recently C++, act as tools to enable computers to be given instructions. Microchips communicate in highly complicated machine code. For the Altair to be commercially successful, a more convenient way of programming it than machine code needed to be available. At the time, the most common programming language was BASIC. It was also the easiest to learn, and therefore the most attractive to the hobbyists that the Altair targeted. Nobody, however, had developed BASIC for the 8080. Gates and Allen decided that they could develop a working BASIC for the Altair. Gates telephoned Roberts and claimed that they already had a working copy of BASIC. Despite not even having an Altair (Allen emulated it on a mainframe computer), they managed to program a working BASIC in just two months.

Partnerships

The partnership agreement with Altair taught the young entrepreneurs lessons about working with others that would influence their long-term business strategy. At its heart was a commitment by MITS 'to use their best efforts to license, promote, and commercialise the Program (BASIC). The Company's failure to use its best efforts ... shall constitute sufficient grounds and reasons to terminate this agreement.' There were many similarities between this approach and the eventual arrangement with IBM but the arrangement was firmly capped and Microsoft's potential earnings were limited. The company had, however, learned that partnerships like this would be the key to long-term growth in the new economy. This way of thinking contrasted sharply with conventional management wisdom in the 1970s which tended to emphasise the value of operational integration and control. The giants of the 1960s and 1970s – like General Motors and ITT – grew by internalising operations and strengthening their controls.

Microsoft also learned to use the soft architecture of the market that was promoting the growth in computing. This soft architecture took three basic forms. First, there was the enthusiasm of (largely amateur) users of the new technology. Gates understood and related to their passions – he could also tap their commitment to stimulate interest in BASIC and his ideas. Microsoft recruited extensively among these enthusiasts. Their commitment and energy contrasted sharply with the conventional view of Corporation Man. Second, there was the general failure of public bodies to appreciate the value of their computer assets.

Gates' first brush with authority occurred when Harvard University discovered the extent of his use of its computing facilities for commercial purposes while he was still studying. While Microsoft was in Albuquerque, the company made a deal with the local school system that gave it 'virtually unlimited hours for a ridiculously low monthly rental.' Third, Gates understood the value of intellectual property rights and fought to defend his rights – even when it produced conflicts with customers. Microsoft's defence of its intellectual property rights contrasted sharply with the approach of other companies. These firms were surprisingly (in today's terms) casual about the way others – including Microsoft – adopted and adapted their work and ideas.

Buttoned down collars

Partnership based development, tapping the enthusiasm of workers, breaking down market boundaries and defending intellectual property rights were key sources of leverage in a new business environment. They contrasted sharply with the corporate environment that dominated most of the century. The predominant approach was based on internal development and the efforts to integrate as much as possible within the firm. Companies like General Motors had their own components, producers, engineering shops, tool makers – activities that would be progressively unbundled over the next thirty years. Personnel and human resource strategies were preoccupied with maximising control over staff and getting them to work in increasingly standardised ways. Market definitions became increasingly important with segments and sectors reduced to numbers and formulae. Physical assets were paramount while business leaders and analysts emphasised the capital costs of market entry and the importance of scale and weight. The epitome of this corporate culture was the IBM that sought out Microsoft in 1980.

That IBM was the ultimate buttoned-up corporation was symbolised by the blue shirts with buttoned down collars that IBM staffers were (according to legend) expected to wear. In contrast Microsoft people ' with the exception of Gates, who looked like a high school freshman, … looked more like part of a Berkeley peace march in the 1960s than employees in a computer software company.' The stereotypes were unfair. IBMers at the *skunk works* that initiated the work on its personal computer could be as casual in their appearance as anyone at Microsoft, while key members of the Microsoft team could look as formal as any US corporate executive when necessary. There was, however, a difference in corporate culture that made the link between the businesses important for both. IBM needed Microsoft's creative energy while the latter need IBM's market power and respectability for its corporate breakthrough.

Gates was so convinced of the value of the link that he even decided to buy a tie to wear at the key project meeting at IBM's facility at Boca Raton. This tie – probably the most valuable article of clothing in history – helped to cement a relationship that transformed the computer industry during the 1980s and 1990s. The industry shifted from being dominated by large well-established firms that controlled large machines like IBM, Honeywell, Burroughs, DEC and ICL, to a sector dominated by new business like Microsoft, Intel, Netscape and Yahoo. They dominate the software that makes the machines operate. Even successful manufacturers like Dell identify their success with the way they work rather than what they build.

IBM's own Manhattan Project

IBM dominated the industrial landscape of the late 1970s and early 1980s. Its growth, sales success and profitability were unrivalled. Surveys of the most admired companies in the world regularly placed IBM at the top. The management literature of the early 1980s was dominated by talk of the IBM way and importance of emulating

IBM's way of doing business. *In Search of Excellence*[5] the first of a new generation of management books placed IBM and its way of doing business as the lodestone of this search for business excellence. 'The company is IBM. With one act ... IBM reaffirmed its heroic status.'[6] The company's own sense of worth was symbolised by the unofficial name for the task force to work on the development of the IBM PC – The Manhattan Project. IBM was going to produce its own version of the atomic bomb and finally win the computer wars.

Even within IBM, there was a realisation that the hero needed help. Bill Lowe, the IBM executive driving the PC project, initially managed to get approval for his plan to produce a personal computer quickly and efficiently, with the use of outside contractors for parts and software. This use of contractors to get non-exclusive technology was a major factor in the standardisation of PC technology. The IBM team recognised that an important feature of their machine would be an operating system. The inclusion of an operating system – the user-friendly buffer between the computer's hardware and its software – would significantly widen the appeal of IBM's product. '...forcing people using PCs to learn the equivalent of Sanskrit [i.e. computer programming language] was limiting their usability enough that IBM had decided to include an operating system.'[7]

IBM contacted Microsoft, believing that they could provide the new PC with an operating system. Gates initially referred IBM to a company called Digital Research Interactive. Microsoft were specialists in programming languages, DRI produced operating systems. For one reason or another, however, IBM failed to close a deal with DRI to use their CP/M operating system – at the time the industry leader. They instead returned to Microsoft who agreed to produce an operating system, plus four programming languages, for the new PC. Microsoft had only a few months to produce the operating system which would be shipped on new PCs.

A series of decisions was made by different parties that symbolised the shift from one way of doing business to another. Each of these decisions played its part in helping Microsoft achieve the breakthrough, from being an interesting, relatively successful specialist firm, to a dominant force in the market. The first was IBM's decision to outsource most aspects of the PC's components and system. There was an implicit assumption in IBM that the market for PCs would be broadly the same as the market for traditional computers. The key feature of this market was the search for security by purchasers. The IBM name provided that security – after all 'no-one ever got sacked for buying IBM.' IBM would control the market because its name guaranteed that security.

Another company's decision provided the opportunity for Microsoft to get close to IBM. Digital Research was a larger, stronger company than Microsoft. For a number of reasons – which are largely lost in time and controversy – Digital's top management were reluctant or unable to sign the type of contract that Microsoft were able to agree with IBM. In many ways the terms were punitive – especially concerning the time allowed to develop and perfect the operating system. The decision to accept these conditions and meet the punishing production schedule was crucial to the Microsoft breakthrough. At the time, the decision seemed reckless to many – including colleagues at Microsoft – but Gates was in tune with the type of thinking that would reshape not only the computer industry but many others.

Knowledge equals power

The ability to adopt and adapt was essential if this project and countless others were to meet the telescoped time scales which came to characterise the new economy. Gates adopted elements of other operating systems, adapted others to meet IBM's needs while creatively filling in any gaps. At almost every stage in the project, IBM seemed to call the shots but Gates ensured that he controlled the key elements of the project – the intellectual property rights. He understood the value of these intangible assets far more than anyone at IBM. Gates simultaneously achieved another breakthrough based on the truism that 'knowledge equals power.' He ensured that Microsoft stood between IBM and other companies contributing to the development of the operating system. This meant, for example, that Seattle Computer (whose operating system was a vital component in MS-DOS) signed a copyright agreement based on the number of individual companies taking a sub-licence not the size of the end user market.

Microsoft's agreement with IBM meant that they would be paid a royalty for each PC that IBM sold. More importantly, however, Microsoft retained full rights to the operating system which had become MS-DOS. This meant that they could license it to any other manufacturer. 'In effect Microsoft controlled the exploitation of the market, so long as the firm controlled access to the operating system. The company achieved this when it bought the rights to Seattle's 86-QDOS operating system – the operating system on which MS-DOS was based. 'For only $50,000, Gates bought all rights to 86-QDOS previously owned by Seattle Computer Products. It was the bargain of the century.'[8]

IBM created the opportunity when it decided it was not interested in controlling the software system. Seattle Computer also operated in ways that reflected established business norms, by selling the rights. Microsoft itself had operated along these lines until the IBM project. The breakthrough occurred when Microsoft spotted a fundamental shift in the way the market operated, far earlier than anyone else. IBM – like everybody else – underestimated the skill with which a relatively tiny firm like Microsoft could construct a deal to its advantage and convert this to market power. IBM's focus was on sales of the PC itself.

The advance of the clones

IBM's thinking was firmly in line with existing business orthodoxy. Computer buyers wanted the reassurance that the IBM name provided. These consumers might buy other machines but IBM's prosperity would lie in expanding the overall market while holding on to market share. The brand was so strong that, not only could IBM charge a premium, but buyers of other PCs would aspire to trade up to its machine. IBM completely underestimated the pace of change, the growth of the market and nature of the customer market. By losing control of the operating system, the giant allowed rivals to enter the market offering the same features. These smaller rivals could innovate faster, introduce new features quicker and adapt themselves to new customer groups more efficiently, while matching IBM's basic systems. Scale without market power rapidly became a disadvantage in the new market, especially as IBM could not focus its attention wholly on the PC market.

The initial success of IBM's PC led to a host of other companies emulating and undercutting the price of IBM's product. These computers were marketed as IBM compatible, which meant that they could run the same software as an IBM machine. Software for IBM's PC, such as the successful spreadsheet Lotus 1-2-3, was written to be compatible with MS-DOS. This meant that the manufacturers of 'compatibles' had to license MS-DOS for their own machines in order to run the popular software packages. The low point for IBM occurred when the 'clones', offered by firms like Compaq, were seen as so superior to its machines that they could charge a premium over the IBM price.

The same forces drove Microsoft forward. The IBM PC transformed the personal computer market from a 'wildcatters' paradise' – of different machines working in different ways to different rules – to an industry with a standard. It was no longer possible for Wang to dominate the word processing market with a dedicated machine, or Commodore's Pet to run good games. The pressure to conform was driven partly by a market seeking security, and by software producers searching for scale. Much of the demand for personal computers was driven by clever new applications. VisiCalc was the first successful spreadsheet. WordStar was a word processing package that did not need dedicated equipment. Customers wanted immediate access to these applications, while producers did not want to spend time adapting their software to the peculiarities of different machines.

The pinch point was the operating system. MS-DOS was the point at which customer demand for compatibility, and software supplier demands for standardisation, came together. Microsoft won on every count. When IBM wanted upgrades, it was forced to come to Microsoft. Other companies improved their technologies, produced smarter, more up-to-date machines but still came to Microsoft. The faster the industry grew, the faster Microsoft grew. Its role was like that of the hub of a wheel – nothing could turn without involving Microsoft. Gates and his team recognised the potential of their control earlier and faster than any of their partners or suppliers. Gates and Allen moved quickly to exploit their advantages; first by reinforcing their control through constant upgrades of the operating system; second by keeping prices low and third by fiercely protecting their intellectual property rights.

No one else was as obsessive about improving MS-DOS than Gates and Allen. One Microsoft engineer commented that 'software engineering was not a job with us, it was an obsession.' This focus was an especially important characteristic, as demand for PCs was stimulated by a flow of innovative software products. These ranged from improvement to spreadsheets, like Lotus 1-2-3, and new word processing, graphics, presentational and database packages, and games software. Each drew on the capabilities of MS-DOS while stretching these further. Microsoft's continuing strength turned on its control and focus on the system and its underlying technology. This position was reinforced by an aggressive pricing policy which left no room for rivals to undercut Microsoft's market position. The only threat came from a wholly different way of handling personal computing.

An Apple a day

This threat came from a major innovation by Apple Computers with the introduction of the Apple Lisa computer and the Mac. These machines replaced the existing text based computing systems with powerful graphics-based user interfaces. Gates spotted the opportunity and the threat very quickly, commenting in 1983 that 'What the new graphics technologies represents is a revolution in user interface. The bottom line is that graphics are going to become a standard part of all computers.' The future of Microsoft would depend on its ability to absorb and control the new technologies and retain its control over computer operating systems. Control over existing operating systems for personal computers gave Microsoft massive leverage in developing new, graphics-based operating systems.

Building on this initial advantage required that the company was fully focused on realising this advantage. This focus was vividly illustrated in the collaboration between Microsoft and Apple in their work on graphical interfaces. Gates seemingly listened, learned and acted while Steve Jobs – Apple's CEO – talked, taught and advised him that he was wasting his time concentrating on operating systems. Gates, however, was determined to ensure that Microsoft would dominate the next generation of operating systems as completely as the current generation.

The tactics learned in the early development of MS-DOS were refined and developed. This was vividly illustrated in the pricing policies adopted for the new operating system. Microsoft virtually gave the system away while rivals were charging OEM[9] manufacturers up to $1000. Gates was playing the long game in his dealings with potential rivals like Apple, partners such as IBM and end-users. Control and focus were turned into massive dividends by Gates' use of his growing leverage to generate massive returns. One person observed 'Bill has a tremendous way of leveraging ... dealing with Bill is being willing to return technology to him, you give it to Bill, and then you buy it back.'

Microsoft was a new generation company that understood the new economy but was able to use classic business strategies with unrivalled skill. The use of existing, profitable systems as cash cows to underwrite potential stars recurs in the company's history. The company's original mainstay – BASIC – was used to underwrite the development of MS-DOS. Once MS-DOS became the industry standard, its revenues underwrote the development of Windows. The ability to think long while acting short, was also shown in the development of the new generation of applications software that Microsoft initiated. The typical approach was to build in new features – many of which were not actively sought by customers – while fiercely protecting copyright.

The learning company

At each stage, Microsoft was showing another feature of the new generation companies – a willingness to learn. Gates and Allen seemed to see every partnership as a learning opportunity. MITS and Seattle Computer were their teachers during the early stages of the company's development. They'd outgrown these relationships by the time the IBM link developed. The lessons absorbed from IBM project the company into the 'big time' but it took the relationship with Apple to transform the company from a follower to a leader. Two aspects of the Apple relationship were especially important. First, there was the confidence to lead the market technologically. Second, Microsoft learned the value of mass, high profile marketing with the launch of first *Windows* and then *Windows 95*. The Windows launch was especially important as Microsoft was facing a series of challenges to its market leadership. Several OEM producers – even IBM – were ready to chose alternative products for their graphics-based operating systems.

Microsoft rewrote the rules of the software marketing game when it bypassed the manufacturers and promoted its system directly to consumers. From then, the company's market power grew as software companies targeted their developments on Windows to tap the rapidly growing end-user market. This ability to understand the way the new economy and its emerging markets will develop has been the key to each breakthrough that Microsoft achieved. The key decisions made by Allen and Gates generally reflect their understanding of the way the market would develop. In the development of MS-DOS, Gates appreciated more than anyone else the way the PC market would grow, and the shift from dominance by manufacturers to dominance by software companies. The decision to risk short term fees for long term revenues highlighted this insight. Later, the same insight prompted Gates to invest massively in the development of graphics-based operating systems. His confidence and determination to retain control of the operating systems market prompted Microsoft to use heavyweight consumer marketing to offset the efforts of other companies to weaken or break the company's lead.

At the heart of the Microsoft's success, and the breakthrough it has achieved, is a vision of the nature and development of the information technology and knowledge industries. Gates doesn't see computers as tools to be used by specialists. His vision, which Microsoft has been successful in bringing to fruition, is computers being used by everybody. Computer ownership and access is becoming more and more widespread. Windows allows people with little or no knowledge of computers to use them intuitively, and productively. Information technology, and in particular the Internet, are gaining a greater and greater influence. It took television 13 years to achieve 50 million viewers, it's taken the Internet 4 years to achieve 50 million users.[10] Microsoft has played a huge part in these breakthroughs, by making computers accessible to all.

Further reading

Gates, B. (1995) *The Road Ahead*, Viking, New York.
Manes, S. and Andrews, P. (1994) *Gates*, Touchstone, New York.
Wallace, J. and Erickson, J. (1993) *Hard Drive*, John Wiley and Sons, New York.

Notes

1 Manes, S. and Andrews, P. (1994) *Gates*, Touchstone, New York.
2 Carroll, P. (1993) *Big Blues*, Orion, London.
3 Davis, W. (1996) *The Innovators*, HarperCollins, London.
4 Wallace, J. and Erickson, J. (1993) *Hard Drive*, John Wiley and Sons, New York.
5 Peters, T.J. and Waterstone, R.H. (1982) *In Search of Excellence*, HarperCollins, New York.
6 Peters, T.J. and Waterstone, R.H. (1982) *ibid*.
7 Carroll, P. (1993) *Big Blues – the unmaking of IBM*, Orion, New York, p. 18.

8 Wallace, J. & Erickson, J. (1992), p. 202.
9 OEMs are Own Equipment Manufacturers like IBM and Compaq.
10 Source: *Yahoo, Internet Life*, January 1999, p. 87.

Chapter 9

Running Ahead

Nike and the Growth of the Leisure Industries

Who's Mike?

Every year thousands of students in universities across the world undertake projects as part of their studies. In business schools these projects often explore business opportunities, ideas for innovative products or market opportunities. One such project by Phil Knight, a graduate student at Stanford University, eventually changed the shape of the sports apparel industry and much of world sport with it. *Fortune* magazine later commented that 'a whole new industry – a phenomenon, really was born thirty years ago on the athletic fields around Portland Oregon.'[1] Phil's project, like thousands of others, reflected his interests outside his studies. He decided to examine the market for running shoes in the light of the comment by one of the USA's top coaches that 'the then state-of-the-art track shoes, manufactured by Adidas – then the world's leading producer – were simply not good enough.'[2]

The coach, Bill Bowerman, had trained Knight when he was a student at the University of Oregon. Knight was good athlete who had developed a strong rapport with his coach while on the track and field team at the University. Knight knew of Bowerman's belief that better running shoes would improve performance. Bowerman taught his athletes to seek a competitive edge in every aspect of their work, from their physical fitness to their sportswear. The coach was known to make running shoes himself by hand if necessary. Neither had a high opinion of the products produced by Adidas, the then dominant producer of sports shoes.

The thinking behind Knight's student project was simple. The best that Adidas produced were in Bowerman's eyes 'not very good but very expensive.' Knight set about testing whether there was a market for lower price shoes that were as good in quality and finish. This was in the early 1960s when the first waves of good quality, low price Japanese products were gaining success in the US market. Knight's basic thesis was that a country that could produce quality cameras at a low price could surely produce good running shoes cheaply. His project achieved good grades but initially Knight behaved like thousands of other business students. He left his project behind and went to work for one of the giants of modern accountancy – Coopers and Lybrand. It did not take long for a career in accountancy to pall and, on a trip to Japan, he followed up the ideas in his project by tracking down a Japanese sports shoe manufacturer, the Onitsuka Company.

A business built simply on cheap if good quality imports was unlikely to make a massive impact on the US sports market, much less challenge Adidas. The driving force behind the company's growth was the partnership that was renewed between Knight and Bowerman. The coach, with his desire to improve the footwear, and the ex-business student with a flair for selling, formed a natural partnership. The first stage in the development of their business was an order for 500 pairs of track shoes from Onitsuka. These sold quickly and the new business, then called Blue Ribbon Sports, was soon winning orders across the state and beyond.

We are athletes

One of the key features of Nike emerged during these early years. The company actively recruited its staff from the athletic community. The first recruit, for example, was a keen athlete who wanted a job that he could combine with this running. As Phil Knight says, he wanted 'to continue a lifestyle and still make a living.' Until recently

Nike emerged originally as an unusual partnership between a graduate student from Stanford University and his track coach. In the mid-1960s both were unhappy because of the price and quality of the track shoes then produced by the leading manufacturers. Phil Knight, the student, resented the high prices and Bill Bowerman, the coach, did not think they added much to performance. The student and the coach came together to design, produce and market sports shoes that not only improved performance but pushed prices down by widening the market for sports shoes. Their investment in design for comfort, support and consumer appeal encouraged the development of a vast new market of buyers who wanted the product but had little intention of competing in track or field. This new leisure market drove up demand and allowed Nike to expand its markets internationally. Nike's distinctive anti-authority marketing, allied to its links with players and athletes, underpinned its breakthrough into new markets, while securing its position in its core market.

During the 1980s, the Nike name and its symbol, the Swoosh, joined the ranks of the most familiar brands in the world. The growth of the company was not without setbacks. Nike failed to spot the growth of the women's market, and faced a serious threat from Reebok. Its extensive use of offshore production, especially in Asia, led to criticisms of its labour practices and its mark-ups. Gradually, however, the company responded to these challenges and reinforced its market position by the end of the 1990s. In 1999, Nike outsold Reebok by a factor of three to one with sales of $9553 million against Reebok's $3224 million.

the Nike Web site *Nike.Com* had a cover page which stated:

WE ARE INNOVATORS
WE ARE ATHLETES
WE ARE RISK-TAKERS
WE ARE COMMUNICATORS

The notion of being innovators, risk-takers and communicators could fit into the mission statement of most, but Nike places being athletes into the same category. This link with athletics created the momentum that drove Nike towards the breakthrough that would transform the sporting goods industry.

Bowerman's belief that better shoes could help people win races prompted him to experiment with different materials and types of shoe. His first modification was to move away from the leather uppers which were typical of running shoes. Blue Ribbon Sports asked Onitsuka to produce a different type of shoe with a nylon upper, rather than the traditional leather product and modified the sole to add cushioning. The shoes were an immediate success, and the elements were coming together around which long term success would develop.

The final components, the distinctive brand name and logo emerged in 1971, five years after the first shoes were imported from Japan. The origins of the brand and the logo lie in the company's determination to build a strong, simple and easy to recall image. The name Nike comes from the winged Greek goddess of victory, while the symbol was produced for $35 by Carolyn Davidson a local graduate student. Initially the name posed problems, as customers wanted to know 'who's Mike?'

Jocks with attitude

It takes more than a student project, inexpensive, imported running shoes, and employees who are athletes to create a $10 billion company. The breakthrough occurred because Nike established a public partnership with athletes and other sports people that was rooted in a genuine interest in their needs and a desire for improved performance. This partnership was especially important as it was based on the decision by Knight and Bowerman to publicly challenge the hypocrisy that surrounded amateur sports at the time. Until Nike went public, sporting goods companies regularly sponsored and financed amateur athletes. The sports governing bodies largely connived in this activity – even in amateur events – by turning a blind eye as money was exchanged.

Nike's partner in challenging this position was Steve Prefontaine, an outstanding middle distance runner. Prefontaine was not only a great athlete but he shared Nike's disdain for authority. He accepted financial backing from Nike and publicly acknowledged this by wearing the Nike logo on his shirt. Knight describes Prefontaine as 'a rebel from a working-class background, a guy full of cockiness and pride and guts. Pre's spirit is the cornerstone of this company's soul.' One expert described the ideal sports star partner for Nike as 'outlaws with morals' or 'jocks with attitude.'

The partnership with Nike allowed athletes like Prefontaine to achieve their own breakthrough. Until Nike arrived, sports administrators, sporting goods companies and the owners of sporting businesses had effectively controlled world sports to their advantage. Vast numbers might watch athletes and sportspeople at the Olympics, in soccer stadiums, on tennis courts and golf courses but the performers received relatively little reward. The sporting links that Nike established and wanted to sustain made this situation untenable. The 'jocks with attitude' included people like John McEnroe, Andre Agassi and Eric Cantona 'as the company sought out the strong personalities that fans and potential customers seemed to like.'

Nike was the first company to recognise that many top athletes were non-conformists (at least in a sporting context), very self aware and conscious of the temporary nature of their success. My own first contact with Nike came in the mid 1970s through Brendan Foster – one of the greatest distance runners of his generation. Brendan confounded virtually every myth about sports people especially those put out by sports administrators.

The latter like to portray athletes as unthinking performers with little awareness of the wider world. Brendan was acutely aware of the challenges he and his sport were facing. He identified strongly with the focus on performance and the willingness to challenge the status quo that Nike represented. Brendan was for a time CEO of Nike's operation in Britain. He knew his career was coming to an end and while nothing would ever match the buzz of being the best in his sport in the world, he could learn 'to be the best' by working with a company that understood him.

A company owned and controlled by a coach and an athlete, employing largely athletes was not likely to connive with the exploitation of sports people. This was especially important, as Nike was determined to achieve its next breakthrough in active partnership with the athletes themselves. Product design, in particular, was driven by the belief that the footwear athletes wore, should reflect the way they ran and where they ran. Bill Bowerman drove much of this development. He and Knight decided that the basic design of the running shoe should be fundamentally redesigned to reflect the needs of longer distance runners and off-track use.

Knight decided to build up the intensity of the sports team within Nike. This extended far beyond merely recruiting former athletes as employees and sponsoring stars. Team spirit was emphasised. Managers were encouraged to compete and strive constantly to get ahead. There was an intense environment within the company that people compared with a top sports team chasing titles and success. Knight said he wanted to be surrounded by 'magnificent bastards and wonderful goons.'

Waffles

Bowerman's interest in design was partly stimulated by his observation that the majority of injuries and fitness problems occurred off-track and outside competition. The footwear athletes used should support them during intense periods of training as much as during competition. This decision lay behind the series of innovations that drove the early development of the Nike product. The first such development – the famous waffle sole – was initially stimulated by staring at the squared recesses of his breakfast waffles. This innovation was followed by a series of related development as soles, foot, ankle and arch support were redesigned around the shape of people's feet and the way they ran and walked. This emphasis on a shoe for training created the focus of footwear development. The new shoes would need to be robust while providing a great deal of support.

The first generation of newly designed running shoes was made for off-track use. Middle and long distance athletes like Knight and Prefontaine did most of their training off-track, on roads, pavements, sidewalks and cross-country. These surfaces are harder than most tracks, which means that cushioning and support are especially important if injuries are to be avoided. Bowerman's new designs combined the traction athletes needed for better performance – through the newly designed sole – with comfort. Wider, more public use by young athletes encouraged Nike to pay greater attention to the appearance of their shoes. The bright blue, yellow-swooshed Nikes of the late 1970s were very different to the products offered by Adidas and Puma.

Nike's origins in individual sports like athletics moved the company in different directions to those followed by Adidas and Puma. Both these latter companies were originally manufacturers of soccer boots. There was an impression that their footwear for other sports was largely an adaptation of their soccer boots with leather uppers and hard soles. Nike's original focus was firmly on running (and eventually other sports that did not involve kicking).

Just as their products were breaking with tradition, Nike were determined to be iconoclasts in other ways. In 1972 not only did Bowerman persuade the top US marathon runners to wear Nike shoes but the company aggressively promoted its shoes as 'worn by four of the top seven finishers in the US Olympic trials.'

Jogging to the top

Not only did this approach to promotion – selling the sizzle as well as the sausage – change the rules of good sporting promotion but it took Nike out into a vastly larger market. It is hard to say which came first, the explosion of interest in jogging and keeping fit, or the development of Nike's lightweight sports shoe with its waffle shaped sole. It was, however, a marriage made in heaven. Bowerman was an important influence in the interest in jogging. His book *Jogging: A Physical Fitness Programme for All Ages* was a best seller that won features in influential magazines like *Life*. There was little doubt that the comfortable, lightweight feel of the Nike shoes made jogging a more accessible, enjoyable experience for the new generation of joggers. It is hard to imagine people getting the same pleasure jogging on hard city or rural streets in the relatively heavy, hard, unshaped running shoes of the pre-Nike days.

Nike had earlier decided to introduce a set of business systems that made the breakthrough into the new market relatively easy. These included:

- far more attention to fitting than previous producers;
- consumer education programmes targeted on the non-expert;
- pricing strategies that recognised the increasing affluence of the baby boomer generations in the USA and Europe;
- retailer support strategies that opened up the new market to more, non-specialist outlets while supporting them with staff training and 'smart' inventory management; and
- aggressive promotion.

Together, these took the sports shoe market out of the realm of the expert – whether specialist buyer or retailer – into a mass market.

An international icon

The links with Asia, especially Japan, were crucial to the long-term development of Nike besides producing some of the most intractable problems, as market success coincided with widespread criticism of its use of low wage production. Nike is almost unique among major US corporations in having strong connections with Asia from its earliest years. The first running shoes sold by Blue Ribbon Sports were made in Japan. Its manufacturing history in Asia started long before most US and European companies were aware of the 'Asian economic miracle.'

Fig. 9.1 Well worn waffles. (Credit: Rowan Cannon.)

Production links with Asia went hand-in-hand with marketing links into the continent. Sales to Asia-Pacific in 1998 were over $1.25 billion dollars despite the overall slowdown in Asian economies.

Growth

Nike's emphasis on support for the non-expert – whether user or retailer – gave Nike a massive advantage over established producers, especially when combined with a vastly superior product. Between 1972 and 1980 the company's growth surged ahead. At the Olympic trials in 1972, shortly after the company's formation, Phil Knight was printing Nike T-shirts and handing them out to athletes and spectators to create awareness of the company. Four years later, sales had reached $14 million. By 1979, the company was well on the way to being an international icon with over 50 per cent of the US running shoe market and international recognition for its brand and image. In 1980 Nike went public with almost 3000 employees and a turnover of almost $300 million. The previously dominant producer, Adidas, saw its market position collapse from almost 70 per cent of the US market to less than 5 per cent.

The stimulus for much of Nike's growth was the powerful rapport between the company's leadership team and the markets they serve. Knight and his colleagues understood the interests and concerns that drove not only the athletic community but the new generation of baby boomers who wanted fitness with style (and if the fitness was not available, they'd take the style). Nike was a market driven company because the leadership team internalised the aspirations and anxieties of the markets it served. It is claimed that Knight decided early on that the company's four great passions would be the shoes, the athletes, the consumers and the teams. This set of priorities has driven the company over the twenty years during which it has led, dominated or influenced the sporting goods market. Control of each of these has shaped Nike's development.

The marathon

Nike's core strategy can be compared to the approach adopted by top athletes, especially long and middle distance runners, to winning in competition. The company seeks to get a psychological edge over its rivals. Aggressive promotion, innovative product development and determination to rewrite the rules are part of this. This attitude was vividly illustrated in the early 1980s when Nike publicly committed itself to overtaking Adidas as the dominant player in the sports apparel market. At the time Adidas outsold Nike by a factor of around ten to one. This aggressive attitude put Adidas on the defensive, prompting it to respond to Nike's game plan rather than playing to its own strengths. Adidas became the establishment while Nike was the young contender where 'even the heads of the company wore blue jeans and played frisbee on the big green lawns.'[3]

This psychological advantage was reinforced by the decision to focus efforts on building technological innovation and novel designs into the core of the company's operations. The success of the waffle sole was the first indication of the power of this approach but its real vindication came with the Nike Air system.

The air-cushion system was initially developed by Frank Rudy, a NASA engineer. He was interested in both the use of inert gases and footwear. Rudy saw his air bags as a means of protecting athletes' feet, by distributing the impact when foot hit track or road in a way that no solid material could match. The gas added cushioning with movement. Rudy's first approach was to the then dominant sports shoe manufacturer – Adidas. As in so many other cases, the dominant company turned down an innovative technology leaving it to a relatively minor player, with lots of ambition but little to lose, to grasp the opportunity. Knight, the athlete, tried Rudy's prototype shoes 'and was amazed by the "ride" the cushioning offered.'[4] The introduction of this new technology provided Nike with a technological edge and market coverage that its rivals are still battling to match. For example, Reebok, Nike's great rival, initiated the latest stage in this technological battle in 1997 with the introduction of its DMX Series 2000 shoes, that contain ten gas pockets to move the gas through every part of the sole, depending on where the pressure from the foot is greatest.

The brand of athletic performance

Technological innovation is only one aspect of Nike's determination to achieve breakthroughs by rewriting the rules of the market from a position of control. The links with top sports stars, its strong brand presence and technological edge meant that by the late 1980s Nike effectively controlled the sports footwear market. This competitive advantage allowed the company to focus its attentions on moving into new markets and getting the maximum leverage from its competitive advantages.

The link with Michael Jordan in the USA symbolised many of the strengths of this approach. Jordan held a unique position in the US sports market while his sport, basketball, was booming in popularity. The relationship with Jordan took Nike into team sports while the link was a vital step in transforming the economics of sports – at least as far as the athletes themselves. By the end of the decade the wealth of sports stars could be measured in tens of millions of dollars. The richest of these, Michael Jordan, Tiger Woods, Andre Agassi had fortunes estimated at over $100 million each[5] and all were sponsored by Nike.

The company had sustained this focus despite facing two massive challenges to its position during the 1980s. The decline in the US jogging craze coincided with the emergence of a new powerful rival – Reebok – to challenge Nike. Just as Nike grew on the back of an intuitive understanding of the predominately male or 'jock' interest in competitive sports, Reebok's growth was driven by the new market for women's trainers, sneakers and sports shoes. Reebok's sales overtook Nike in 1987, but Knight survived by focusing on its core strengths, especially the powerful link with sports stars and most especially the link with Michael Jordan. Within a few years, Knight's decision was vindicated as Nike won back market leadership, widened its product base and improved its performance. By 1993, Nike had sales of $3.9 billion against Reebok's $2.9 billion.

Nike's growth during most of the 1990s confirmed the value of an approach based on a virtuous circle of market control built on design-based innovation, powerful brand marketing and rapport with top athletes. An acclaimed series of advertisements reinforced this strength. One marketing expert said, 'these ads are legendary' while another said, 'these ads changed the economics and mechanics of everything we do.' The campaign confirmed 'Nike as the brand of athletic performance.' Nike used this control to focus its efforts on gaining maximum leverage through moves into new markets, for example, team sports like soccer, and retailing such as its Niketown concept retail stores.

The surge in new growth posed new challenges to a company that had managed to retain its core strength through two decades of remarkable development. Knight acknowledged in Nike's latest annual report that 'we were facing some serious issues' with the size and shape of the business under the microscope as the firm expanded from 9500 employees to 21,800 with a 'structure [that] was essentially the same, just a lot bigger.' The firm had achieved worldwide sales of almost $10 billion but was battling to retain the distinctive corporate ethos that had created a business breakthrough that had transformed an industry.

Further reading

Greenberg, K.E. (1992) *Bill Bowerman and Phil Knight : Building the Nike Empire*, John Wiley and Sons, New York.

Katz, D. (1994) *Just Do It*, Adams Media Corporation, Holbrook, MA.

Vanderbilt, T. (1998) *The Sneaker Book: Anatomy of an Industry and An Icon*, New Press, New York.

Notes

1 Labich, K. 'Nike vs Reebok' *Fortune*, 18 September, 1995.
2 Katz, D. (1994) *Just Do It*, Adams Media Corporation, Holbrook, MA.
3 Becklund, L. (1991) *Swoosh*
4 Katz, D. (1994) *Just Do It*, Adams Media Corporation, Holbrook, MA.
5 *Forbes*, 22 March, 1999.

Chapter 10

Pale with Excitement

Littlewoods and the Pools Business

Spend, spend, spend

T he football pool is a distinctively British phenomenon that established itself as a national ritual in the 1920s, and even today retains a special place in the national psyche. For decades, the ritual of sitting by the radio – television results never gripped in the same way – listening to the football results was shared by the vast majority of households in the UK. Everyone knew how eight draws or 24 points could transform their lives. This was especially true on Saturday nights, when home and away wins dominated the football results. The big winners could become celebrities in their own right like Viv Nicholson. She summarised her life after winning the pools as *Spend, Spend, Spend!* Even today, despite the success of the UK national lottery, TV and radio still summarise the number of draws, score draws and other results which determine whether this week's winner will get a big win or jackpot.

The origins of this phenomenon lie in the inventiveness of one man and the determination and marketing skills of another. The inventor was John Jervis Barnard, an ex-Guards officer who decided to give people an easy method of gambling on Association Football or soccer. At that time (1922) soccer in Britain was going through a surge of popularity after the end of World War I. The game was largely professionalised. The vast majority of today's major clubs were already established. The basic league structure of a first, second and third division was in place with the third division divided into northern and southern sections. The third division south was created in 1920 and the third division north was formed in 1921. This structure would remain largely unaltered until the late 1950s. The game was being driven along by a surge in support for leading clubs like Everton, Arsenal and Manchester United.

Barnard spotted an opportunity to link this interest in the game with a chance to gamble on forecasting results. Barnard's Pari-Mutual Pools started in Birmingham, England with a single pool, which asked people to forecast six winning teams across the divisions. His first forays into the game produced poor returns but his invention was spotted by the man who would turn this idea into a giant business. Pari-Mutual Pools struggled through their first year in operation with very little success. Income was insufficient to pay the postage to distribute coupons and prizes. Barnard came close to abandoning his efforts at the end of this first season but he persevered – changing the name from Pari-Mutual to Jervis, and gaining some modest success.

Three young gamblers

The real success story, however, occurred eighty miles away in Liverpool. Three young telegraph clerks working for the Commercial Cable Company tried Barnard's pools, liked the idea and decided they could do better. They pooled some of their savings to set up Littlewoods Football Pools. John Moores described later how 'they were all "pale with excitement" as they met at the bank, each to draw out his £50.' He said, 'As I signed my own cheque, my hands were damp. It seemed so much money to be risking.'[1]

Initially they had no more luck than Barnard. At first, they distributed the coupons by hand. This expedient was forced on them by the distribution company they chose first. This company – The Manchester Bill Posting Company – was run by a fervently anti-gambling Methodist who treated John Moores as 'a visitant from hell,' and refused their business. The only way the three friends could reach their potential customers – fans attending a game at Manchester United's

The football pools were a peculiarly British invention that grew into a national institution during the 1930s. This lottery is based on the results of soccer games played in the English and Scottish Leagues (and in Australia during the summer) and combines excitement and big prizes with attempts by the gamblers to predict results. The original inventor failed to build a major enterprise from his idea but John Moores, a telegraph clerk, used the football pools to build one of the largest private companies in the UK through his company Littlewoods. The company's success grew from a mixture of the appeal of the basic proposition and brilliant marketing. Moores spent very little on mainstream marketing or advertising but used press and media relations to generate excitement especially as the prize money soared during the 1930s, 1940s, 1950s and 1960s. The company expanded into other areas using its mailing lists and merchandising expertise. The launch of the UK national lottery has, however, posed a major challenge to Littlewoods and its football pools. Revenues have declined, whilst its prizes are overshadowed by those won on the Lottery.

ground – was by getting 'boys to run round and hand them out.' Despite their enthusiasm and willingness to innovate, Littlewoods found customers in Manchester no more enthusiastic than people in Birmingham. They distributed 4000 coupons but received only 35 back. Wagers totalled little more than £4 and the first dividend was just over £2. Their resilience in the face of difficulties was tested a week later. This time 10,000 coupons were printed but only 1 was returned.

It will never work

The new business was a drain on the limited resources of the three partners. Their initial investment of £150 (£50 each) reached £600 before two of the partners lost their confidence. Bill Hughes, one of the original partners, called an emergency meeting and proposed that they cut their losses and drop the idea. Bill said 'let's face it, we've lost nearly £600 between us. It sounded like a good idea, but obviously it will never work. I vote we cut our losses and drop the whole thing.' Only John Moores retained his original belief in the viability of the business. He refunded the losses of his former partners and ploughed on alone.

Times were pretty grim with costs increasing. Sales started to improve; they increased to almost £80 at their peak but were down to less than £60 in the last week of the season. There seemed little prospect of the new business earning an adequate return while Moores paid out well over half the income in prizes and tried to meet all his expenses and take a profit from a commission of ten per cent.

The initial breakthrough came at the start of the next season. John Moores recognised that very large sales were needed to make the commission system produce profits. He decided to switch from a pure commission system to a mixture of cost recovery and commission on the advice of his printer. This decision produced two important benefits. It stopped the haemorrhaging of funds; his costs were met before prizes were paid. It also gave him far more control over his operations. The search for greater control led to other changes. He stopped using schoolboys to distribute coupons. All too often, these young boys would take their wages and dump the coupons in some convenient place. Moores also turned to his family for help. Family members played a vital part in the early years of the growth of the new business. They were dedicated workers, who could be trusted not to take advantage of a fledgling business still learning its trade.

John Moores made other decisions during these early years which produced long-term returns. He decided, for example, to use, build and maintain a strong mailing list. He spotted that a good mailing list could be the cornerstone of his business. He was following one of the classic routes to business success – thinking long and acting short. The success of the entire enterprise was largely determined by the ability of Littlewoods to reach and retain new customers. He linked his own lists – created from pools subscribers – with those bought in from newspapers and others.

Increased professionalism, better control and a stronger focus on the market paid its first dividend during the soccer season 1925/1926. Sales grew steadily, so that takings at the end of the season were almost £10,000 with an income of £258 on the last day. This was almost a sixfold increase over the season and a fivefold increase on the same day in the previous year.

Growth accelerated into the next year and family members were increasingly supplemented with paid staff. John Moores was still working part-time for the Commercial Cable Company, but he spent a great deal of time on staff recruitment. He wanted good quality staff who could follow instructions, exercise discretion and be trusted. This emphasis on quality bore fruit during a series of attempts by anti-gambling groups and the police to force the company out of business. The law at the time forbade cash-based gambling. Bets could be placed on credit or payment could be made by postal order or cheque. Various attempts to trick staff into taking cash bets were thwarted by vigilant employees. The same approach helped the company successfully appeal against a conviction for illegal gambling. After facing up to these challenges, Littlewoods' growth surged. Total income for 1926/1927 grew to over £50,000 and the following year revenues doubled again.

Success produced its own problems. The most immediate of these was the greater risk of fraud. Moores' 'walk about' management style, and commitment to good quality management controls helped him recognise both the risks and possible solutions. One blatant attempt to smuggle in a 'winning' coupon prompted him to make two changes. The first was to strengthen his management team. The second was to introduce innovations which transformed the firm's operating systems. Among the operational innovations was the decision to transfer the point of delivery and collection of entries from the company's own offices to the Post Office. This was combined with the introduction of technology to date-stamp every entry. These decisions shaped both the short-term success of the company and its operational philosophy in the following year. John used innovative technologies to increase his operational control while freeing him to focus on the growth of the business and in later years to develop important diversifications.

Smashing all previous records

Marketing and public relations were relatively new disciplines in the 1920s and 1930s but John Moores decided to use both to achieve three business breakthroughs. First, he wanted to escape from the hole-in-the-wall, slightly disreputable image of most gambling – especially that associated with the working classes. Littlewoods actively courted media coverage for its winner. The immense popularity of the Sunday newspapers in particular was a boon. Every record win was announced with a flourish. Headlines about smashing records and vast returns from small bets, like the one quoted below, drove up interest and stimulated awareness.

Every aspect of this type of cover was carefully designed to change the image of gambling, and the football pools in particular, while reaching the companies key target groups. The coverage was very public – allaying fears about the type of people involved in the pools business. Mr P. Woods, for example, had his prize cheque given to him by Sir Michael Bruce. Sir Michael was 'a descendent of the King Robert the Bruce, the hero of Bannockburn (and) Sir Michael served with distinction in the Great War.' The full address of Mr Woods was given. This reassured punters – members of the *Littlewoods Happy Circle* – that anyone could have their lives transformed by a pools win. Littlewoods soon provided financial

LITTLEWOOD'S AGAIN SMASH ALL PREVIOUS
RECORDS
THE WORLD'S LARGEST PENNY POOL
Mr P. Woods
326 Dundyvan Road, Whifflet, Coatbridge,
LANARKSHIRE
wins
THE WORLD RECORD DIVIDEND
OF
£28,130 for 1d.

advisors, to help their often unlettered winners to cope with their new fortune.

John Moores second goal was to stimulate demand among his key customer groups by holding out the image of vast wealth. There was constant pressure to break new records with wins. The highest dividend paid out before World War II was the £30,780 paid to R. Levy of London. This fortune (worth over £500,000 at 1999 values) was soon eclipsed after the War when the famous £75,000 prize became synonymous with Littlewoods' pool. Even this was exceeded in 1950 when Mrs Knowlson of Manchester won £104,990. The £1 million barrier was exceeded in 1987 and wins of more than £1 million soon became part of the battle against the UK's National Lottery.

For over sixty years, however, Littlewoods and John Moores managed their media campaign to focus on the top prize, the single biggest win. Other winners were publicised at a much lower level. This campaign linked massive wins with tiny bets and caught the public imagination so much that films, books, radio plays and other forms of mass entertainment took the pools and the pools winner as themes and backgrounds for plots, sketches and songs. John Moores recognised intuitively that the big win pulled in potential gamblers faster than any other promotion. He also recognised the principle that now guides lottery operations around the world. This principle is that a single winner of a giant prize generates far more interest and enthusiasm among regular users than lots of smaller prizes – even if the latter produces a higher chance of winning.

The third aim of the promotion effort was to distinguish Littlewoods from the competitors who joined the market in the late 1920s and early 1930s. Although rivals carved out specific niches, none came close to challenging the dominance of the market achieved by Littlewoods. John Moores controlled every aspect of the company's operations so well that he was able to make bigger profits and produce larger prizes than his rivals. He'd also learned how to 'sell the sizzle as well as the sausage.' This focus on promotion that highlighted the image of the pools (the sizzle) as much as the substance (the sausage) drove up demand.

Growth

By the end of the 1920s, the total amount wagered came close to £20,000 a week – a 75-fold increase in three years. Two years later, it had doubled again. By the middle of the 1930s, the average weekly income was £200,000. The virtuous circle of large amounts waged, producing large prizes and stimulating yet more people to gamble, drove growth throughout the 1930s. The Great Depression, which saw unemployment reach record levels had no noticeable negative effect. In practice, it probably stimulated demand as the low price of entry attracted desperate people who saw the big win as solving all their financial problems.

The growth of the pools business was associated with increasing efforts to strengthen internal control and integrate the business. Short-term security problems were solved by the links with the Post Office, tighter policing and careful vetting of employees. Across the company, greater integration of activities became a central aspect of the company's efforts to increase control over costs and operations while maximising profits. The decision to deduct fixed costs – instead of relying on commission – delivered additional benefits as the business reaped immediate gains from any cost reductions.

The biggest single external cost was printing. In 1928, the vast bulk of printing work was transferred to the in-house printing operation – J. & C. Moores. Although overall control was vested in two members of the Moores family, John employed the printer who had advised him to introduce the new costing system to manage the company. The in-house printing operation allowed the company to focus its efforts on building the market, especially filling the part of the year when football was not played in Britain. A series of experiments made some headway against this dip in demand especially the move into horseracing. Nothing, however, came close to having the same appeal.

All a fluke

The gap was only filled when the firm focused on the capabilities that had been created in managing mailing lists and direct mail operations. The vast bulk of the pools business operated through people sending their coupons in regularly and getting a fresh coupon in return. This vast operation reached millions of homes during the 1930s. This access was a major asset that Littlewoods controlled very effectively. It was, however, largely under-utilised as each transaction was limited to a specific item and dealt in relatively small sums of money.

John Moores decided to focus attention on getting a better return from this asset. There is also a belief within the Moores family that John was concerned that his success was just a matter of luck. His brother Cecil recalled a conversation in which John asked 'Cecil, do you think we've been rather lucky? Was it all a fluke? If we'd gone into any other sort of business, 'd'you think we'd have done as well?' Regardless of the source of the drive to widen the business base, the outcome was a major breakthrough. This breakthrough took Littlewoods into new areas that would convert the company's control of, and focus on, its core capabilities into catalogue-based mail-order retailing.

The decisions which led to this breakthrough had much in common with the decision which led to the success of the football pools business. Initially there was a decision to build on existing strengths like the mailing list. Equally important was the decision to use outside experts instead of learning from mistakes. This produced the type of serendipity that often produces business breakthroughs.

Mail-order retailing was a creature of the railway age. Nicholas Faith[2] points out that 'railways brought the whole universe of capitalism to previously self contained regions.' The first mail-order business was the Army & Navy Co-operative Society Limited (1871) which supplied goods to members – most of whom were serving in the British Army. The best known pioneer of mail-order retailing and the person who took this approach to mass markets was Aaron Montgomery Ward. He started the company that bears his name in

1872. He saw the potential of bringing quality merchandise to the disparate communities that had grown up around the US railway network. Montgomery Ward, and later the even more successful Sears, developed catalogue-based mail-order retailing into the form which still exists today.

Leveraged growth

There was less demand for mail-order goods in Britain. The much smaller distances allied to the ready access to major retail outlets in cities undermined the competitive edge which Montgomery Ward and Sears achieved in the open spaces of the USA. The 1930s, however, produced circumstances which encouraged the development of several major mail-order businesses notably Littlewoods and Great Universal Stores. In part, their success grew out of the recession. This encouraged people to come together in buying clubs.

Equally significant were the tallymen who sold bedding or clothing by collecting money from clients on a regular basis. The tallymen then provided vouchers which customers could exchange for goods in selected stores. This was an expensive way to shop offering little choice. The client received no interest on the money saved with the tallyman and the selection of stores was very limited. Despite these drawbacks, this was often the only means of saving enough to buy significant items like bedding and clothes in poor households.

John Moores drew these elements together in his mail-order business. First, he organised clubs around agents or organisers. The organiser would receive catalogues and promote the goods to club members. Second, the organisers were responsible for processing the orders and collecting payment in return for either a small commission or discounted goods. The catalogues generally offered far better choice and lower prices than the stores used by the tallymen. The mailing lists for the initial promotion were drawn from those used by the pools business.

Littlewoods was moving into a new industry by building on the control systems created in the pools business. John Moores focused his efforts on getting maximum leverage from the assets created by the core business. These included the mailing list and the skill in handling mail-based transactions. The marketing and promotion skills developed during the growth of the pools business were equally important. Littlewoods had established a reputation for honesty in creating the football pools. This reputation was used to reassure those buying mail order that their money and goods were safe.

Throughout these developments, John Moores learned to spot the pinch points in the businesses he ran. The first pinch point lay in the struggle to combine reasonable prizes with meeting operating costs. It was impossible to break even without deducting costs before allocating prizes. This emphasis on costs made the founder very conscious of the importance of both cutting costs and getting maximum returns from each investment. This emphasis helped him overcome the second pinch point – access to the market. He invested in building up a strong mailing list. This was an important decision in its own right and later provided the platform for his breakout into new markets. His sensitivity to the dynamics of markets drove the business forward. He was a pioneer in the use of press relations to boost business growth. Moores focussed his effort on maximising his market share through heavy promotion of big wins. He knew the leverage that could be earned from the good luck of winners. The same principles were equally important when the company moved into departmental store retailing. These skills enabled Littlewoods to remain the largest private firm in the UK for over a quarter of a century.

Further reading

Clegg, B. (1993) *The Man Who Made Littlewoods*, Hodder and Stoughton, London.
Hunter, W. (1996) *Football Fortunes*, Oldcastle Books, London.

Notes

1   Clegg, B. (1993) *The Man Who Made Littlewoods*, Hodder and Stoughton, London.
2   Failth, N. (1990) *The World the Railways Made*, Pimlico, London.

Part III

Grabbing the Moment

T here is a powerful link between opportunism and the type of enterprise needed to achieve a business breakthrough. Few people, however, show the type of opportunism demonstrated by Ray Kroc when he spotted the potential in the McDonald Brothers' hamburger restaurant. He did not fit many of the stereotypes of the opportunist who will grab the moment. Ray was in his early 50s. His sales franchise for the Multimix milk shake mixers was in trouble. Ray admitted that 'it wasn't easy to be cheerful' but he spotted the potential of McDonald's.

Ray did not just grab the opportunity to develop the national franchise for McDonald's, he recognised that major social and economic forces were in play that could transform the prospects for the company. New road systems, new communities were being created for a newly mobile, middle-income America. The people who were living in these communities, travelling on these roads, exploiting the new prosperity, wanted eating experiences that they could rely on. They did not want to pay the prices of expensive restaurants but they wanted reliable standards. The new franchise provided this consistency. Every McDonald's offered the same prices, the same mix of products of the same quality. Ray Kroc was determined to ensure that his franchisees delivered the promise he made to his customers.

Ray Kroc grabbed the moment created by the transformation of America society during the 1950s and 1960s. Mayer Rothschild grabbed a moment created by the turbulence created by the Napoleonic Wars.

The legend of the way he risked his fortune to save the Elector of Hesse's greater fortune may not be true. It is true, however, that Rothschild saw the opportunity to create an international financial institution against the background of the Napoleonic Wars. He skilfully solved the security problems of those with liquid assets, especially the Elector of Hesse, while solving the cash problems of the warring nations. Through his sons, he established a network of financial intermediaries that continues to play an important role in international finance.

War can create many opportunities for those able to grab the moment. Robert Woodruff spotted the opportunity to link Coca-Cola with the wave of patriotic fever that was sweeping the USA during World War II. Other things worked in his favour. Eisenhower admitted that Coca-Cola was his favourite drink. Other generals preferred soldiers to drink Coca-Cola instead of beer or other alcohol. Despite this, there was opposition within the company to the high cost of meeting Woodruff's promise that he would deliver 'Coca-Cola for five cents, to the American soldier, wherever he is.' The long-term returns were immense. Coca-Cola became part of the American way of life. More immediately important, bottling plants followed the US Army across the world and after the war were bought by Coca-Cola.

It did not take a war for Cubby Broccoli to spot the opportunity offered by Ian Fleming's novels about James Bond. Broccoli, however, grabbed the moment in the early 1960s to link his films with the way of life that emerged during that decade. Opportunism characterised every stage in the development of the film series. Cubby spotted the potential of a relatively unknown British actor (internationally at least) and wedded Sean Connery's image to Ian Fleming's creation.

The story of Gillette started with King Gillette's search for an opportunity. He eventually grabbed the moment when he 'stood there with the razor in my hand ... In a moment I saw it all.' Almost a century later, Gillette as a company was under massive pressure from rivals and predators. The company grabbed a moment created by innovative production technologies to transform the company's prospects. The Sensor changed the firm's direction, enabling it to carve out a new and distinct niche in its markets.

Chapter 11

An Exemplary Life

Mayer Rothschild

Legends

T here are many stories and legends about the decision and actions that led to the business breakthroughs that created the House of Rothschild. The existence of the stories is not surprising. For much of the nineteenth century the Rothschilds occupied a place in European and world finance that has never been matched before or since. Two stories symbolise their position. The first is linked to Guttle Rothschild, the mother of Amschel, Nathan, Carl, Salomon and James Rothschild. It is said that a neighbour came to her saying that the news was terrible and war was breaking out. Guttle, it is said, replied 'Don't be afraid. There will be no war. My sons will not provide the money for it.' Even later, it is said that at the start of this century some people believed that war would not break out in Europe because the Rothschilds would not permit it.

It is hard to imagine how a small, Jewish coin dealer, restricted to the ghetto of one of the most restrictive cities in Europe, could transform his family within a generation to the most powerful banking concern in the world. Of all the business breakthroughs in this collection, this is in a real sense the most remarkable. Not surprisingly, there are legends about the source of the breakthrough. A popular story focuses on Mayer Amschel Rothschild's ability to plan for the long term and risk a little to get a lot. Mayer was the husband of Guttle, father of Amschel, Nathan, Carl, Salomon and James. Mayer created the financial base which his sons developed so well.

One legend about the origins of the Rothschild wealth focuses on the relationship between Mayer, and Wilhelm the Landgrave of Hesse. Wilhelm was at the time the richest ruler in Europe with a fortune estimated at over 40 million gulden. Wilhelm's mistake in 1806 was to choose the wrong side when war broke out between Prussia and Napoleon's France. French forces defeated the Prussians at the battle of Jena and on the direct orders of Napoleon marched on Kassel, the Landgrave's home with very clear instructions.

'You will seal up all treasures and stores and appoint General Lagrange as Governor of the country. You will raise taxes and pronounce judgements in my name. Secrecy and speed will be the means through which you will ensure complete success. My objective is to remove the House of Hesse-Kassel from rulership and strike it out of the list of powers.'[1]

Wilhelm's palace was one of the largest, most beautiful and luxurious in Germany. He also kept part of his fortune at the palace plus details of his investments, annuities, deposits and loans. In his haste to escape Napoleon's forces, it is said that the Landgrave was forced to send much of his wealth to Mayer Rothschild for safekeeping.

Not long after, however, the French captured Frankfurt. This was Mayer's hometown. Troops immediately started looting the ghetto. Mayer's critical decision, it is said, was to put the protection of Wilhelm's vast fortune ahead of the defence of his own, much smaller fortune. He did this by hiding the Landgrave's wealth behind his own riches. The troops found the latter and did not search for the rest.

The legend has it that the Landgrave was so impressed by Mayer's acumen and honesty that he gradually gave the management of his entire fortune over to the Rothschilds. This story and other similar tales were useful to the Rothschilds. They often alluded to the legend, and hinted at secret links or ties between the family and their wealthy patron. At one dinner in London, Nathan described how 'The prince gave my father his money, there was no time to be lost; he sent it to me. I had £600,000 arrive unexpectedly by the post;

Trapped in the Jewish ghetto in Frankfurt with few advantages, Mayer Amschel Rothschild built a financial empire that has outlasted the other empires of his era. He started as a coin dealer but built links with powerful potential allies. Mayer's home was looted by Napoleon's troops but his money helped finance Wellington's campaigns in Spain, France and eventually Waterloo. Rothschild achieved his business breakthrough by a mixture of patience, planning and a determination to overcome every setback. Patience was needed to build and confirm the links with his aristocratic patrons, especially the Elector of Hesse. Careful planning underpinned the decision to despatch his sons to the major financial capitals of Europe and create a financial network that spanned Europe. Every setback became a vehicle for further growth and innovation. The Rothschilds' interests grew throughout the nineteenth century. Even today, the successor companies' reputation for innovation, quality and sound advice underpins their strength in financial markets around the world.

and I put it to such good use that the prince (after the war) made me a present of all his wine and his linen.'[2]

Nathan's elder brother Amschel added to the picture by commissioning two paintings by a famous Frankfurt artist. In the first, Wilhelm leaves his wealth in the hands of Mayer. In the second, the fortune is restored to a grateful Prince.

Break-out

The truth is more prosaic, but gives more valuable insights into the decisions that allowed the Rothschilds to break out of the physical and commercial ghetto that enclosed them in eighteenth century Frankfurt, and emerge as the most powerful bankers in Europe. Eventually Amschel Mayer Rothschild (1773–1855) controlled the Frankfurt bank, Salomon Mayer Rothschild (1774–1855) operated from

Vienna, with Carl Mayer Rothschild (1788–1855) in Naples, James Mayer Rothschild (1792–1868) in Paris and Nathan Mayer Rothschild (1777–1836) working first in Manchester, then in London.

Mayer Rothschild, their father, who masterminded this international network of financial interests, worked for years to build up the relationships, links and reputation that allowed him to capitalise on the turmoil in Europe in the later years of the Napoleonic Wars. There is some dispute about the extent to which the creation of this network was part of a carefully designed masterplan to break out of the limits imposed by the family's location and the prejudices they faced.

Wilson,[3] for example, is largely dismissive of the carefully crafted plan argument. He sees Nathan's move to London as a reaction to the tensions of a large family of powerful and talented individuals, living and working together. Wilson claims that 'Nathan was, first and foremost, escaping from the claustrophobia of the ghetto to a more open society.' Elsewhere it is argued that there was a plan behind the move first of Nathan abroad, and then of his brothers, to the other main financial centres of Europe. Elon talks of Mayer's 'evolving dynastic scheme.'

More likely than either of these explanations is the view that the moves out of Frankfurt to London, Paris, Naples and Vienna were specific decisions to resolve specific problems, but within a general pattern. There was a clear and consistent desire or plan to match their business's development to the needs of their clients, notably Wilhelm. This would be difficult without footholds in the main industrial and financial centres. The timing of Nathan's move, first to Manchester and then London, might have been prompted by impatience with his circumstances but it was inevitable. In no other way could the Rothschilds exploit the Landgrave's growing links with Britain or the UK's increasing economic power. Similarly, the Paris office was essential to the family's bullion trade. There is, however, no doubt that Mayer was determined that the family would stick together. His final injunction to his eldest son was 'Amschel, keep your brothers together and you will become

Fig 11.1 The shadow of a great man. (Credit: Rothschilds Archives.)

the richest men in Germany.' The vision and determination existed, and key decisions were made to deliver these goals.

The relationship with the Landgrave was crucial but the family's breakthrough occurred because they realised an opportunity,
years in the making. Mayer had built up his relationship with
Wilhelm for over 40 years. It started when Wilhelm was crown
prince and heir to the principality (Landgrave) of Hesse. He lived
in Hanau, near Frankfurt. The young nobleman was an avid collector or coins, and Mayer was an astute trader in coins and an-
tiques. Wilhelm was soon impressed by Rothschild's intelligence
but despite Mayer's many offers 'to stand ready to exert all my

energies and my entire fortune to serve Your Lofty Princely Seren-
ity whenever in future it shall please you to command me' the commercial links between the two grew slowly. The young nobleman
was not short of suitors from established banks and financial agents.
The growth of the relationship relied on Rothschild's long-term
view of the link, and his willingness to concede short-term earnings
and profits for long term returns. Their surviving correspondence
abounds with reference to 'low prices', 'discounts', and competitive 'interest rates.'

There was a constant search for interesting collections or coins
that would interest Wilhelm, and offers to obtain and supply them
'even at a small loss, in the hope of more profitable business in the
future.'[4] Eventually Rothschild became one of Wilhelm's honorary
Court-Factors and a firm friend of Wilhelm's trusted financial advi-
sor Carl Buderus. There were several, identifiable stages in the relationship between Mayer and the Landgrave. During the first phase,
Rothschild was a petitioner offering special deals, lower prices and
first refusal 'in deepest submissiveness and in highest consideration.'[5]

Later, Mayer became one of a number of bankers invited to
trade in the bills of exchange paid by the British for Hessian troops
to fight in the American War of Independence. Bills of exchange[6]
were vital components in both the development of banking and the
trade between people and states. This was an important phase in the
relationship because it linked Mayer with Carl Buderus – the official
who would cement links with Wilhelm. Although the Landgrave was
an important client, he was just one of several noblemen with whom
Rothschild worked.

Changing circumstances

The relationship changed when the crown prince inherited the title
from his father. There were three significant elements in the change.
Most immediately, Wilhelm became the richest ruler in Europe with
a fortune of between 40 and 120 million gulden. Inevitably, this
meant that powerful, more established banks competed vigorously

with Mayer for access to the Landgrave. It would have been easy for the scale of competition and the extent of anti-Semitism that underlaid this rivalry to deter the newcomer. Instead Rothschild decided to build on his links, especially with Buderus, and use his ability to compete on price to play the long game. At this early stage in his business breakthrough, Mayer Rothschild was thinking far more long term than his rivals and decided to swap short-term profits for long-term returns. He was determined that Wilhelm would see him as the source of the best prices, quickest payment and best returns. This was, however, a waiting game as tradition and prejudice worked against a Jew from the Frankfurt ghetto.

The French Revolution and the rise of Napoleon changed this world, but not immediately. Revolutionaries might declare that all men were equal but these attitudes do not shift the attitudes of the burgers of Frankfurt. Even the City's occupation by French troops led to no immediate improvement in conditions. The law of 1791 annulling 'all adjurnments, restrictions, and exceptions (to the rights of full citizenship) affecting individuals of the Jewish persuasion' was not implemented in Frankfurt until 1810, despite frequent French occupations and effective French control for much of the intervening period. The turmoil of war, and Britain's willingness to pay others to fight the French, was more important.

The first major opportunities, which emerged with the outbreak of the first French revolution, were in 1792. Wartime difficulties made it hard for the Landgrave's traditional bankers to handle his dealings with Britain so he turned to new traders, notably Rothschild, whose links with Buderus gave him an edge. The first major tranche of dealings between Hesse and Britain handled by Rothschild (1794) was followed by Nathan's move to Manchester (1796). The importance of this move, and the value placed on trade with England, was illustrated by the decision to transfer roughly half the family's wealth with Nathan. The business he built partly mirrored the enterprise in Frankfurt – straddling general trade, dealing in bullion and bills of exchange and handling the investments of key clients. Earlier, however, than his father and brothers in continental Europe, Nathan specialised in finance.

The carefully cultivated links with Wilhelm and Buderus were vital to the continuing growth of the business. Wilhelm's vast wealth made him a crucial client at a time when capital and liquidity were in short supply, as nations either fought wars or prepared for them. It was important for the Landgrave to keep his role in many of these transactions secret from the major warring powers and factions. This increased his dependence on intermediaries, especially those with a reputation for discretion like the Rothschilds. The scale of the trade between the new bank and the established ruler grew. During 1801 it totalled over half a million gulden but for the entire period 1801–1806 it grew to over five million gulden. This growth was fed by the success of the Rothschilds, first in developing trade in textiles between Britain and mainland Europe and then by the success of the banking services.

Loyalty

Even before 1806, and the final crisis in relations between Napoleonic France and Wilhelm's House of Hesse-Kassel, Mayer had established himself as Buderus' key partner and one of the Landgrave's main bankers. The capture of Wilhelm's palace and his subsequent flight to neutral territory changed the nature of the relationship. The Rothschilds remained loyal to Wilhelm and, in return, won increasing control over his assets. The shift in the nature of the partnership is vividly illustrated in the tone of the correspondence between the Landgrave and his bankers. His grumbles, complaints and threats grew, but he knew that only the Rothschilds could satisfy his requirements. In one letter he states that:

> 'I am increasingly worried about this matter [delays in delivering to him certificates of the debts and bonds taken out using his money] and am most eagerly waiting to hear what you have to say. In the meantime you are to cease making any further payments in respect of these stocks, neither are you to invest in them any further English payments ... in spite of all the confidence which I have in Rothschild, I cannot tolerate this delay any longer.'

The final breakthrough

Within months, however, Nathan in London was using the prince's wealth to lever the transactions that would transform the family's position. The final stage in the breakout was growing out of the control that had been achieved through the decision to cultivate the link with Wilhelm and the subsequent decisions to build up the relationship with Buderus. Mayer's focus on the long term had seen short-term losses in individual small transactions turn into large profits in large transactions. The basic pattern was the same when Wilhelm was under pressure from Napoleon. There were overtures and threats from Napoleon's agents to the Landgrave's favourite banker. The Rothschilds were offered bribes to betray their client. Later, Mayer and his sons Salomon and Jacob were arrested and pressured to provide details and access to Wilhelm's riches. By this time, the Rothschilds were clear in their decision not to betray their client and used this to gain increasing control over the disposal of his assets. This control became focused on their determined effort to use their international links to capitalise on the opportunities that emerged first from Napoleon's Continental Blockade,[7] then the British campaigns in Spain and Portugal and eventually the collapse of Napoleon's empire.

The Continental Blockade sharply increased the prices of British goods (especially textiles and manufactured products) in mainland Europe. The Rothschilds with their operations on both sides of the Channel and ready access to capital were well positioned to capitalise on the opportunities created. They could then focus their wealth and that of their major clients on exploiting the opportunities created when the European wars started turning against Napoleon. The points of maximum leverage occurred when the British government needed gold to pay Wellington's troops during the Peninsular War which followed Napoleon's invasion of Portugal (1807), and the rebellion of Spain from French rule (1808). The international nature of their trading interests paid its first massive dividends when the Rothschilds acquired, at large discounts, bills of exchange issued by Wellington in Portugal during the early stages of his Peninsular Campaign. Nathan was able to trade these in at face value in London at a substantial profit. The British government was sufficiently impressed to employ Rothschild to ship gold to Wellington's army in Portugal and Spain.

The careful groundwork, long-term view, and astute decisions of the last 20 years now paid off. Control over a massive share of the Landgrave's wealth had projected Nathan into a leadership position in London financial circles. The Rothschilds were happy to acknowledge the debt. 'The Prince made our fortune, if Nathan had not had the elector's £300,000 (around £15 million at today's prices) in hand he would have got nowhere.' The scale of Wilhelm's investments grew as Nathan showed his skill in squeezing increasing returns from his new clients in London. Between the spring and winter of 1808, four tranches of around £150,000 were put at Nathan's disposal. Nathan's growing links with the British government and his increasing role in securing payment for Wellington's army was now made easier by the next stage in the expansion of the Rothschilds' mainland interests beyond Frankfurt.

Mayer sent one of his younger sons to Paris to establish a local trading operation. Initially, this enterprise was, apparently, set up to take shipments of British gold shipped from England by trading partners wanting to escape an economy on the verge of collapse. The French authorities welcomed these shipments, partly as evidence of declining confidence in British victory and partly as an indication of inflationary pressures in England. In practice, however, much of this gold was shipped on to Wellington and his armies. 'It has been claimed that between 1811 and 1815 almost £20 million was shipped by the Rothschilds to Wellington and to England's allies on the continent.'[8] The leverage gained from their increasingly strategic role in shipping bullion around Europe was immense. This probably gave rise to the claim that in the latter stages of the Napoleonic wars the Rothschilds were simultaneously financing Wellington and his allies through Nathan in London, and Napoleon through James in Paris.

Mayer died in September 1812 before the final returns from his decisions could be seen. He had, however, seen his family break free of the ghetto. His sons were established in the major banking centres. Nathan was already one of the leading financiers in the world's major banking centre – London. It is impossible to estimate their wealth, but total assets of about £5000 in 1750 had been built up to around £100,000 by 1800. Over the next decade, he and his sons converted this to a fortune of £500,000 and when he died two years later this had doubled. By the end of the Napoleonic Wars 'the Rothschild banks in Frankfurt, London and Paris had accumulated immense capital assets and had established between them a unique clearing house system for international bills of exchange.'[9] During the post-war settlement, the Rothschilds were able to confront and defeat an attempt by the victorious powers to exclude them from handling any of the settlement transactions. Wilhelm regained his throne in 1813 and died a decade later, richer than ever.

His fortune by this time was eclipsed by the combined wealth of the Rothschild brothers. The French National Archive calculates that 'their combined capital grew from 3,332,000 francs in 1815 to 118,458,332 francs in 1828.'[10] The structure of the bank tried to balance out their individual wealth. It is hard to arrive at precise estimates of their wealth but they are likely to be of the order listed in Table 11.1 (at 1999 values).

Only at the end of the century would capitalists emerge in the USA, to match their success in breaking out of the boundaries they faced, by making decisions that would create comparable wealth.

Table 11.1 The combined wealth of the Rothschild brothers.

	1818	1825	1828
	$m	$m	$m
Nathan	85.8	192.5	201.3
Amschel	55.55	135.3	140.8
Salomon	55.55	135.3	140.8
Carl	55.55	135.3	140.8
James	55.55	135.3	140.8
Total	308	733.7	764.5

Further reading

Elon, A. (1996) *Founder: Meyer Amschel Rothschild and His Time*, HarperCollins, London.

Ferguson, N. (1998) *The World's Banker*, Weidenfeld and Nicholson, London.

Gray, V. and Aspey, M. (1998) *The Life and Times of N.M. Rothschild 1776–1836*, N.M. Rothschild, London.

Morton, F. and Cooperman, N. (1998) *The Rothschilds: Portrait of a Dynasty*, Kodansha Globe, New York.

Wilson, D. (1988) *Rothschild: A Story of Wealth and Power*, André Deutsch, London.

Notes

1 Quoted in Wilson, D. (1988) *Rothschild: A Story of Wealth and Power*, André Deutsch, London.

2 Quoted in Elon, A. (1996) *Founder: Meyer Amschel Rothschild and His Time*, HarperCollins, London.

3 Wilson, D. (1988) *ibid.*

4 Elon, A. (1996) *ibid.*

5 Letter to Le Prince hereditaire Landgrave de Hesse from Mayer Amschel Rothschild quoted in Ferguson, N. (1998) *The House of Rothschild*, Weidenfeld and Nicholson, London.

6 A bill of exchange would be issued by, say, the British government for the use of Hessian solders in North America. This government would promise to pay the bearer the identified sum on a fixed future date. A recipient such as Wilhelm would want to convert this bill to cash as soon as possible. The trade would pay a discounted sum (less commission) and eventually present the bill for payment to the issuer.

7 The Continental Blockade was Napoleon's attempt to counter the British Navy's blockade of French maritime trade by imposing a ban on the import of British goods into those parts of Europe that he controlled.

 8 Elon, A. (1996) *ibid.*
 9 Wilson, D. (1988) *ibid.*
10 Elon, A. (1996) *ibid.*

Chapter 12

An American Dream

Linking Coca-Cola and the American Way of Life

A way of life

Coke is the most heavily consumed beverage in the world after water. It is estimated that if all the Coca-Cola consumed by the human race by the year 2000 was poured over Niagara Fall, the falls would flow at their normal rate for over 40 hours. Coke is served almost 1000 million times every day of the year in almost every country in the world. A year's consumption would fill one of the towers of New York's World Trade Centre almost a hundred times. The statistics of Coke production, distribution, promotion and consumption, themselves, could fill their own sets of record books.

Much of the success of Coca-Cola comes from its close identification with the American way of life. This has produced phrases like Coca-Cola diplomacy – the Atlanta Olympics were even dubbed the Coca-Cola Olympics. Serious studies of US diplomacy linked US foreign policy to the spread of Coca-Cola.[1]

This bond between the USA and Coca-Cola was highlighted in 1985 when the leadership at Coca-Cola's headquarters in Atlanta decided to replace the traditional, hundred-year-old product with a new formula. The US media exploded with criticism.[2] One columnist said 'next week they'll be chiselling Teddy Roosevelt off Mount Rushmore.' Another writer attacked the company because 'I love Coca-Cola. It is the finest product produced in the United States, and America's most noble ambassador to the world.' A New York paper said that 'the new drink will be smoother, sweeter, and a threat to a way of Life.'

In the aftermath of the attempt to replace the traditional formula with New Coca-Cola, the company's bosses concluded that 'the passion for original Coca-Cola – and that is the word for it; passion – was something that caught us by surprise ... It is a wonderful American mystery, a lovely American enigma, and you cannot measure it any more than you can measure love, pride, or patriotism.' His words echo comments made by Nancy Mitford 40 years earlier when a character in her novel *The Blessing* says 'When I say a bottle of Coca-Cola, I mean it metaphorically speaking. I mean it as an outward and visible sign of something inward and spiritual, I mean it as if each Coca-Cola bottle contained a djinn [spirit], and as if that djinn was our great American civilisation ready to spring out of each bottle and cover the whole global universe with its great wide wings.'

One dollar for half of it

The foundations for the success of Coca-Cola were well established before the decision that transformed the nature of the relationship between Coca-Cola and the American way of life. It was in 1942, just after Pearl Harbour, that Robert Woodruff (Coca-Cola's chief executive) issued the order that 'we will see to it that every man in uniform gets a bottle of Coca-Cola for five cents, wherever he is and whatever it costs our company.' The decision was a brilliant mixture of patriotism, insight and commercial good sense. There is little doubt that Woodruff wanted to do his bit for the morale of Americans serving overseas during World War II. A year earlier he'd responded positively to a request from the US press corps in London for supplies of Coca-Cola. The reporters had wired:

> 'We, members of the associated press, can not get Coca-Cola anymore. Terrible situation for Americans covering battle of Britain, know you can help, regards.'

From 1886 when John Stith Pemberton first developed his new drink and sold an average of nine servings a day, to today when the Coca-Cola company sells one billion servings of its drinks every day, the history of the company and its most famous drink has seen massive and generally consistent success. The early years saw considerable turmoil as changes of ownership and disputes about rights slowed down development. First, Alfred Chandler bought control in 1894 for $2300, then Ernest Woodruff paid the then astonishing sum of $25 million for control in 1919. Under the control of Ernest and his son Robert, the company and its most famous product – Coca-Cola – grew into the largest soft drinks company in the world.

The Coca-Cola brand is regularly identified by the Guinness Book of Records as the most well-recognised or most powerful brand in the world. The success of the brand has allowed the parent company to diversify with considerable success into related products. The firm's marketing successes are now linked with increasing investments in sponsorship. Coca-Cola's $100 million sponsorship of the Atlanta Olympics is the largest sponsorship deal in history. Consumption continues to grow despite increasing competition from its main rival Pepsi, which overtook Coca-Cola itself for US sales in the 1990s (largely because of its greater penetration of US retailers). More immediately, the brand's image has been affected by problems with its Belgian bottling company. The success with which Coca-Cola responds to this and other challenges will determine whether its achievements in the 21st century will match its triumphs in the 20th.

Woodruff was a natural marketer and immediately spotted the opportunity to make friends in the media. Supplies were sent immediately.

The outbreak of war saw supplies of Coca-Cola disappear from American bases across the world – just when solders, seamen and airmen wanted to retain their links with home. Shortages pushed up prices. One soldier wrote home saying 'one real bottle of Coca-Cola, the first I have seen here. It was pulled out from under the shirt of a pilot ... He caressed it, his eyes rolled over it, he smacked his lips at the prospect of tasting it. I offered him one dollar for half of it, then two, three and five dollars.' The standard US price was five cents. Lonely young men and women couldn't get home to watch baseball, visit the movies, see their families but the familiar look, feel and taste of Coca-Cola could be taken to them. Robert Woodruff spotted the opportunity to link his product with the wave of patriotic fever that was sweeping the USA.

It was a shrewd move. Coca-Cola faced two uncomfortable problems with US entry into the war. The most pressing difficulty was the introduction of sugar rationing. The more worrying was the success of its business in Nazi Germany. Sugar shortages were the immediate threat. The company had enjoyed rapid growth in the years immediately before the war. This meant that the introduction of quotas of sugar based on the average of sales in the *three* previous years hit the company hard. They were cut back by more than fifty per cent of their previous year's consumption. To make matter worse, the stocks of sugar that had been accumulated to face this type of crisis were under threat from the War Production Board which wanted to take all such reserves under its control.

The only exemptions to these cuts were goods supplied to the armed forces. In June 1942, the US Army's quartermaster general intervened to exempt Coca-Cola from rations on products supplied to troops. The early origins of Coca-Cola as a temperance drink helped persuade the military leadership that it was a good alternative to alcohol. Woodruff also sponsored the publication of research which showed that soldiers and munitions workers were far more productive if they had frequent rests and cooling drinks. These research arguments were skilfully linked with more emotional messages about Coca-Cola being ' a part and symbol of a way of life for which a war is being waged.'

The decision by the War Production Board to relax quotas of goods sold to the military and defence industries solved only part of the problem. Shipping the product overseas was neither cheap nor without its critics. Some journalists suggested that guns and planes were higher priorities for scarce space on military transports. Woodruff resisted the pressure from the finance people inside the company, who said it cost far too much to deliver his 'bottle of Coca-Cola for five cents, wherever he is' promise, and outsiders who criticised the space given to shipping Coca-Cola. Woodruff was backed by those within the Company who wanted the product to 'be an inseparable part' of the war effort. Woodruff wanted to create an affection for Coke that 'will carry through the lives of the young men now in the Army and through them will be reflected in generations to come.' Woodruff was following his instincts for immediate action but thinking about the long-term benefits for the company.

American Cola

The core strategy worked but it required major changes in Coca-Cola's way of doing business. The most immediate need was to establish bottling plants, deliver syrup and establish production facilities in the different theatres of war. Plants were soon constructed in most of the main war zones where there was not already some production capacity from pre-war overseas expansion. In developing these facilities Woodruff and Coca-Cola were determined to establish and maintain strict standards of control. In Britain, the company ceased all operations when the UK Ministry of Supply ordered it to combine its operation with Pepsi to produce a generic product called American Cola. Elsewhere, the Army agreed to appoint company employees as 'technical observers' so that they could quickly get to their destinations and set up their production facilities.

Senior generals were often Woodruff's strongest supporters. Eisenhower, Patton and Bradley were among the product's most famous supporters. In one famous article describing Ike's (Eisenhower's) preferences it is said that he asked, 'Could someone get me a Coke?' After polishing off the drink, the General said he had one more request, Asked what he wanted, he answered, 'Another Coke.' Ike's belief in the value of Coca-Cola to the war effort was so strong that after the North Africa invasion by allied troops he asked the company to set up sufficient production facilities to provide 'three million bottled Coca-Cola (filled)'. The priority he gave to this operation led to the construction of ten bottling plants in North Africa.

This pattern of following the movements of the troops with new production facilities delivered a series of tangible benefits to the company. It ensured that the company could retain control of its production standards while reaffirming its image and presence in the minds of the troops. This control confirmed the psychological link between the brand, the troops and their images of home. This became a powerful focus for the company and its customers.

A massive correspondence confirms this link in the minds and eyes of forces personnel who wrote that 'it's the little things not the big things that the individual solder fights for or wants so badly when away. It's the girlfriend back home in a drug store over a coke.' Equally, the soldier who wrote that 'the crowning touch to your Christmas present was the bottled Coca-Cola' was embedding the product in the minds of people back in the USA. Coca-Cola was 'a godsend' or a 'vaguely remembered nectar, reminiscent of some far-off paradise land.' These images were not lost on the locals. Sometimes the sexual energy of US forces personnel was linked to a hoped for, or assumed aphrodisiac in the drink itself. More prosaically, the new plants gave Coca-Cola a massive competitive advantage when they were purchased from the US government after the war.

The combination of this powerful and positive image and a well-focused production and distribution system gave Coca-Cola massive leverage in international markets after the War. Coca-Cola was linked with American wealth and prosperity in an impoverished postwar world. This was not the first time the company had moved overseas. Before the outbreak of the war, Coca-Cola had successful operations in several countries. The business in Germany had been

"Congratulations. You're the 100th soldier who
has posed with that bottle of Coca-Cola.
You can drink it."

Fig. 12.1 Cartoon circa 1944. (Credit: Copyright Bill Mauldin, 1944, reprinted with permission.)

so successful that it could easily have damaged the company's reputation if the brand had not been so closely linked with the war effort. Coca-Cola's trademark had survived in every German occupied country. The substitute product that had been produced – Afri-Cola – had done no harm to the franchise. More importantly, the German company had developed an alternative product – Fanta – that became a useful part of the portfolio of products and brands that emerged with the Coca-Cola franchise after the war.

Brand power

At the end of the war the Company had 63 overseas bottling plants and a vastly increased brand franchise in the USA and internationally. Coca-Cola was preferred to its only serious rival Pepsi by a margin of 8 to 1 among solders and by only a smaller margin among the wider public. 'Coca-Cola's place in American Life seemed as secure and tightly woven as the Stars and Stripes in the flag.'[3] Apart from chewing gum, no product was as closely identified with the American way of life in the minds of millions of potential consumers around the world than Coca-Cola. By the 1960s more of the product was being consumed outside North America than within the USA. During the company's centennial celebrations in 1986, 12,500 bottlers came to Atlanta from all over the world. Coke's market share internationally was far stronger than its powerful US rival Pepsi.

In the USA the two products were neck and neck but in international markets Coca-Cola outsold its rival by three or four to one. Even in the USA, the company's market share among older consumers – who remembered the war – was far greater than that among young consumers. Uniquely among brands it occupies the same ranking for recognition and awareness in the UK, Europe, the USA and the World – top. This brand recognition extends beyond the brand itself to its logo – the Coca-Cola script, its packaging – the original 5 cent bottle and its distinctive colour scheme.

Table 12.1 The world's most powerful brand names – ranked.[4]

UK	Europe	USA	World
Coca-Cola	Coca-Cola	Coca-Cola	Coca-Cola
Marks and Spencer	BMW	Marlboro	Sony
Kellogg	Adidas	Pepsi-Cola	Mercedes Benz
Gillette/Guinness/Mars	Mercedes Benz	McDonald's	Kodak
	Philips	Miller	Disney

Fig. 12.2   The world's most powerful brand. (Credit: Rowan Cannon.)

The magic formula

Robert Woodruff's involvement in Coca-Cola came through the acquisition of the company by his father Ernest Chandler, for the then vast sum of $25 million in 1919. At the time, this was one of the biggest business transactions ever undertaken in the southern USA. The scale of this transaction highlights the reputation and strong market position that the company had already established, especially in the southern USA where its reputation as a cure for headaches and dyspepsia had gradually been transformed into a popular drink at Soda Fountains. Ernest was a determined and skilled financier who wrestled control of the company, the secret syrup formula and the brand, from the different groups who claimed ownership of each.

Ernest recognised his son's skills in sales and promotion as clearly as he spotted the potential of the core product. Robert built up the brand, established national sales and distribution systems and underpinned this with a powerful advertising programme. His links with the D'Arcy advertising agency led to a series of innovations in marketing and promotion. These ranged from his emphasis on sales of the bottled product – giving him direct control of prices – to presentation and quality control. Together Woodruff and the agency chose the colour scheme – white for purity, red for energy and green for coolness. They chose the best illustrators of the day to build images of the product that became intrinsic aspects of America's self image.

A patent medicine

The vehicle for this growth was written in a formula that was kept in the safe of a New York banker. The formula was originally devised by a pharmacist-cum-patent medicine designer called John Sith Pemberton. Pemberton was a talented designer of new drinks at a time when the USA's increasingly prosperous population was looking for ways to keep healthy, socialise and avoid alcohol. Pemberton was, however, always short of money. This was partly because of his ill health and partly because of his morphine addiction.

Pemberton and his partner Frank Roberson introduced the 'Refreshing! Exhilarating! (and) Invigorating!' drink to the new Soda Fountains that were opening across the USA. These temples of 'crystal, marble and silver' were ideal outlets for the new drink. Pemberton was torn by his ambitions for the product and his need for funds as his health declined. The latter pressures predominated and he sold many of his rights to the product – without consulting Robertson.

This produced the first in a series of legal wrangles and crises that marked the early development of Coca-Cola. Neither Pemberton, his new partners nor Robertson had effective control over the product, its distribution or promotion. Effective control was only achieved when Robertson turned to Asa Chandler for help in his struggle with Pemberton. By this time, Pemberton was near death and soon collaborated with Chandler's efforts to win effective control of Coca-Cola's operations. Chandler and Robertson worked together to build up the franchise but effective control lay with Chandler. Pemberton's death in 1888 left Asa Chandler (in his words) 'in bad health, $50,000 in debt and with Coca-Cola in my hands.'

Over the next 20 years, Chandler's drive and Robertson's promotional skills built Coca-Cola up to be one of the most successful drinks in the USA. This growth, however, was not without its problems. In an ironic twist on its future success, the product was banned from US army bases during the early years of the century because of the claim that it contained cocaine and was addictive. Only when the chief chemist of the US department of agriculture cleared the product of containing any cocaine was it reintroduced to army bases. Even then the legal debate continued about the product. These wrangles persuaded Chandler that, although he was now the richest man in Atlanta, he wanted to sell his rights to the product. The battle for control was wearing him down; he could no longer focus on the product's success. He was ready to withdraw when the business was sold and control passed to Ernest Woodruff. This transfer established the dynasty that would lead Coca-Cola for 60 years, and complete John Pemberton's dream of breaking out of its southern US market and transforming itself from a questionable health drink to America's (and the world's) favourite cold drink.

Further reading

Allen, F. (1995) *Secret Formula*, HarperCollins, New York.

Elliott, C. (1982) *Mr Anonymous*, Cherokee Publishing Company, Atlanta. (Originally published as *A Biography of 'The Boss'*, copyright Robert W. Woodruff, 1979.)

Friedman, K. (1996) *Elvis, Jesus and Coca-Cola*, Bantam, New York.

Greising, D. (1998) *I'd Like the World to Buy a Coke: The Life and*

Leadership of Roberto Goizueta, John Wiley, New York.

Hoy, A.H. (1986) *Coca-Cola: The First Hundred Years*, The Coca-Cola Company, Atlanta.

Prendergast, M. (1993) *For God, Country and Coca-Cola*, Phoenix Books, London.

Notes

1 Freedam-Smith, R. (1994) *The Caribbean World and the United States; Mixing Rum and Coca-Cola*, Twayne Publications, New York.

2 Quotes from Allen, F. (1995) *Secret Formula*, HarperCollins, New York.

3 Allen, F. (1995) *Secret Formula*, HarperCollins, New York.

4 *The Guinness Book of Business Records*, Guinness Publishing, London.

Chapter 13

How Far Could I Go on Kroc Burgers?

Ray Kroc at McDonald's

I've got to get involved

T he achievements of the McDonald's hamburger franchise provide one of the most vivid success stories in modern business. The key elements of the story are familiar. The McDonald brothers started the ball rolling with their drive-in hot dog bar in Pasadena (California) in 1937. Their business grew so they moved to new outlets in San Bernardino (California). Almost 20 years after their first restaurant was opened the brothers met Ray Kroc. He held the national marketing rights to the mixers that the brothers used for making milk shakes. Kroc was so impressed by their operations that he decided 'I've got to get involved in this.' His way in was to get the rights to franchise their business across the USA. Kroc was a marketing perfectionist and passionate advocate of quality fast food. This combination of promotion, quality and specialisation with the franchise form of trading and the post-war boom in the USA led first to McDonald's dominance of the US fast food industry and then to its global leadership.

KISS

Less well known parts of the McDonald's story are the setbacks that the people and the firm faced on the way to the global success, and the decisions – culminating in a major strategic shift in approach during the mid 1950s – that led to the real business breakthrough behind McDonald's success.

Maurice and Richard McDonald, the founders of the first McDonald's, authors of the core approach to fast food and designers of the golden arch, started their first drive-through restaurant after they failed in the movie business. They had arrived in California from New Hampshire hoping to make it big in films. After years working on the back lots of film companies and failing in their first business – operating a cinema – they opened their first drive-in restaurant.

Later accounts of their success highlight the lack of baggage they carried into their new business. This apparent weakness encouraged them to try new ideas and approaches. In a sense this was essential. New drive-ins were opening right across California. New companies had to be creative to survive. Growth in the local population and expanding job opportunities allowed the brothers to build their business. Gradually, however, the same forces eroded their profits as staff costs grew and labour turnover increased. They wanted a way out of the vicious circle of increasing costs and reducing profits.

Their answer was a classic example of the oldest business principle – Keep It Simple, Stupid (the KISS principle). They streamlined their product range – concentrating on hamburgers for the first time. They replaced traditional cutlery and crockery with disposable products. They invested heavily in a new facility designed to speed service while reassuring customers about quality and hygiene. From a slow start the business boomed. The company's reputation spread so far that it attracted the interest of an equipment salesman from Illinois – two thousand miles away.

Ray Kroc was facing his own crisis when he came across the McDonald brothers. He held the national sales franchise for Multimix milk shake mixers. But, 'it wasn't easy to be cheerful about my business in the early 1950s. Al Doty (a colleague) once told me that he liked to have lunch with me because he always learned something about his own business trends. "You seem to be able to see further into the future than the rest of us," he said. I believe I did. And what

The McDonald name, the Golden Arches, Ronald McDonald and the hamburger itself are among the most easily recognised business images of our era. The company has spread from a single location in California to a global business. The company has sustained its success in the face of powerful rivals and local resistance because of the strength of the core proposition. McDonald's originally offered its newly affluent and mobile customers in the USA total reliability and quality. The post-war baby boom in the USA boosted the economy while creating new demands from parents and children. Internationalisation emerged naturally as the brand became linked with the aspirations of customers across the world. Sustaining growth was a massive challenge that the company solved through an ingenious financial instrument.

Continuing growth is sustained by one of the most skilful marketing operations in the world. The marketing effort is still rooted in Ray Kroc's commitment to consistent quality standards. Programmes as diverse as the McDonald's University (for training potential franchisees) to the heavyweight advertising and promotional effort, sustain the company's position in the marketplace as the world's most successful fast food retailer and one of the best known brands.

I saw made me very unhappy. It was clear that Multimix's days were numbered.'[1]

The grim prospects for his existing business persuaded Kroc to book his 'fifty two year old bones into the red-eye special and fly west to meet my future.'[2]

The combination of Ray Kroc – a natural salesman desperate for a new business idea – and the booming McDonald's business was just beginning. He was excited by the potential of the business.

'It was a restaurant stripped down to the minimum in service and menu, the prototype for legions that would spread across the land. Hamburgers, fries and beverages were prepared on an assembly line basis and, to the amazement of everyone, Mac [Maurice] and Dick included, the thing worked. Of course the simplicity of the procedure allowed the McDonalds to concentrate on quality in every step, and that was the trick. When I saw it working that day in 1954, I felt like some latter-day Newton who'd just had an Idaho potato caromed off his skull.'[3]

Ray was a novice in the fast food business but his work for Multimix had taken him across the US in the search for business. He knew this enterprise operated by the McDonalds was special and he wanted part of it.

Franchising

Franchising was not a new idea to the McDonalds. Their popularity and success had drawn admirers from across the state. Some had come and simply copied. Others wanted access to their expertise so had entered into franchise agreements. These had not been very successful. They took up more time than they were worth to the brothers, who were already running a very successful small business. Ray Kroc had no such problem. He could also see the potential in an America that had discovered prosperity, travel and parenthood. People were eating out in increasing numbers but traditional restaurants catered largely to more mature markets, teens or casual travellers. No one had established a leadership position in the new growth market of young, affluent (but not rich) families wanting to eat out together.

Ray Kroc was the perfect partner for the brothers. He was hungry for the business – so he accepted a deal stacked in favour of the McDonalds. The franchise fee was held down to $950 while franchisees had to pay a service fee of 1.9 per cent of sales. The brother took 0.5 per cent of this fee and Kroc had to operate the entire business out of the remaining 1.4 per cent. Not only was he hungry but he was determined. Kroc spotted the potential and he was determined to make the business succeed.

He recognised the importance of control early in the development of the franchise. In part, this was forced on him when he arrived

Fig. 13.1 The Golden Arches sign. (Credit: Rowan Cannon.)

back in his home state and found that the brothers had already re-leased the franchise for his local market. He bounced back from that setback by buying out the franchisee rights for $25,000. This gave them a $15,000 dollar profit in a matter of weeks and forced Kroc into debt.

Rolling Green Golf Club

His next setback was personal. He'd opened his own restaurant in Des Plains modelled on the McDonald's business. Fred Turner, one of the first grillmen at the new Des Plains restaurant (and future chairman of the corporation) describes it 'as so clean, so bright, so colourful. It was demonstration cooking. All the food preparation was out in the open. There was all that glistening stainless steel. And the uniforms of the crew were white and clean.' The new restaurant was an immediate success.

Despite this success, there were few established restaurateurs chasing up franchises. Kroc turned, instead, to his friends and the Rolling Green Golf Club. Although many took up the franchise opportunity, hardly any met the standards that Kroc was determined to impose on his franchisees. The breakthrough did not occur until a stranger – Sandy Agate – took up the franchise, operated it to Kroc's standards and was a success. Agate's success, and his willingness to show people his accounts, was the platform the franchise needed for growth. The perfectionist could show others how to make money from perfection.

Ray Kroc puts much of his success down to the persistence with which he battled against difficulties. His most well-known quote is a paean of praise for persistence and focus:

> 'Nothing in the world can take the place of persistence. Talent will not; nothing is more common than unsuccessful men with talent. Genius will not; unrewarded genius is almost a proverb. Education will not; the world is full of educated derelicts. Persistence and determination alone are omnipotent.'

Despite his determination, however, the franchise business continued to struggle. New franchisees came forward in increasing numbers. The chain's restaurants prospered. They achieved sales of over $75 million in 1960 but the corporation's profits were less than $200,000. This was less than the estimated profits of half a dozen franchisees. It certainly did not justify the $2.7 million dollars paid to the McDonald brother for total rights to the name. Kroc's determination that 'YOU MUST BE A PERFECTIONIST!'[4] was stimulating demand but doing little for profits.

His love of the business and determination to grow it in partnership with franchisees closed many traditional sources of profit. He wanted the franchisees to buy the best equipment and materials so he did not force them to buy through the corporation or build sweetheart deals himself with suppliers. Kroc refused to weaken his control by charging larger territory fees so that franchisees would open new operations. The man who still collected litter when he visited a McDonald's rejected the easy route to profits. Without some form of breakthrough, the company would grow itself to death.

Franchise Realty Corporation

The solution was a 'stroke of financing genius' by Kroc's alter ego at McDonald's – Harry Sonneborn. Harry's stroke of genius was to underpin the growth of the business by setting up a real estate company called Franchise Realty Corporation in 1956. The proposition had the simple win–win base of many of the greatest business decisions. Franchise Realty operated by leasing or buying potential store sites and then sub-letting them to operators. This was a win for the franchisee because it released them from one of the toughest problems of any new business, i.e. finding premises. Franchise Realty constantly scouted for locations that met their needs; close to new developments, handy for the highways and good access. Franchise Realty would then lease or purchase the site and sub-let the premises to the new operator.

This was a double win for McDonald's itself. It produced a larger and more reliable source of revenues. The income came in three forms. First, the franchisee was obliged to pay a refundable security deposit for the site. Initially this was $7500 but it has since grown significantly. Second, the franchisee's money could then be used as a down payment of the lease or land purchase. The third advantage of the system was that it increased earnings because the franchisee was obliged to pay a monthly rent based on fixed premium on the rent i.e. 20–40 per cent more than McDonald's were paying. The franchisee was obliged to pay this or a rent based on the outlet's turnover *whichever was the higher*. These improved returns transformed the Corporation's finances and provided a powerful financial base from which to extend.

Sonneborn's strategy required increases in the company's financial support to buy property. Initially, this meant tackling bankers or savings and loans in the localities of the new operation. This, however, was massively time consuming even for the team of young Turks recruited by Sonneborn. The scale of their finances had to be increased if the monies available to the business were to keep pace with demand. They were facing a major cash-flow crisis at the end of 1958. This was made worse when the company fell victim to a defaulting intermediary who took a number of franchisees' security deposits, entered into a series of mortgage agreements on McDonald's behalf and then disappeared. Faced with this crisis, the core strength of the company's approach saw them through. A group of major suppliers, who by now believed in its prospects, purchased a series of debentures to solve the immediate crisis. This difficulty forced McDonald's to increase its search for a much larger financial backer.

Sonneborn's patience and Kroc's enthusiasm eventually persuaded E.E. Ballard, president of All-American Life and Casualty, to provide a major injection of finance. Ballard described his encounter with Kroc. 'It was Ray's fire that really got me interested. I'll never forget his knowledge of the details of the business. He knew exactly what he was going to do and how he was going to do it. I liked his neatness. The way he stood and talked.'[5] Ballard admits that McDonald's lacked the assets to back their borrowings but he decided to back the loan at a mere 6 per cent. This new financing was only the start. The new focus on property created an opportunity for a breakthrough in financing as the company secured additional support from another Chicago-based insurer, Central Standard Life. The real breakthrough in financing came later when, after several false starts, the company won backing from financial groups such as John Hancock, First Boston and eventually State Mutual in partnership with Paul Revere.

This final partnership was especially important in the history of McDonald's as it provided the firm, not only with new finance in excess of a $1 million,[6] but it illustrated the synergy between the real estate operation and the core business. It is hard to imagine these financial institutions considering a loan of this size without the security offered by the property portfolio. It is, however, clear that 'If the parking lots had been dirty, if the help had grease stains on their aprons and if the food wasn't good, McDonald's never would have gotten the loan, regardless of what Harry Sonneborn said about real estate.'[7] This loan transformed McDonald's standing. New financial backers were happy to come in behind these investors. The loan simultaneously transformed McDonald's standing in the fast food industry. This was the first major loan provided by significant financial institutions to a fast food operation.

Buying out the McDonalds

Without access to this type of finance it would have been impossible to embark on the next stage in Kroc's strategy for control. He was determined to buy out the McDonald brothers. Their price was high in terms of current earnings. The brothers wanted $2.7 million for all their rights. This was almost 15 times the royalties they had earned the previous year ($189,000) and over 30 times the profits of Kroc's company that year ($77,000). Kroc's only levers were the real estate deals that would make it hard for the brothers to replace Kroc's company, his growing reputation and the brothers' desire for a one-off deal that would give them long-term security without the difficulties of running a growing and complicated business.

The funds to buy out the brothers came from a consortium of educational institutions, trusts and charities that become known in McDonald's as the 12 apostles. They included Princeton, Howard and Syracuse Universities, Colby and Swarthmore Colleges and the Good Will Home Association. Their returns more than justified their investment. More importantly for McDonald's the company could go for growth with concerns about ownership, finance and revenues firmly on the back burner. They could concentrate on exploiting their business breakthrough.

Growth accelerated, especially as Ray could combine his control over the operation with his clear focus on the business's core strengths and the leverage he had from the real estate business. The description of Kroc as the Henry Ford of the restaurant industry was amply justified by his determination to routinise production, maintain quality and cut costs. He was furious when people diverged from the standard he set. Some, at least, of his anger with the McDonald brothers emerged from their lax control over their local franchisees. His control over property provided a powerful weapon in the battle over standards. The lease offered to franchisees included the clause that 'if at any time McDonald's System Inc. notifies Franchise Realty Corporation that the Corporation does not conform in every way to the McDonald's standards of quality and service, this lease will be cancelled on thirty-day notice.' This was the club with which the Corporation forced up standards and enforced compliance.

Ronald McDonald

Like Ford, Kroc was reluctant to change the basic format. There were no Pizzas, Chicken Legs or any of the other variations that crept into the fast food industry during the 1950s, 1960s and 1970s. This did not preclude creativity. It merely focused innovation around the core business. Lou Groen, a Cincinnati-based franchisee, developed, promoted and eventually won corporate support for his fish sandwich in 1962. Ronald McDonald emerged a year later initially in Washington but eventually across the USA. The Big Mac and Chicken McNuggets appeared in the mid-1970s. The source of 'all the major new products can be traced to the experimentation of franchisees.' Kroc's determination to establish a genuine partnership (albeit on his terms) with his franchisees continues to pay off.

The asset base created by the real estate business allowed the business to exploit its breakthrough. In his autobiography, Kroc comments that 'we started Franchise Realty Corporation with $1000 paid-in capital, and Harry parlayed that cash investment to $170 million worth of real estate.'[8] By the mid-1990s the net book value of McDonald's real estate exceeded $10 billion and over three-quarters of the corporation's profits come from its real estate business. The core business grew rapidly so that there were 750 outlets by the time McDonald's went public in 1965. Their firm broke through the 1000 outlet barrier a few years later and achieved 2000 in 1971. The 3000th store opened in London in 1977 and the 4000th store was added less than a decade later with the firm creeping inexorably towards Ray Kroc's target of 12,000 sets of golden arches. The arches and the underlying brand now ranks with Coca-Cola, Marlboro and Ford as one of the most powerful brands and symbols in the USA and the world. Despite Harry Sonnerfield's role in the decisions that transformed McDonald's from interesting new business to a global symbol, he did not survive long at McDonald's. Harry left in 1967 to be replaced at the top by Ray's surrogate son Fred Turner. The breakthrough had happened and a new team would use this leverage to build the global company.

Further reading

Kroc, R. (1977) *Grinding It Out*, Contemporary Books Inc., New York.

Love, J.F. (1995) *McDonald's Behind The Arches*, Bantam Books, New York.

McDonald, R.L. (1997) *The Complete Hamburger: McDonald's Behind the Arches*, Birch Lane, New York.

Vidal, J. and Nader, R. (1998) *McLibel: Mc Donald's On Trial*, New Press, New York.

Notes

1 Kroc, R. (1977) *Grinding It Out*, Contemporary Books Inc., New York.

2 Kroc, R., *ibid.*

3 Kroc, R., *ibid.*

4 The McDonald's Franchisee's operating manual.

5 Love, J.F. (1995) *McDonald's Behind The Arches*, Bantam Books, New York.

6 State Mutual and Paul Revere provided a $1.5 million loan at 7 per cent and between the loan offices and the companies they obtained 22.5 per cent of McDonald's stock. Within five years this gave them a capital gain of $20 million while their loan was paid off at the end of its 15-year term

7 Fred Fidelli, chief loan negotiator for State Mutual, quoted in Love, J.F. (1995) *McDonald's Behind The Arches*, Bantam Books, New York.

8 Kroc, R., *ibid.*

Chapter 14

A Close Shave

Gillette

The cover story

R azors, and the companies that make them, do not often feature on the front covers of magazines – not even those like *Forbes* that look at business. This unusual accolade went to Gillette's Sensor razor in 1991. The success of the Sensor was an especially vivid illustration of the ways in which a global brand can transform a deceptively simple technology into a powerful franchise. The Sensor itself was the culmination of years of technological developments, production and marketing decisions that confirmed Gillette's market power and achieved a breakthrough that transformed the company's prospects.

The Sensor was an important product in many ways for Gillette. It affirmed the company's technological advantage over its rivals while confirming its leadership in global markets. The breakthrough the Sensor achieved was based on decisions that exploited Gillette's core strengths in production, branding and global marketing. These decisions often flew in the face of conventional wisdom but were rooted in an understanding of Gillette's core strengths, and built on its ability to control production and marketing while focusing on ways to get maximum leverage from assets. The apparently simple technology – twin, separately moving blades – was remarkably difficult to produce at volume. The high production speeds tested Gillette's manufacturing systems to the full. The success of the product and the related technology changed the direction in which Gillette was going at an especially important moment in its history.

A premium product

Until the success of the Sensor, Gillette seemed to be moving inexorably away from its position as a leading producer of premium branded products into a manufacturer of relatively cheap disposable razors. In fact, the entire shaver market seemed to be moving away from the branded products, which were Gillette's strength, into low-price disposables. Gillette continued to be the dominant force in advertising and promotion, but little of this expenditure seemed to distinguish its offerings from those of its rivals. The implicit threat of disposable razors was that their success would force producers to see their products increasingly as commodity items, selling at the lowest prices through mass retailers.

The premium image of Gillette would be hard to sustain, especially as key product features such as the use of steel in handles was unsustainable in disposable razors. Key members of Gillette's team, especially in the Safety Razor Division (SRD), 'believed that ... Gillette should dedicate its best technology and marketing efforts to disposable razors ... Gillette's best hope was to adapt its technological advantages in a superior line of disposables to hold off Bic and Schick.'[1]

In contrast, others in Gillette were arguing that the company should turn away from disposables and re-establish their commitment to premium shaving systems based on new technologies and strong brands. Twin blade technologies were at the heart of this approach. The company had pioneered volume production. Its control of these production processes had created Gillette's global leadership. The most successful innovation grew out of a clear focus on better products using better technologies. The first twin blade – the Trac II Razor – had moved the company away from the double-edged blade towards shaving systems that linked a metal or plastic handle with a disposable shaving cartridge. Gillette was also a pioneer in global marketing. Its brands were in the small cluster of globally recognised images. These

Gillette was founded in 1901 to a very simple dream for an unusual man. King Gillette was inspired by his friend William Painter's success in inventing the crown cork bottle stop. This earned a fortune for Painter and he advised Gillette, who was anxious to rebuild his family's fortune, to invent a simple product that 'people can use just once and throw away.' In a sense the history of Gillette is a combination of that apparently simple proposition and three distinct twists that were added by King Gillette. The first was King's discovery that apparently simple products often require complex technologies and constant innovation to make them work. It took the best part of a decade, for example, for King to turn his idea for the safety razor into a product that could be patented and then produced in quantity.

The history of Gillette has seen the same pressure to innovate either in products like the famous blue blade or in production itself. Flexible shaving heads, twin blades, pivoting heads and, now, the triple blade system put massive pressures on manufacturing systems when 1.2 billion people around the world use a Gillette system every year. King was a natural salesman who recognised the importance of promotion and branding. He set a pattern of active promotion that prompted the company to pioneer radio advertising in the 1930s and television in the 1950s. Gillette is now ranked among the top ten most valuable brands in the world. This international success can be traced back to the opening of the company's first oversead operation within a few years of its creation. Now global sales amount to over $10 billion, with production facilities in 25 countires, sales in over 200 countries and territories around the world. The Sensor drew together each of these core strengths. Its simultaneous launch on both sides of the Atlantic was an especially vivid illustation of the ways in which a 'throwaway' product can still have meaning in a corporation with a market capitalisation of over $53 billion.

brands were heavily supported by advertising that emphasised the brand, its reputation and the underlying technology.

Raiders at the gates

In the competition over the way forward between groups within Gillette, both could claim to represent the company's traditions and core competencies while representing a breakthrough for the business. A major success built around a business breakthrough was especially important, as Gillette was under intense pressure from investors and the financial community. For several years Gillette had been under attack from corporate raiders who were at the peak of their power in the second half of the 1980s. Gillette had been under some form of stock market pressure or attack for most of the late 1980s. It had all the characteristics that made it attractive to corporate raiders. Its control over technologies and brands had been built up over decades. There was a wealth of value in both that 'could be released' to profit a few smart investors.

These assets included a portfolio of strong brands that generated large amounts of cash. There was little in the way of corporate debt, but sales, profits and dividends had stagnated over the past decade. Advertising expenditures, research and development were significant but neither seemed able to produce dramatic commercial breakthroughs. The firm's international position was strong but it was sustained through a range of businesses that had little in common but the strength of their brands. Top management seemed complacent and lacking ambition. Control seemed to exist but there was apparently little focus on efforts to get maximum leverage in markets or for investors. Raiders could see ways to acquire large amounts of stock, sell off key businesses, 'realise value' and generate substantial profits – albeit in the short term.[2] A model was established at firms like Phillips Petroleum, Beatrice, Revlon, and eventually giants like RJR and Nabisco that seemed to offer massive profits through realising the accumulated value of companies with long traditions and strong brands.[3]

The attacks on Gillette had turned management's attention away from its core businesses, forced it to retrench its operations and drained the corporate treasury. Focus on the core business could easily be lost as the company struggled against predators. At the start of 1986, Gillette was cash rich with virtually no debt but a target for several acquirers. Two years later, it was in debt after being forced to buy off the predators and restructure its business. The core business was sound but lacked a strategic focus on which to base the choice between disposables and systems.

Something like crown cork

Disposables offer many attractions. They are relatively easy to produce, and seemed to take the company back to its basics. The origins of the company lay in the search by King Camp Gillette for a product that would restore his family's and his own personal fortune. Both had been lost in the great Chicago fire of 1871. Ideally he wanted to follow in the footsteps of his friend William Painter who had invented the 'crown cork' bottle stop. He advised Gillette how to go about this: 'Concentrate on just one thing –something like crown cork – that people just use once and throw away'.

It took Gillette four years to come up with his vision of this something – the disposable razor. It is said that he came to this realisation in 1895, while trying to shave with a dull straight razor. As he put it, 'As I stood there with the razor in my hand, my eyes resting on it as lightly as a bird settling on its nest, the Gillette razor was born – more with the rapidity of a dream than by a process of reasoning. In a moment I saw it all.'[4]

Gillette saw the potential but he lacked the technical skills to produce the product. His patent for a double-edged, sharp piece of steel, held in place by two metal plates, attached to a handle was registered in 1901. Although the patent was registered, Gillette had no means of manufacturing the product until William E. Nickerson got involved. Nickerson's technical skills allowed the dream to become a reality. After being shown a model of Gillette's idea, he wrote, 'It is my confident opinion that not only can a successful razor be made on the principles of the Gillette patent, but that if the blades are made by the proper methods a result in advance of anything known can be reached.' The language was little different to that used almost a century later when the Sensor was first discussed. The idea of two independently moving blades was as impractical in 1979 as Gillette's disposable blade in 1900. The principle of getting the idea right and 'worrying about how to produce it later' was remarkably similar.

Nicholson solved the technical problems and the company went into production in the summer of 1902. There was very little initial interest and at the end of Gillette's first year's trading only 51 razors and 168 blades had been sold. Sales took off in 1904 when over 90,000 razors were sold and over 10 million blades were consumed. Control of the company soon moved from Gillette to his old friend John Joyce who gradually built up the firm's business. The symmetry was repeated as John Joyce gave Gillette the stability to focus on its strengths in sales, promotion and market development. Warren Buffett's decision in 1988 to acquire $600 million worth of shares provided similar stability. Once again the company could focus on its strengths and deliver leverage in markets and technologies.

The smooth shave

From the outset, The Gillette Safety Razor Company emphasised marketing and international sales. There were early decisions to avoid promotion based on price and concentrate on promotions that emphasised the 'manliness and sexiness of the smooth shave.' Intensive promotional efforts advanced the brand, and its distinctive green packaging, through retailers. Equally important was the decision to make product presentation, packaging and most promotion common across international markets. The company moved quickly into international markets. By 1915, Gillette had eight sales subsidiaries in North America and parts of Europe. Gillette blades were available in Europe, Asia, the Far East and Latin America by the end of World War I. By the middle of the 1920s, Gillette could claim to be a truly global business.

These international developments slowed down between the 1930s and 1960s at Gillette after the company decided to concentrate on product improvement, the intensive development of its core markets and diversification. Perhaps the most important technical development during this era was the famous 'Blue Blade' and later the 'Super Blue Blade.' These became the company's standard products until the 1960s, when the UK's Wilkinson Company rewrote the technological rules of the game with its steel blades.

The diversification programme added such products as the Toni range of haircare products, Paper Mate Pens and Right Guard deodorants. In 1965, two-thirds of Gillette's sales and earnings were generated in the USA. European operations were declining, with Gillette's share of the European shaving market down to 30 per cent. This situation was changed by a series of decisions that transformed the company's international operations by passing down marketing and sales-making decisions to local operations while retaining strategic decisions at a higher level. This illustration of Tom Peter's famous tight/loose approach to policy – tightly defined strategies but loose control over implementation – did not extend to advertising or promotion. Factories were modernised, especially through the development of mini-mills that could produce high volumes to good standards but with low initial set-up costs. By the time the control crisis emerged in the 1980s, Gillette had re-established itself once again as a global business with a powerful corporate culture.

The corporate culture was based on a commitment to treat employees and customers equally, regardless of local market conditions. This vision of the global corporation with the same core systems, regardless of location, was well ahead of its time when introduced in 1967. US managers were encouraged to work overseas while training, and development programmes for international managers enabled them to move easily between worldwide posts. In the 1970s operational power was devolved across the company to its local units. Gillette became a textbook example of the global company as it delivered its founder's vision of a simple, easily disposable product that anyone, anywhere could use.

Six per cent of the world's population

There was fierce drive during the late 1970s and early 1980s to move the company into parts of the world where Gillette did not yet dominate the market. Colman Mockler, the then CEO, decided to build business where the markets existed. He complained, 'Look at our business – most of it is with 6% of the world's population.' Steve Griffin, President under Mockler, claimed that Mockler maintained that Gillette's long-term growth was totally reliant on the growth of second- and third-world countries. Even during the takeover turmoil, Mockler initiated a company-wide reorganisation reflecting the steps made over the last 20 years to promote the globalisation of Gillette. He decided to centralise product strategy to ensure control of the key processes, whilst increasing the power and resources of local managers.

The drive to internationalise was combined with pressure for innovation on existing products, and diversification. The shock caused by Wilkinson's success had forced Gillette to review its approach to research and development and invest heavily in product development. The most tangible success of this strategy occurred with the arrival of the Trak II. This was the world's first successful twin track blade. It was based, in part, on the hysteresis effect produced during shaving. This means that the first pass of the blade draws the bristle out for an instant. The second pass or blade could, therefore, achieve a smoother shave. Effectiveness depends on the distance between the two blades being finely calculated and no material getting stuck between the two blades.

The diversification programme was also continued, but many of the moves into new markets were relatively unsuccessful. Failures were particularly marked as Gillette went far beyond its core franchise of low-price personal care products. Many acquisitions were quickly discarded but the company held on to Cricket disposable lighters, Oral-B Laboratories and Braun electrical products. The Paper Mate Division also produced a significant success, with the introduction of its Liquid Paper correction fluid. Overall the 1960s and 1970s reaffirmed the company's strengths and highlighted its weaknesses. The strengths made its attractive to a potential acquirer while the weaknesses made it vulnerable.

The four takeovers that the company fought off between 1986 and 1988 gradually weakened the company until major commercial success was essential to the company's long-term survival. 'We held on to the company, in part, by promising a big winner,' says Robert Murray, a Gillette vice-president. 'Sensor was a symbol of the "new Gillette". If it failed to deliver, we would have been vulnerable all over again.'[5]

Preparing the ground

Disposables reflected one part of the Gillette tradition but the Sensor represented another aspect of the company's culture. This was a culture that emphasised strong brands that could build up a powerful franchise based on technology and innovation. The first disposable blade was based on the innovative technology used by William Nicholson to produce and manufacture products at high speed. The 'Blue' and 'Super Blue' blades were equally demanding of contemporary technology. Survival against Wilkinson and the success of the Twin II relied on the company's ability to manage innovative technologies. The Sensor was a natural evolution from these products. It had the added advantage for Gillette of building on a new direction in brand development while being capable of establishing a powerful franchise.

Across the company, there was a shift to a much stronger brand development focus. The shaving products division had rationalised its advertising into a small number of advertising agencies with a more cohesive, common campaign built around the theme 'the best a man can get.' This campaign grew out of a series of decisions that reaffirmed the company's commitment to strong brand messages based on premium products. The marketing team saw themselves losing control over their core markets. This loss of control was caused by a series of distractions that meant the company was responding to others while dabbling in peripheral products. Clear decisions were made to shift the company's emphasis towards systems and away from disposables, combined with a determined effort to concentrate advertising where it did the most good for Gillette.

Out-of-stock

The Sensor represented the fulfilment of the advertising promise. It was, however, a technologically advanced and highly complex product. The essence of the product lay in three features:

- independently moving twin blades;
- a cartridge based shaving system; and
- a steel handle.

The combination of these three features gave shavers a superior result while delivering a feeling of quality and weight that disposables could not match. There were, however, massive production problems. Most of these difficulties centred on manufacturing the cartridges at high speed. The cartridge had to contain the two blades held in place by tiny springs and bonded using advanced laser technologies. Volume production had to be achieved while prices of the blades had to remain competitive with disposable razors. It took the best part of five years and over $150 million in development costs before the product could reach the market. The initial promotional programme was budgeted at around $200 million. Altogether the development and launch costs were close to $400 million, up to and including 1990 (around $1 billion at current prices).

Success was almost instant. Sales of over 24 million units in the first year were over a third higher than forecast. At one point, demand so far exceeded supply that advertising was cancelled to dampen sales. Out-of-stock signs appeared across the company's distribution system. Within a year, the Sensor had won almost half the market for non-disposable blades. The Sensor was so markedly superior to its rivals' offerings that almost all those who tried the product remained loyal. The threat from disposables was pushed back for the foreseeable future. Gillette was back in control of its future and could focus on developments in its markets.

Further reading

Adams, R.B. (1978) *King C. Gillette: The Man and His Wonderful Shaving Device*, Little, Brown and Company, Boston, MA.

McKibben, G. (1998) *Cutting Edge: Gillette's Journey to Global Leadership*, Harvard Business School Press, Boston, MA.

Notes

1   McKibben, G. (1998) *Cutting Edge: Gillette's Journey to Global Leadership* Harvard Business School Press, Boston, MA.

2   Stewart, J.B. (1991) *Den of Thieves*, Simon and Schuster, New York.

3   Burrough, B. and Helyar, J. (1990) *Barbarians at the Gate*, HarperCollins, New York.

4   Davis, W. (1996) *The Innovators*, HarperCollins, London, p. 157.

5   Quoted in *The Economist*, 'Management Briefs', 1996.

Chapter 15

Rapture in My Rags or an Arabian Nights Adventure?

Cubby Broccoli and James Bond

The most profitable film series in history

T he 18 James Bond movies to date have combined to create the highest grossing, most profitable film series in history. The gross earnings are hard to calculate but the best estimate puts the total sum at over $6 billion at current prices. This dwarfs the earnings of the biggest grossing single film – *Gone with the Wind* – at $1250 million. Its nearest contemporary rivals – The *Star Trek* series and the *Star Wars* series – have earned just over $2 billion each. Even the combined earnings of Steven Spielberg's blockbusters fall short of the Bond earnings.

The format and high recognition for the films has translated these earning to high profits. Even the special effects that have been employed in the later movies have done little to dent the returns, which are estimated at 30 per cent of the gross earnings – before merchandising.

The success of the James Bond films contrasts sharply with the inauspicious beginnings of a series of films that would eventually be seen by half the people on the planet. The series idea was initially squeezed between two different proposals. Albert (Cubby) Broccoli was working on a script for a film called *Arabian Nights Adventure* with Wolf Mankowitz when he grew increasingly disillusioned with the project. In his autobiography he comments that 'the more I turned the pages [of Mankowitz's script] the less I liked the idea.' This left a major gap in the programme of work for his production company Warwick Films.

Rapture in My Rags

The idea of a James Bond film was not new. Broccoli had tried to buy the rights earlier but found they were already owned by an independent producer – his future partner, Harry Salzman. Broccoli's initial approach to Salzman established first that Harry still owned the rights but seemed more interested in promoting another project for a film called *Rapture in My Rags* about a scarecrow. Some of the greatest business breakthroughs and best business decisions involve hard choices. It is, however, clear from Cubby's autobiography that he did not face this kind of dilemma when he chose between James Bond, *Rapture in My Rags* or an *Arabian Nights Adventure*.

This specific choice might be easy but getting the Bond project off the ground was tough. In retrospect, it sometimes seems that breakthroughs are obvious and the best business decisions are easy but that is seldom the case. The components of a successful business decision recur, even in the entertainment industry. Typically there is the groundwork. This usually involves hard work building up knowledge, expertise and understanding. The father of the modern, electronic entertainment industry, Thomas Edison, expressed this with his view that success was 99 per cent perspiration and 1 per cent inspiration. The groundwork is usually followed by an intensive search for a solution, answer or way forward. Eventually these developments crystallise around a specific decision or choice.

The authors of the James Bond success – Harry Salzman and Cubby Broccoli – followed each of these stages. Harry started in theatre before moving into cinema. In sharp contrast to the Bond films, his early films were gritty, down-to-earth British films like *Look Back in Anger*, *Saturday Night and Sunday Morning* and *The Entertainer*. Some elements of the Bond success can, in retrospect, be discerned. There is the attention to detail, the awareness of actors and the touch of snobbery. Cubby Broccoli had a Hollywood background. He'd worked with people like

The ability to spot an opportunity is a vital business skill. Cubby Broccoli saw potential in Ian Fleming's stories and turned them into the most successful film series in history. Broccoli's business breakthrough lay in turning a successful film series into a powerful brand that could survive changes in its leading man, style, format and, eventually, its roots – as new material replaced the Ian Fleming originals. There had been successful film series before, like the Andy Hardy films, and many built around the same characters, but these disappeared when the stars moved on. The James Bond films are the first global film brand. The Star Wars series, Star Trek and others have built their success around the format pioneered and sustained in the James Bond films.

Howard Hughes before setting up Warwick Films with Irving Allen. His links with stars like Alan Ladd gave him a sense of glamour. He also knew the US film industry and the major sources of finance. Despite their track records, the dim prospects facing both men were illustrated by the projects they dropped for James Bond.

Three characters in search of a plot

The other element in the success of James Bond is the novels of Ian Fleming. Even before the success of the films, these were popular. President Kennedy was a fan. He listed *From Russia With Love* among his top ten favourite books. The popularity of the books was, however, restricted to the fairly narrow audience for spy, espionage or thriller fiction. Their basic strength lay in the character of James Bond, the underlying glamour and the flexibility of the plots. These elements could be transformed by the right production, actors and treatment into a powerful and long-run success. Fleming himself seems to have combined a strong sense of plot with a willingness to work with the production team to make good movies rather than film his books.

Between Broccoli, Salzman and Fleming there is a sense of three characters looking for a plot. The breakthrough required several further components. The most immediate issue was the basis on which Broccoli and Salzman could work together especially as Salzman owned the option of the films. Broccoli's only tangible contribution, at this stage, was his belief that he could get sufficient backing to make the films and reach the audience. Here again, one of the recurring aspects of the best business decisions emerges. Outstanding decisions are typically made up of a series of separate choices. The starting point was Salzman's decision to hand over half the rights to Broccoli and Broccoli's decision to accept 'half a cake'. Cubby describes the meeting[1] and subsequent discussion:

> ' "Look, Mr Salzman, Wolf Mankowitz told me that you might be interested in selling me your option on the Fleming Books" ' is Broccoli's opening.
>
> 'Harry hedged around, then finally said, "Listen, I don't need the money, I'm in good shape: I've just finished *Look Back in Anger* and ..."
>
> 'I let all that pass. What mattered to me was following my hunch that Fleming's books, James Bond, had great film potential. I could see that the only way I could proceed with the project was by going into partnership with Harry ... I agreed to go into business with him.'
>
> ' "We'll make a deal," he said. "We'll draw up a piece of paper now."
>
> 'He said cheerfully, "You'll have forty-nine per cent, I'll have fifty-one per cent."
>
> 'I said less cheerfully, "No, Mr Salzman. If you want to make the deal with you having fifty-one per cent, forget it ..."
>
> ' "All right, we'll have it drawn up. Fifty-fifty." '

In a short exchange, the first set of decisions that was to lead to billions of dollars of earnings and transform a number of lives had been made. Both men decided to put aside their egos. They decided to concentrate on the real issues – making a deal that would work. They committed themselves to a partnership that would hold them together for over 15 years and initiate the longest running series of films in cinema history. The two partners had the vision but they still needed the finance and backing from a major company. Their search for this led to the next set of decisions.

$1 million

Broccoli approached two major studio bosses – Arthur Krim of United Artists and Mike Krankovich of Columbia Pictures. Another recurrent theme of business breakthroughs emerged in these discussions; that is, the notion that for every winner, there is often a loser. The mantle of loser falls with surprising frequency on those with the initial edge. Broccoli had a prior agreement with Columbia but they were quick to release him when he wanted finance for his new partnership. Krim's reaction was sharply different. His team recognised the potential and agreed an initial investment of $1 million in 'no more than thirty-five or forty minutes.'

The first building block for the breakthrough was in place. The partners had the key property – rights to all the James Bond novels, with the exception of *Casino Royale*. They created a company called EON Productions to manage the projects. They had also raised the finance and won the backing of a major US company. There were, however, still a series of important decisions to make before their vision could become a tangible product. Broccoli recounts the difficulties they faced in deciding which novel to feature first, the right scriptwriter and the actors for the key roles.

The initial choice of film was *Thunderball* but the rights to this film were entangled in a legal argument between Ian Fleming and a one-time collaborator, Kevin McClory. Salzman and Broccoli quickly decided to avoid this entanglement and opted to film *Dr No*. They invited Wolf Mankowitz, who had played a part in bringing them together, to write the script. In his autobiography Cubby describes how Mankowitz originally suggested that the Dr No character should be 'a little marmoset sitting on his (the villain's) shoulder, and the monkey would be Dr No.' Deciding to reject this treatment was easier than deciding who would play the lead role. The leading actor's success would ultimately decide the fate of the film and the series.

A Limey truck driver

The partners faced the classic dilemma of decision-makers starting on a new project with few clues about the right way forward. It was clearer what they should not do than what they should do. There were many options and lots of advice. Even Ian Fleming made it clear that the character should not be too English. An international audience would not accept a Bulldog Drummond- or Biggles-like character. The greatest fear was that the wrong decision would alienate key audiences, especially in North America. There was some pressure to use a leading US actor – superficially disguised as a Canadian with Scottish-Swiss parentage. Although this option was rejected, it recurred as first Cary Grant, then Patrick McGoohan, James Fox, Roger Moore and David Niven were considered then rejected. The impasse was resolved by the choice on an actor whose main claim to fame was his part in *Darby O' Gill and the Little People*. It was footage from this movie that prompted the production team, first to talk to Sean Connery and then to choose him for the role.

There are two different views of the decision made in casting Connery. On one side are those who emphasise the risk. They see Connery as an unknown actor whose only claim to fame was a series of poor movies such as his latest with Lana Turner. Broccoli, for example, describes him as 'an uncut diamond' and notes his wish to cast 'a virtually unknown actor'. The protagonists of this view highlight the risk taken by the production company and, ultimately, the lack of gratitude shown by an actor with such an 'unmemorable' past. In sharp contrast, other writers highlight Connery's track record. He already had a contract with 20th Century Fox. He had a powerful reputation in the UK based in part on his success with major television series such as *The Age of Kings* and one-off productions

```
                                         8/23/61
        L/T


        Harry Saltzman - Warwicfilm - London


        Blumofe reports New York did not care
        for Connery  feels we can do better


                        CUBBY
```

Fig. 15.1 New York says 'No' to Connery. However, Broccoli stood firm.

like *Anna Karenina*. *The Times* commented about one performance that 'the part had found the young Olivier it needs'. His immediate peers and contemporaries were Michael Caine, Roger Moore and Alan Bates – whose careers also blossomed. Even the *Daily Express* poll to choose the perfect James Bond placed him at the top. His interview for the job seems to have impressed everyone. John Parker, Connery's biographer, claims that 'Salzman thought the man came alive when he moved and possessed an impressive litheness for one so tall. "He bounced across the street like he was superman," said Broccoli.'[2]

Regardless of the balance of opinion, the decision was made to cast Connery. This decision was the rock on which the initial success and long-term strength of the films was based. Initially, it was useful that Connery's fees were low. He was paid around £7000 for the first film – a large sum in UK terms and understandable with an initial budget of £1 million. In the same year, however, Elizabeth Taylor was paid the first $1 million fee in the film industry while the likes of Warren Beattie and Natalie Wood were paid over $250,000 for films that had nothing like the impact of the Bond series. The low initial fee fits well with the basic principle of husbanding your resources before the breakthrough so that success can be fully exploited.

Dr No opened successfully in London but United Artists were cautious about its prospects in North America. Their concerns were understandable. Few British movies had succeeded in the USA. Those that worked were either historical epics or built around classical English actors like Lawrence Olivier or Leslie Howard. There was little confidence about a spy film with 'a Limey truck driver playing the lead.' The film did not open in a major US city but was shown initially in Oklahoma and Texas. The enthusiastic receptions of these audiences convinced United Artists that they had a potential success and they moved the film to the major centres where it received favourable reviews from the press.

The central format of the series was established in the first film. Besides Bond himself, there are other recognisable characters: M, Bond's boss; M's secretary, Moneypenny; Q, the genius with gadgets; and Liter, Bond's CIA contact. The actors, even the gender of the main actors, can change, but their roles and their quirks are familiar and reassuring to audiences. There is enough familiarity to provide comfort with sufficient change to avoid staleness. The greatest challenge to this formula was Connery's desire to end his link with the Bond persona. There must have been some temptation to kill the role or the series with his departure. The producers, however, showed the confidence and belief in an idea that characterises business breakthroughs. They built the strength of the series around the character not the actor. The credibility of the series could hardly have survived 33 years with 69-year-old Sean Connery in the lead. The five different actors have won support for their ways of playing the role and have generally added new dimensions and new interest in the films.

Shaken not stirred

Bond is a human superhero. He studied languages at Cambridge (*You Only Live Twice*), but is an expert on cars, gems, guns, wines, sports, riding, gambling – even electronic games. Despite his success, he is human and vulnerable. He is usually in the villain's grasp at least once during a film and at least one of his male or female partners perishes. Even the more dated aspects of the formula, those that owe more to the 1960s, add to the character and the film's appeal. In part, this reflects the decision not to take the series too seriously but never to mock itself (or its audience).

Audiences identify not only with Bond but with the plethora of characters. It is this continuity from film to film that gives the series instant recognition and a feeling of involvement. There is, however, situational continuity as well. Bond's vodka Martini is 'shaken but not stirred', Q's gadgets are expected and anticipated by the audience. And of course, the Bond music, when judiciously used, enhances the dramatic moments and is instantly recognisable.

The use of subtle humour within the serious setting of an espionage drama has never been done better than in these films. This may take the form of an offhand quip or a double entendre (Pussy Galore). In the best of the films, the humour is subordinated to the action and the remainder of the dialogue so as not to interfere with the involvement of the viewer. These films are also enjoyable as travelogues. There are lush images of Istanbul and Venice in *From Russia with Love*, of the Swiss Alps in *Goldfinger* and of France in *Diamonds are Forever*.

Finally, most impressive is the pacing of the action. Unlike so many so-called 'action films' today, the Bond films do not rush ahead from scene to scene without regard for a developing story line. Rather, they tend to linger over an exciting confrontation, an interesting character, or a humorous moment. And they are not above laughing at themselves. Rarely do they take themselves seriously.

The central plot seldom shifts much beyond Bond challenging the power of an all-powerful foe. Sometimes a master criminal like Goldfinger is the enemy, elsewhere it is a powerful secret organisation like SPECTRE (Special Executive for Counterintelligence, Terrorism, Revenge and Extortion). Even these bizarre people and organisations are played straight, with the producers determined to avoid the temptations to make them figures of fun. An early and important decision was made to avoid using a nation or national organisations as the enemy. Even before glasnost Bond was co-operating with his equivalents in the Soviet bloc to foil enemies of mankind.

Locations, heavies and lovelies play an important part in Bond plots. The Caribbean, Florida, The Middle East, The Russian Steppes, Venice and Istanbul are classic locations. The villain usually employs a heavy to take on Bond. Oddjob, Jaws, Red Grant all seem invincible until they challenge James. There are typically three female leads, one of whom dies in the middle of the film, sharpening Bond's desire for revenge. In more recent movies the female leads have become stronger, more able to support, even save Bond before succumbing to his charms. The pacing and the special effects add to the popularity of the series. The pace allows the characters to fit into their prescribed roles while bringing them up to date. The special effects are important but never drown the plot. These careful balances can be traced back to the original decision to build the plot around the groundwork invested in series research. There was the refusal to compromise on the James Bond character. The producers still keep things fairly simple with a solid, central framework to the plots. The original partnership between Broccoli and Salzman collapsed in the mid-1970s but the integrity of the approach was maintained. Cubby Broccoli remained the driver until his recent death. Perhaps more so than most producers, Broccoli emphasised the way in which business breakthroughs and the best business decisions are driven forward by the belief and commitment of the initiator(s).

1962–1965:

- *Dr No*
- *From Russia With Love*
- *Goldfinger*
- *Thunderball*

1967–1973:

- *You Only Live Twice*
- *On Her Majesty's Secret Service*
- *Diamonds Are Forever*
- *Live And Let Die*

1974–1981:

- *The Man With The Golden Gun*
- *The Spy Who Loved Me*
- *Moonraker*
- *For Your Eyes Only*

1983–1989:

- *Octopussy*
- *A View To A Kill*
- *The Living Daylights*
- *Licence To Kill*

1995–present:

- *Goldeneye*
- *Tomorrow Never Dies*

Future

- *Bond 19*

Further reading

Balio, T. (1976) *United Artists: The Company Built by the Stars*, University of Wisconsin.
Broccoli, C. (1998) *When the Snow Melts*, Boxtree, London.
Freeland, M. (1995) *Sean Connery*, Orion, London.

Notes

1   Broccoli, C. (1998) *When the Snow Melts*, Boxtree, London.
2   Parker, J. (1993) *Sean Connery*, Victor Gollancz, London.

Part IV

Defying Convention

T he willingness to defy convention is closely linked with some of the biggest business breakthroughs. Walt Disney faced opposition inside and outside Walt Disney Productions when he decided to create a new type of amusement park that was totally different to the 'dirty, phoney places, run by tough-looking people' that he found across America. It was not easy for a cartoonist running a successful but small movie studio to defy every piece of accepted wisdom in operating amusement parks. He was told that he could only survive by selling concessions to people looking for a quick return. The best advice available said that once built he should avoid change to get a return on his investment. Specialists warned him against rural developments that people would not travel to.

The scale of his planning, his preparation, his insistence on quality and his determination to create 'something live, something that would grow' confounded every aspect of conventional knowledge. His proposals were so radical, so expensive that his own company refused to back them. Walt was forced to sell a house and cash in his insurance to get the project off the ground. The result was a spectacular success that transformed the leisure sector.

Allan Lane faced similar opposition inside his own company, The Bodley Head, when he proposed his new style paperback. Other publishers objected to his ideas, not even replying to his letters. The first publisher to sell Allan Lane the rights to publish its list in paperback only did so because 'I thought you were going bust, and I thought that I'd take four hundred quid off you before you did.'

Michael Dell defied convention in a different way when he decided to build his computer business through the direct model. This approach meant missing out the retailer and dealing directly with the customer. Even after his success in North America, industry experts argued that this approach might work in the USA but would fail in Europe and Asia. Dell's success in these markets highlights the continuing success of its policy of defying convention.

The challenge to convention initiated by the Roddicks and the Rochdale Pioneers went even further in defying accepted social and economic thinking. The Body Shop offered a new way of retailing alongside a different way of thinking about the social and environmental role of business. Anita and Gordon Roddick refused to accept either the conventions of retailing or established practices in the soaps and cosmetics industry.

The Rochdale Pioneers defied convention on many levels. Most profoundly, they challenged the conventional motives of starting a business. They created a giant enterprise without seeking any significant personal rewards. In building this business they challenged accepted ideas about relations with customers and the role and nature of profit. They refused to exploit their poorer customers, insisting on quality and returned profits to their members through the 'divi'. The success of their enterprise is perhaps the clearest evidence that the willingness to defy convention can prove a powerful route to business breakthroughs.

Chapter 16

When You Wish Upon a Star

Walt Disney and Disneyland

An epitaph

hen Walter Elias Disney died the *New York Times* ran the headline:

Walt Disney, 65, dies on coast;
Founded an empire on a mouse
(*New York Times*, December, 16, 1966)

The prospect of this image had haunted Disney in his later years. During his final illness he talked about his worries over this narrow view of his work and achievements.

The comment highlights the two sides to Walt Disney's work. There was the empire builder whose enterprises continue to grow. There was also the creative film maker – probably the first of the 'imagineers' who were so important to the long-term success of his businesses. The two sides to Disney and the reactions they provoked remain part of any portrait of Walt and his achievements. *Time* magazine summarised many of these views in an obituary, which said; 'when he died ... Disney was no longer simply the fundamental primitive imagist ... but a giant corporation whose vast assembly lines produced ever slicker products to dream by. Many of them, mercifully, will be forgotten ...'[1] The businessman, the visionary and the planner were closely interlinked in Disney.

The *Wall Street Journal* drew out some aspects of this in the oft-quoted comment, 'Disney's land; dream diversify – and never miss an angle'.[2] Or as expressed by Roy O. Disney, 'Walt always has operated on the theory of making today pay-off tomorrow'.[3] All these aspects of Walt's personality came into play with the business breakthrough that transformed his enterprises from niche players in a crowded marketplace to a major leisure conglomerate setting standards for others far beyond the confines of movies, even entertainment. The key to this breakthrough was Disney's decision to create Disneyland or, as one commentator described it, 'the world's biggest toy for the world's biggest boy.'

Dirty, phoney places, run by tough-looking people

There are many aspects of the creation of Disneyland and later Walt Disney World that mark them out as both major business breakthroughs and exemplary decisions. Disney was, for example, surprisingly old when he decided sometime around 1952 to create an alternative to the 'dirty, phoney places, run by tough-looking people' that passed for amusement parks when he went out with his daughters. Not many successful people make a major detour in their career in their early 50s. The decision was even more surprising given the success of his current enterprises and the opposition from within his existing company led by his brother Roy.

The Disney Company had had a difficult few years following World War II. In 1949 the firm reported losses, but the next year saw the start of a major turnaround. In 1950 turnover exceeded $7.3 million with net profits of $720,000. A year later it was creeping towards $10 million with profits of $1 million. This new-found success was rooted in three major innovations that were already underway while Walt was dreaming of his new kind of leisure facility. The first was the move to live action film productions with films like *Treasure Island*, *Rob Roy* and *The Story of Robin Hood*. These were successful and produced more immediate profits than many of his classic cartoons. The

It is hard to change direction after you've built a business and achieved fame in one industry. It was doubly hard for Walt Disney when his film production company refused to back his ideas. He was, however, so committed to his ideas about transforming the leisure industry that he risked everything to develop Disneyland. His ideas are familiar today. He emphasised quality, saw perfection in every detail, embedded continuous change and sought excellence in service. Disneyland produced a revolution in people's expectations that created not only the new phenomenon of theme parks but redefined the relationship between entertainment and leisure.

successful move into live action coincided with the development of even more successful nature films such as *The Living Desert, the Vanishing Prairie* and *White Wilderness*. The third element in this transformation of the core business was the company's move into television.

Disney was the first significant film production company to embrace television. The move was a triumph with the *New York Times* describing the alliance as 'the most important development to date in relations between the old and the new entertainment forms'.[4] Commercially, both Disney and ABC prospered. The *Disneyland* TV series was an immediate hit. It was propelled to and stayed at the top for years. It helped to transform ABC from an also-ran among TV companies to a leader while Disney got a new platform for old and new properties. *Disneyland's* Premier series captured 52 per cent of the audience and leapt into the top ten rated television shows in the USA.

Dreaming, diversifying and making sure that today paid off tomorrow

In the middle of these developments, Walt decided on a wholly new initiative. It was a project that would put him at odds with his fellow directors, notably his brother Roy. The confrontation was so serious that Walt was forced to take the project outside of his original firm, Disney Productions, and start a new company, WED. It seems that Roy was especially hostile to this new distraction, especially as Disney Productions seemed to be turning the corner after some difficult years. Mosely claims that Roy 'was against Disneyland, against Disney World and against EPCOT, all of them'. In the face of this opposition Walt decided to dream, diversify and (he hoped) make sure that today paid-off tomorrow.

The risks behind the decision were enormous. The costs were far greater than even the most expensive Disney film. The biggest of these films cost $2 million, but it was expected that the creation of Disneyland would cost between $15 and $20 million to get off the ground. He managed to squeeze $10,000 out of Disney Productions but most of the initial costs came out of Walt's own pocket. He cashed in his insurance policies, sold his second home (he secured his family home by transferring the rights to his wife). Disney was risking almost everything he had built up over the years since *Plane Crazy* had introduced Mickey Mouse to the world.[5] This decision and its implementation highlight key aspects of a breakthrough decision. There was the powerful sense of belief in the rightness of the project. Disney was also determined to implement his vision in full, avoiding easy compromises and demanding perfection.

He built up a small team of designers, architects and engineers who soon became known as his 'imagineers.' He paid the Stanford research Institute to review the possible sites. He was determined that the new park would avoid the mistakes of traditional facilities. It had, for example, to be open all year to cover costs and draw in customers. This excluded areas of Los Angeles that were affected by fog. The San Fernando Valley was too hot. Poor access excluded other sites. His park would be vast by contemporary standards: 'a place of fun and fantasy, neat and clean, relaxing – neither noisy and dusty nor rank with greasy fumes, nor peopled by grizzly barkers and hard characters. This amusement park would be more like a park, with trees, benches and flowers … The rides would carry the "guests" through storylands peopled with the characters from Disney's most popular movies.'[6]

Fig. 16.1 Disneyland. (Credit: Rowan Cannon.)

Something live, something that would grow

In Disney's own words 'I want something live, something that would grow. The park is that. Not only can I add things to it, but even the trees will keep growing. The thing will get more beautiful year after year. And it will get better as I find out what the public likes. I can't do that with a picture. It's finished and unchangeable before I find out if the public likes it.'

His initial research was discouraging. Other amusement park operators said it was impossible to succeed without the type of traditional rides that Walt was determined to avoid. The scale of his proposals was daunting, not least because he wanted to have five distinct areas within the park – Main Street, Fantasyland, Frontierland, Adventureland and Tomorrowland. He consistently decided to avoid compromises that that stood in the way of his vision. The rides would be themed with Alice in Wonderland's Teacups in Fantasyland competing with Tom Sawyer's Rafts in Frontierland. He was determined to live up to Michaelangelo's dictum that 'details make perfection and perfection is no detail'.

The difficulties with his brother and the other directors did not stop with their objections to the proposals and the costs. His decision to establish a separate development company WED caused a new set of arguments. At one point Roy threatened Walt with legal action over any use of the Disney name. In response, Walt threatened to stop all creative work for the studios. An impasse was close when another innovation achieved the breakthrough in finance that was needed. Walt decided to go outside the normal sources of finances – bank and insurance companies – and seek money from those in the entertainment industry who understood his vision. He achieved a double breakthrough in this way.

His initial plan was to make a series of films especially for television. The networks could have these in return for finance for Disneyland. This approach was rejected by the major networks but accepted by the head of NBC. This success even persuaded Roy to come behind the project – even to the point of carrying and distributing a special leaflet that Walt prepared about the Disneyland. The final distribution of shares gave Walt Disney Productions 34.48 per cent of the shares in Disneyland with ABC-Paramount getting the same amount. Walt himself, through WED, kept 16.56 per cent, an established partner company of Disney, Western Printing and Lithographing, bought 13.8 per cent and a few small investors acquired the rest. The conclusion of this complex financial deal coincided with the choice of the site for Disneyland.

Involvement and partnership

The location chosen was Orange County. This was, at the time, one of the less densely populated areas around Los Angeles. More importantly, a new freeway would link the chosen location – Anaheim – with the main population areas in the region. This meant that the original vision of an extensive parkland within easy reach of people could be delivered. In his determination to break out from the bounds of conventional thinking, Disney took a series of decisions that still affect thinking within The Walt Disney Company. These included the following:

- A determination to link traditional imagery with advanced technology.
- A commitment to accessibility, which went beyond physical access to, for example, building slightly smaller than full scale – 'the railroad running around the perimeter was built on a five-eighths scale … while the buildings on Main Street shrank from nine-tenths on the first floor to eight tenths on the second'.
- Every effort was made to engage partners in the projects. Sometimes these were sponsors but often the partnership went deeper at Walt's insistence.
- Customer service was made a paramount priority in everything from the quality of the eating facilities to the presentation of 'the cast'. The latter term encouraged the feeling among those working at the park that they were not employees but players in a complex play.
- Walt also made it clear that in his view the park would never be completed.

The link between technology and imagery occurred on several levels. Most of the major rides and virtually all of the exhibits used (and still use) the latest technology to build up their effects. The 'imagineers' sought out new technologies and built them into the operations of the rides.

Key exhibits, such as the display of President Lincoln, use advanced three-dimensional imaging technologies. The technology itself is the exhibit in rides like the monorail – one of the world's first working monorail systems. Disney decided from the start to take the risk with technologies that extended the capabilities of the park. This was often essential to the scaling down of features to make them accessible and child-like while still exciting and interesting. The bobsleigh run around the Matterhorn works because the proportions feel right. The ride is not terrifying but the mountain does not seem diminished. This is achieved by a mixture of the artist's eye – Walt's legacy – and the engineer's skill – Disney's commitment.

It's a Small World

Investment of this scale was only possible because Disney extended notions of involvement and partnership far beyond his contemporaries. Initially this meant finding sponsors for exhibits and rides. He soon moved on to developing rides and exhibits that were initiated by other companies. One of the most popular and enduring features – It's a Small World – was created because Pepsi-Cola and UNICEF wanted an exhibit created for the 1964 World's Fair. The project was initially rejected by the park's staff, but Disney intervened, saying 'I'll make the decisions. Tell Pepsi I'll do it.' Ford initiated proposals for the Magic Skyway while General Electric came up with the Progressiveland Pavilion.

There was no sense of the 'not invented here' phenomenon that can inhibit partnership-based innovation. The alliance between Disney's park and leading US technology companies enabled Disneyland to get access to the latest innovations and these corporations had the chance to try out their ideas in a relatively controlled environment. Disney was building his breakthrough on an ability to use his control over a concept, to focus his creative energies while getting leverage from the science and technologies of America's business giants.

Living above the fire station

Being compulsive came easy to Walt. He'd had a compulsive streak all through his life. He'd shown it in the early years as a cartoon film maker. He hated the haphazard approach that characterised early cartoons. Stories were made up as the cartoonist worked. Incidents, jokes, even characters were added without any sense of structure.

He left this approach behind when he started the first story department in a cartoon studio. He helped to perfect the storyboard so that he could see ideas develop and plots mature. He left little to chance. This was an essential pre-requisite for the production of the first full-length feature cartoon. He interfered with everything because he was determined that everything would be right.

Walt Disney decided to adopt the same approach at Disneyland. He had a small apartment built for himself just above the fire station on Main Street. He lived there for days on end especially as the opening approached. He inspected everything. When there was no one around to listen to his views, he would leave notes saying 'paint this curb' or 'move this bench', always signed 'Walt.' He was not afraid to roll up his sleeves and solve problems, through the night if necessary. He was an original 'walk the talk' manager.

He did not think that the traditional language and attitudes of the service industries met his needs. He invented a new, more appropriate language. Workers became the cast, visitors became guests and designers became imagineers. Guests were not arriving at an amusement park, they were joining him in his dream. Walt wanted the cast to reflect the youthful exuberance of the characters they played, so university students were encouraged to join. They were schooled at the 'University of Disneyland' in both the basics of customer service and his vision for Disneyland. The image was 'no bright nail polish, no bouffants. No heavy perfume or jewellery, no unshined shoes, no low spirits. No corny raffishness, yet the ability to call the boss by his first name without flinching. That's a natural look that doesn't grow quite as naturally as everyone thinks.'[7]

The physical appearance of the park was especially important. Thousands of plants are replaced every year to keep the fresh appearance. Hundreds of cleaning staff keep the park tidy by day and scrape it clean every night. Every day is supposed to look as bright as an opening day. Disney's designers reviewed every aspect of the traditional amusement park; spotted the things that did not work and redesigned them. Walt hated the notion that his guests would be harassed into spending money so he banned every such effort. Instead, guests were relaxed into spending money. He hated the queues for rides so his designers came up with the lines that were long but snaked back on themselves so people were always moving, feeling they were making progress, never alienated by the wait.

Disneyland will never be completed

The commitment to constant renewal and expansion was clear from the start. Walt said in 1955 that 'Disneyland will never be completed, as long as there is imagination left in the world.' This led him to spend £50 million on improvements and modifications during the first decade of the park's existence. The constant renewal encouraged so much repeat trade that within a few years over half the visitors were returning. The link with the films was a strength initially but during the 1970s and 1980s became a weakness. Michael Eisner, the current chief executive of The Walt Disney Company, commented that: 'The most effective way to attract local customers (for Disneyland in California) back to the park was to regularly introduce new rides and parades and shows, preferably built around recognisable characters from Disney's recent movies. The problem was that few successful new movies were released during the seventies and early eighties, no broadly popular character had emerged since Mary Poppins.'

This was not Walt's problem in 1955 as the opening day approached. He needed to draw together the different aspects of an increasingly diverse project. There were massive problems with the physical development of the site. Rivers dried up, plants died, construction was late, technologies did not work and great ideas – like giant dumbos flying over the park – became threats to life and limb. Getting the construction finished was only part of the problem.

An army of new staff was being recruited. They needed to understand the vision and to be trained to deliver it. Alongside this, Disney had to keep his backers from ABS and Walt Disney Productions happy with new film ideas and the move to a wholly new medium. Even his capacity for control slipped but he remained faithful to his vision and determined to see it through. He rejected all suggestions that the opening should be postponed. The opening was a triumph but was also, in Wellington's words after Waterloo, 'a near run thing'. The TV cameras highlighted the triumph while employees rushed from crisis to crisis to mend leads, restart rides or fix freezers.

Commercially its success was almost instant. Visitor numbers steadily increased from around two thousand visitors a day at the first few weeks to over five thousand visitors a day at the end of six months. Growth continued so that by 1960 almost 30,000 people were visiting the park daily. The amount spent by visitors grew also from $2.50 per visitor in the first year to almost $4 the next year. At the start of the 1950s Disney's turnover was creeping towards $10 million. In 1956, a year after opening, Disneyland achieved this turnover. By the end of the decade, group turnover (at 1950 values) was over $100 million. Much of this growth and the related increased profit was driven by Disneyland and the complementary activities of TV production and merchandising.

Every guest a VIP

Disney had broken out from the confines of his film production company. He had achieved this by making decisions that changed the rules for leisure activities across the world. He changed the nature of customer service. The Disney principle was that 'we love to entertain kings and queens, but the vital thing to remember is this: *every* guest receives VIP treatment.' Walt was determined to achieve his vision.

He was willing to share ownership but refused to slacken his control. His partners in the venture – ABC and Western Printing and Lithographing – made massive profits when they sold up their shares. ABC was paid $7.5 million for their investment of $500,000 in 1960 while Western Printing and Lithographing made an even bigger profit a short time later. Walt's focus on the main issues never wavered and he used his determination to make his vision (for today) pay-off tomorrow never wavered.

He also spotted the weaknesses in his original delivery. He saw the way other developments crept in on Disneyland in California. The locality became crowded with others seeking to exploit his vision. Within a few years of completing Disneyland, he was looking for a new site where there was sufficient space to build without the pressure from rivals outside his gates. By 1965, over 50 million Americans had visited Disneyland but the 'open spaces' of Orange County were increasingly filled with hotels (the number of hotel rooms in Anaheim grew from 100 to 4300) and other attractions (Disney's share of a local leisure expenditure of almost $900 million was less than a third) grew to crowd in on the park.

He chose a new location – Orlando, Florida – to build a new facility on a much larger site that could give him even more control over his vision. Walt Disney attributed his success to his belief in the four Cs – 'curiosity, confidence, courage and constancy'. Many of his colleagues would add a fifth C: control. 'We must have control' was a constant refrain while 'we couldn't control it' was the death knell for a project. He used this determination to retain control as a basis for breaking out of the confines of his original business and made a series of decisions, which delivered his vision and transformed an industry. He died five years before his final expression of this vision, 'Walt Disney World', opened in Florida in October 1971.

Further reading

Miller, Diane Disney (1957) *The Story of Walt Disney*, Holt, New York.
Mosley, L. (1986) *The Real Walt Disney*, Grafton, London.
Schickel, R. (1997) *The Disney Version*, Elephant Paperbacks, Chicago, IL.
Thomas, B. (1976) *Walt Disney: An American Original*, Houghton Mifflin, New York.
Watts, S. (1997) *The Magic Kingdom*, Houghton Mifflin, New York.

Notes

1   *Time*, 23 December 1966.
2   *Wall Street Journal*, 4 February 1958.
3   Quoted in Schickel, R. (1997) *The Disney Version*, Elephant Paperbacks, Chicago, IL.
4   Watts, S. (1997) *The Magic Kingdom*, Houghton Mifflin, New York.
5   The more famous Mickey Mouse cartoon, *Steamboat Willie*, was the third in the first series of cartoons but the first to have sound.
6   Flower, J. (1991) *Prince of the Magic Kingdom*, John Wiley & Sons, New York.
7   Quoted in Schickel, R. (1997) *The Disney Version*, Elephant Paperbacks, Chicago, IL.

Chapter 17

The Remedy

The Rochdale Pioneers and the Development of Co-operative Retailing

Pioneers

Most of the leaders who seek and achieve business breakthroughs succeed, at least in part, through personal ambition. Most research about entrepreneurs highlights the search for independence as a major motivator. When successful they create great enterprises and build personal fortunes. One group, however, built a giant enterprise that dominated retailing in the UK for half a century. Their venture continues to play a powerful role in a host of industries across the world. Despite this, they did not build vast personal fortunes – nor did they aspire to make themselves wealthy or pass riches to their children. These were the Rochdale Pioneers. They created the Rochdale Equitable Pioneers Society. The precursor of the modern consumer co-operative.

The 28 original subscribers to the Pioneers Society created an enterprise that, at its peak, was the leading departmental store, food retailer and wholesaler in the UK. It is still one of the largest store groups in Britain. Its trade is global with tea plantations in India, farms across the UK and major interests in businesses as diverse as insurance, banking and undertaking. Its international network of fellow co-operators covers most of the world with 47,000 co-operatives in the USA, 11,000 in Canada, 3000 in the Caribbean and Central America, 50,000 in Latin America, 70,000 in Asia, 20,000 in Africa and a further 60,000 in Europe. In Japan alone there are more than 600 consumer co-operatives (similar in mission to the UK retail co-operatives). No other retail operation comes close to the co-operative in either longevity or reach. While some of the smartest retailers in the world like Marks & Spencer and Wal-Mart struggle to globalise their business, the co-op has been a global phenomenon for most of this century.

The Rochdale Pioneers, the creators of this trading breakthrough, were not driven by the personal search for success and wealth that features in many breakthroughs. They made a series of decisions that changed the face of trade but took little for themselves. William Cooper, the first cashier who also looked after the initial capital of £28 (a £1 contribution from each of the original subscribers), became known as the 'faithful handyman of the co-operative.'[1] He died of typhus in 1868 with little in the way of personal wealth. Samual Ashworth, the store's first salesman, died a few years later – still working for the enterprise that he had helped to create. None of the original members of the Pioneers received any payment beyond their three pence per hour wages for creating the enterprise.

In 1867 – 23 years after the first shop was opened in December 1844 – the rules were changed to allow board members to be paid a five-shilling (25p) attendance allowance and second-class travel to board meetings. J.T.W. Mitchell, grandson of a Pioneer, led the Co-operative Wholesale Society (CWS) as it grew to become the largest wholesaler in the world; but he died of bronchitis in a cottage in Rochdale. His entire estate was worth £350. Percy Redfern in his history of the CWS comments that they 'gave their lives to establish first local then national co-operative business. They died that the movement might live.'

The line between life and death was real to the original Pioneers. Their hometown of Rochdale was one of the poorest in Britain in the second quarter of the nineteenth century. Rochdale had a population of around 25,000 with another 40,000 living in adjoining villages. The community had been savaged by the effects of the early industrial revolution. This negative effect hit the people of Rochdale in two ways. First, the main occupational groups – notably handloom weavers – were losing out to the new factories and

The Rochdale Pioneers were 12 craftsmen and workers who came together to start a small shop in Rochdale, Lancashire, England, and established a set of principles that underpinned the creation of the world's first global retailer. The Rochdale Principles, such as unadulterated goods, dividends to members, open membership and no credit, were designed to solve specific problems faced by poor people enduring economic hardship. Their success in embedding the notions of quality goods, open access and fair dealings have shaped not only the success of co-operative retailing across the world but most successful retail developments.

their machines. Simultaneously, the economic and political ideologies of the time had no place for displaced workers. Traditional rights, for example over common land, were being set aside so that while their paid employment was disappearing the space to keep some animals for food was taken from them.

Abject poverty on every side

In just 30 years the wages of a hand loom weaver dropped from 151 pence per week in 1797 to 23 pence in 1830. The weavers had tried to stop this collapse in their wages by joint action and the creation of a union, the Rochdale Journeyman Weavers Association. The union had some early successes – even agreeing a fixed rate of pay called the Statement Price with some 'honourable' manufacturers – but their successes were short lived. Others tried more direct action and riots were common. In May 1829 the Manchester *Guardian* reported rioting in Rochdale, Blackburn, Manchester and elsewhere. In Rochdale 'about twenty of the principal rioters were captured and taken to the New Bailey (the jail), an infuriated mob following. When the main body of the military left, the mob attacked the jail and, as the remaining troops opened fire, ten rioters were killed.'[2] This was the second time in 30 years that the jail had been attacked by rioters. On the previous occasion they had succeeded in burning down the building.

The anger and frustration of the weavers was made worse by the speed of the collapse in their conditions of work and life. At the end of the eighteenth century, they had been relatively prosperous – especially when the Napoleonic Wars increased demand for cloth. The introduction of new machinery allied to the post-war recession had shattered their position so that: 'the house of the woollen weaver was [once] almost proverbial for a degree of comfort and plenty such as is now rarely witnessed. The furniture was abundant, always sufficient and not rarely handsome ... Now we see about us abject poverty on every side. Wages so low that many men with full work are compelled to apply to the parish for relief; their houses are unfurnished, possessing neither wardrobes nor garments and their hunger-marked countenances bespeak the terrible wrongs they endure.'[3]

Even the notoriously unsympathetic Poor Law Commissioners were shocked to find John Binns, head of a family of six, with only straw for bedding and no beds, blankets or sheets. He was not unusual in a community in which life expectancy had dropped over recent decades from 35 years to 21 years and five per cent of the population died every year.

31 Toad Lane

The speed of the decline in the weavers and the town fortunes had one positive effect. The relative prosperity of the early years of the century had created a nucleus of people who knew how to organise themselves and others. This group had been radicalised by the experiences of the Rochdale Journeyman Weavers Association and the strikes of 1808, 1827, 1829, 1830 and 1842. This group formed the core of the Pioneers. They recognised that they were not strong enough to stop either the new technologies or the new business owners. They resolved to help themselves through co-operation. Weavers were the largest group within the Pioneers but the group included shoemakers, a clogger, a joiner, a blockmaker, a hatter, a hawker and a cabinetmaker. They were not typical of the destitute weavers whose plight prompted their action. They could at least afford the £1 subscription (ten weeks wages at the prevailing rates). They were literate enough to draw up and understand their principles, take on the lease for 31 Toad Lane, purchase their first stock and set themselves up in business.

Their business breakthrough was not based on being the first co-operative or the original retail or consumer co-operative. They were building on the ideas of others. It was the way they adapted these ideas and learned from earlier mistakes that enabled them to transform the nature of co-operation and build a business that has survived for over 150 years. The founders were prompted by a series of external events to set up their first shop, but the decisions they made in establishing the rules of the co-operative, or The Rochdale Principles, determined their long-term success.

The move into co-operative retailing was prompted by the economic crisis of 1844 and the collapse of an effort to protect the Statement Price for wages through direct action. Some employers had agreed to stick to this rate but only if all their fellow producers agreed. The weavers had tried to force non-compliant employers into line through selective strikes. Workers in firms complying with the agreed rates supported strikers through a subscription of two pence per week. This level of support was inadequate and the strike crumbled.

Workers, however, did not merely face deteriorating conditions at work – they faced a series of other abuses by employers and local traders. Among the worst were Truck shops and the Badger shops. Truck shops were operated by employers who paid their workers in notes that could only be used in the company owned Truck shop. Many of the goods sold in these stores were low quality and high priced. Badger shops trapped workers by offering unlimited credit to the poor. While they were in debt, they were trapped into using the Badger Shop for all their purchasing.

The Pioneers saw their new shop as a more productive use of the two pence subscription than backing more, futile industrial action.

The shop would also offer good quality at affordable prices. It was, however, the decision to add a clear set of trading principles – known now as the Rochdale Principles – that distinguished this co-operative from earlier efforts at co-operative retailing.

The Rochdale Principles

- Democratic control, one member one vote and equality of the sexes;
- open membership;
- pure unadulterated goods with full weights and measures given;
- no credit;
- profits to be divided on the amount of purchase made (the divi);
- a fixed rate of interest on investment;
- promotion of education; and
- political and religious neutrality.

The Principles are an attempt to tackle several issues simultaneously. The most basic were those that tackled the adulteration of products and deception over weights and measures that were commonplace, especially in Truck and Badger shops. The founders were also determined to free people from the credit trap – so all trade was strictly cash.

The 'divi', or the dividend on purchases, was a clever innovation. Users of the new shop would get a dividend – based on the amount that they bought – out of the shop's profits. This was an important incentive and a powerful means of building loyalty. Cash trading was a practical necessity. After spending all their spare time making repairs and fitting out the shop, the pioneers only had £16 for buying stock. With this, they bought 28lbs of butter, 56lbs of sugar, 6 cwt of flour, a sack of oatmeal and some candles. Initially, they only opened part time but soon they were open most weekdays. Membership grew to 75 by the end of their first year and turnover was £710.

The public mind

The early, steady growth reflected the lessons that they had learned from past efforts at co-operation and the support they received from others. Co-operative retailing was not new. Earlier in the century, Robert Owen, the pioneer of workers' co-operatives, had linked retailing to his manufacturing co-operative. Owen generally saw the co-operative stores as a subsidiary activity to co-operative production. Other advocates of co-operation such as Dr William King, who published the influential publication *The Co-operator*, were more open-minded about consumer co-operatives. During the 1820s and 1830s there was a surge of interest, with over 250 co-operative societies being founded.

The first Rochdale Friendly Co-operative Society was opened in 1832. During this early phase, the focus remained on manufacture with the founders of the Rochdale Friendly (mainly weavers) intending 'to start manufacture on an extensive scale in the above business [flannel manufacture] in the confident expectation of support from their fellow co-operators.'[4] The Society even opened a store in Toad Lane but it closed down within two years. In these early co-operatives, retailing was subsidiary to either a wider political goal – creating the Co-operative Commonwealth – or to a producer co-operative. This first high water mark of co-operation was very utopian. The London Labour Exchange, for example, was an idealistic attempt to bring the producers of goods and potential buyers together in a largely co-operative form.

Contemporary observers describe how 'the public mind was completely electrified by this new and extra-ordinary movement.' The Exchange itself took place in a 'great assembly room ... capacious enough to hold two thousand individuals.' There was 'a superb and majestic organ [and] festivals were opened with a short lecture on the subject of social love, universal charity, and the advantages of co-operation.' The exchange itself was a giant marketplace where goods could be bought and sold using specially produced labour notes. The idealism that created the London Labour Exchange foundered with the discovery that 'the beautiful labour notes [the co-operators' own currency] could not by any means be forced into general circulation.' As a result 'the supply of provisions failed' and with it 'one of the most extraordinary movements that was ever attempted in this or in any other country.'[5]

The decline of co-operation in the early part of the eighteenth century coincided with the collapse of two major attempts to organise labour in the face of increased pressure on their wages and living conditions. The more ambitious of these efforts – the Grand National Consolidated Trades Union – was directly influenced by Robert Owen's ideas. Owen announced its creation in October 1833 as 'a giant tree the top whereof shall reach to heaven and afford shelter to succeeding generations' (with King William IV as Owen's candidate for President). The failure of the Union's campaign to defend the Tolpuddle Martyrs led to its decline and collapse within a few years. A more immediate influence on the Pioneers was the National Associate for the Protection of Labour. The Association drew heavily on support from the textile towns of central and east Lancashire, notably Rochdale. It survived for around eight years after its formation in 1829 and embedded some powerful lessons in the experience of the people who came together to open their shop on Toad Lane.

Practical men

The Pioneers were now wary of utopian dreams. They were determined not to overextend themselves. They knew they had to establish effective means of control. They realised that over-ambitious goals had defeated earlier efforts. The National Association's headquarters in London cost too much, Robert Owen's increasingly diffuse philosophy had lost focus, while the original Toad Lane shop gave too much credit. Their new store would be tightly managed, well focused and cash based from the start. The Pioneers drew on other sets of experiences. Ten of the Pioneers had been active in the Chartist movement, so they built key Chartist principles such as one man one vote, secret ballots, regular elections, open and equal membership and political neutrality into the Principles. Others among the Pioneers had been active Owenite co-operators but wanted a more practical, down-to-earth solution to their problems.

Slow early growth was inevitable given the harsh economic conditions of the time. The textile industry was in difficulties and the New Poor Law ended unemployment relief to distressed workers – giving them instead the workhouse. The close control of the founders, however, meant that the membership, turnover, surplus and the capital value of the co-operative continued to grow: from 28 members in 1844, to 74 in 1845 to 140 by 1848. Turnover grew from £710 in 1844 to £2276 in 1848. They ended 1848 with record numbers of members, turnover, assets and surplus. The controls they had built into their business gave them the base to build a breakthrough – on an opportunity that occurred in 1849.

Wilful neglect

Effective controls in any enterprise create a platform from which opportunities can be grasped and exploited. The collapse of the Rochdale Savings Bank in 1849 provided this opportunity for the Pioneers. The Savings Bank had originally been established by a group of local mill owners to encourage thrift on the part of 'working people.' Its day-to-day operations were supervised by George Howarth, a trusted mill owner – one of those who had originally supported the Statement Price. Howarth had embezzled the bank's funds to support his ailing business. Savers initially expected the bank's trustees to make up the shortfall but they failed to live up to these expectations offering only a low percentage of people's original investments in recompense. This failure destroyed what faith remained in the good intentions of liberal mill owners. Depositors accused the trustees of 'wilful neglect' and '[shifting] your own responsibilities on the shoulders of working men.' Former depositors turned in large numbers to an institution run by their peers – the Rochdale Equitable Pioneers Society.

During 1849 membership grew to just under 400, while trade almost trebled and the surplus soared from £118 in 1848 to £561 in

1849. The new members were ideal clients for the new enterprise. Their thriftiness had led them to keep deposits in the Savings Bank – they were just the sort of solid and responsible customers that the new shop needed. The timing was doubly fortuitous. Good controls and an increasing customer base meant that they could focus their efforts on their core business, of quality goods and fair prices, with everyone sharing the profits through the dividend.

The repeal of the Corn Laws[6] in 1846 led to increases in imports and sharp reductions in food prices. Within ten years of opening there were almost 1000 members, turnover was surging towards £50,000 and the surplus was around £1000. Members, who had been so reluctant to shop in the store in the early years that James Daly (an original Pioneer) proposed that non-shopping members be expelled, were spending around £50 per year in the shop ten years after its opening. The decisions to establish strong internal controls and introduce the dividend as a powerful loyalty-building tool had created a basis for growth. The next half-century would show how much leverage could be won from these core strengths.

Initial growth occurred through the classic retail routes of opening new stores and diversifying into new lines. The Pioneers opened additional outlets in and around Rochdale, until there were over 30 shops by the late 1850s. These stores carried an increasingly wide range of products. They moved from food to other basics, then into draperies and the wider range of goods required by an increasingly diverse customer base.

The Co-op soon ceased to be solely a store for the thrifty working class. Clerks, supervisors, and other members of the new middle classes found the shops' guarantee of quality, fair prices and a share of profits equally attractive. There was relatively little competition at this end of the market.

The industrial revolution had changed manufacturing much faster than the service sector. It would be decades before Michael Marks or John Sainsbury emerged to tackle the same markets. At the time, retailing served either the needs of the relatively prosperous with high levels of service, or the poor with ill-trained staff, high prices and poor quality. There was very little to serve the middle market. In 1868 there was certainly nothing to rival the new central store opened by the society in Rochdale.

Co-operative fever

By the late 1860s the Rochdale Equitable Pioneers Society had changed the face of retailing in Britain. Turnover exceeded £250,000 per annum and there were over 5000 members who could expect a 'divi' of up to £5 for every £30 spent. The Society's success prompted others to copy. The Pioneers were great promoters of their ideas and approaches. Within a few years there were societies in local towns like Bacup, Todmorden, Leigh, Salford and Middleton. Even the great cities of Liverpool, Leeds and Manchester were catching 'co-operative fever.' Within a decade of the Rochdale Society's opening, there were almost 1000 other societies in the UK.

The Pioneers went beyond simple advocacy in promoting their approach. They published a monthly magazine, gave regular advice to new societies and, *in extremis*, even acquired failing shops in their locality. More importantly, the Pioneers made two crucial decisions, which transformed the nature of their business. The writer Dorothy Davis suggests in her history of retailing that their real breakthrough came through their decisions to adopt 'two brilliant ideas which had nothing to do with co-operation, namely vertical integration and the branch system.'[7]

Vertical integration is so much a part of contemporary retailing that it is easy to forget the time before Tesco (UK) soups, Carrefour (France) wines, Safeway (USA) beans or the host of other retailer branded goods. The Pioneers' roots in Owenite co-operation made this shift in thinking and their subsequent decision easier for them. They had rejected the idea of retailing as a service to manufacturing, but they expected a link between the two operations. More importantly, their guarantee of quality required them to have close links with producers.

The first steps in the creation of the new structure came with the creation of their wholesale operations. The Co-operative Wholesale

Society (CWS) gave co-operatives direct access to producers, while ensuring that even the smallest society could sustain its commitment to quality at low prices. The advantages of increased vertical integration took the CWS and the societies even further down the production chain, into ownership of farms in the UK, plantations overseas and factories in different areas. Their decisions coincided with the 25 years of prosperity that marked the high water mark of Victorian capitalism between the late 1840s and early 1870s.

The decision to adopt a branch system to reach customers was equally important. Previously great retailers built their businesses by expanding on the same site. John and Ambros Heal, Harry Selfridge and Charles Henry Harrod each grew their business in this way. The railways, better roads, the penny post and increasing urbanisation – especially the growth of new towns around the new industries – required innovative solutions to bringing customers and sellers together, with goods offering consistent standards of quality, similar ranges and comparable service. The branch system allowed the co-operatives to deliver these important customer benefits to a population that had low levels of literacy and were still becoming acclimatised to urban living. The Pioneers also came close to introducing a form of franchising as they helped other societies in their formative years, and gave them access initially to the Rochdale Equitable Pioneers Society's then the CWS's purchasing power.

Some parts of the UK were quick to adopt the co-operative model. Scotland and the North of England were especially successful. Elsewhere, factors other than location were more important. Munitions workers in London had been committed to various forms of co-operation long before the Pioneers started their Society. It is therefore no surprise that these workers came together to form The Royal Arsenal Society in the 1860s. This was long before co-operation became well established in London and the south-east of England. By the end of the century, the breakthrough initiated by the Rochdale Pioneers had become the single most important retail enterprise in the British Empire – perhaps the world.

The Pioneers' decision to concentrate on retailing while ensuring good control of every aspect of their business gave them a basis

on which to build. The determination of the various societies to focus on their core strengths of quality goods, guarantees of quality
and the distribution of profits built up a vast and loyal franchise.
Delivering these benefits prompted a series of innovations, notably
the move into vertical integration and the development of the branch
system. Together, the strong customer base and the core business
strengths gave the societies the leverage to move into new markets
and new businesses. The co-operative movement was not confined
to the British Isles. A year after the Pioneers founded their shop, the
Workingman's Protection Association store was opened in Boston
(USA). In Switzerland the Zurich Consumverein started in 1848,
the same year that a French Society emerged in Hargicourt and two
years later an Italian society in Turin but 'it was only when the promoters in each country discovered the "Rochdale Principles" with
its dividend on purchases that their own movements began to flourish.'[8]

Further reading

Baren, M. (1996) *How It All Began Up The High Street*, Michael
O'Mara Books, London.

Birchall, J. (1994) *Co-Op: The People's Business*, Manchester University Press, Manchester.

Birchall, J. (1997) *The International Co-Operative Movement*, Manchester University Press, Manchester.

Parnell, E. (1995) *Re-inventing the Co-operative: Enterprises for the
Twenty First Century*, The Plunkett Foundation, Oxford.

Notes

1   Birchall, J. (1994) *Co-Op: The People's Business*, Manchester
University Press, Manchester.

2   Cole, J. (1994) *Conflict & Co-operation: Rochdale and the Pioneering Spirit*, George Kelsall Littleborough.

3   Contemporary account quoted in Cole, J. (1994) *ibid.*

4   J.W.T. Mitchell quoting the document in the *Rochdale Observer*, 3 June 1891.

5   Quoted in Thompson, E.P. (1968) *The Making of the English Working Class*, Pelican Books, Harmondsworth.

6   Corn Laws were introduced between the 1400s and mid-1800s to control the price of corn and other grains. The power of the land-owning interests in Parliament meant that the price of corn (and hence bread and other staples) was kept artificially high. Protest against this grew during the first half of the nineteenth century – partly prompted by The Anti-Corn Law League, a group of factory owners and workers who wanted the laws repealed so bread would be cheaper. Parliament repealed the Corn Laws in 1846.

7   Davis, D. (1966) *A History of Shopping*, Routledge, Keegan and Paul, London.

8   Birchall, J. (1997) *The International Co-Operative Movement*, Manchester University Press, Manchester.

Chapter 18

Direct to You

Dell Computers and a Distribution Revolution

Introduction

D ell Computers has emerged over the last decade as one of the most successful producers of personal computers in the world. From a standing start in 1980, when the founder Michael Dell bought his first Apple II, to today's turnover of over $18 billion, with profits of around $1.5 billion, the company has shown dramatic growth. Apple Computers might have inspired Michael Dell to buy his first computer – to take apart to see how it worked – but its sales are less than a third of those achieved by Dell. Dell's continuing profitability contrasts sharply with the losses Apple posted in 1998.

Although there are sharp contrasts between the way Dell and Apple operate, there are also significant similarities. Both companies were founded by entrepreneurs, who were willing to defy convention to achieve success. Steve Jobs at Apple saw the potential of the new technologies long before anyone else. He built machines that changed the world and was determined to continue the changes, through new technologies and innovative machines. He challenged the standards and conventions of the computer industry – refusing to follow the rush into IBM compatibility when everyone else went that way. Apple has paid a massive price for its distinctiveness.

Transforming distribution systems

Michael Dell accepted some of the emerging conventions of the personal computer industry. He started in business selling upgraded PCs. His technological reference point was the IBM PC and the battle for compatibility. He saw the advantages in an industry standard for machines and equipment, but questioned the logic of the existing ways of reaching customers and distributing product. Like so many pioneers before him, he recognised that transforming distribution systems was the key to success for new entrants in growing markets – especially those wanting to compete with well capitalised market leaders. General Motors, under Alfred P. Sloan, transformed automobile industry by building brand ranges, reforming dealer networks and transforming car finance. Michael Dell saw similar opportunities if he could transform the ways PCs and PC-based computer systems were delivered to customers.

T.R. Reed, a Dell manager, summarised this approach in an interview in *Forbes*, when he said, 'what we are selling around the world is the direct model.' It is a 'revolutionary way of custom building computers upon purchase, ignoring the traditional reseller chain where orders for peripherals and special requests have historically been filled.' Michael Dell describes it slightly differently 'Dell sells computers directly to our customers, deals directly with our suppliers and communicates directly with our people, all without the unnecessary and inefficient presence of intermediaries. We call this "the direct model," and it has taken us, to use a common phrase at Dell Computer Corporation, 'direct to the top.'[1]

Competing with IBM

Michael Dell was the first to recognise that the adoption of traditional distribution and retail methods by PC suppliers was initially useful but contained a host of inbuilt weaknesses and inefficiencies. These flaws could be exploited by someone able to design a distribution system around the realities of the market, the technology and

The state of Texas is sometimes seen as one of the most locally focussed of the US states. Despite that, Dell Computers (based near the state capital) has grown into the world's largest direct computer systems company in less that fifteen years. Michael Dell, the company's founder started trading while still a student and is regularly defined in terms of his youth. In truth, he is now the computer industry's longest-tenured chief executive officer, building remarkable growth for his company based on his 'revolutionary' idea of selling personal computer systems directly to customers. The company's success is partly built on the failure of its rivals to adapt their ideas of marketing and selling to the new environment they faced. Dell has also taken the need to rethink marketing, sales, production, inventory and distribution to its logical conclusion within the capabilities of current technologies.

Dell's direct business model allows it to offer the type of virtual business organisation and set of relationships that academics see as the key to future business success within the digital economy. The company offers one-to-one relationships with customers, with Internet purchasing becoming increasingly important. Internet sales are now (1999) worth $30 million per day. The bulk of Dell's sales are to large companies and the public sector. The fit between this approach and the demands of the market has seen sales grow to almost $20 billion from a standing start in 1980. Simultaneously, production facilities have extended across the world from Austin, Texas to Xiamen, China. The value of the company has soared to over $100 billion.

the production potential of the new machines. Computer retailing fell uncomfortably between several established types of traditional distribution system. Many retailers treated personal computers like traditional electrical goods. The product from various manufacturers was on display. Customers were given various different specifications by sales staff who often knew less than the customer. This approach to selling left customers dissatisfied and producers with little sell through for their products. Neither felt that the middleman was doing any more than holding product for display – especially as many did not hold stocks.

Other retailers adopted an approach more akin to traditional car dealers but with no after-sales support or servicing. These promoted a specific make or narrow selection of brands. Despite these links, the stores lacked technical expertise – again showing little more product knowledge than consumers. Other retailers adopted warehousing approaches, while direct-mail based selling was popular among certain producers and customers. Few if any retailers offered any real added value for the supplier or customer. Most companies were operating within structures of traditional markets, while Dell internalised the attitudes and structures of a new market built around smart customers, mass customisation and time-based competition. Before these latter concepts had entered academic or popular literature, Dell was delivering all three in a distinctive and integrated way.

Inventing and engineering

Michael Dell's early experiences as a student highlighted both the relatively low cost of entry into PC production and the opportunities from direct retailing. Working from his student apartment, Dell was able to offer fellow students cut price PCs to a higher specification than any others available locally. He was especially critical of dealers who would 'pay about $2000 for an IBM PC and then sell it for $3000, making $1000 profit (with) … little or no support for the customer.' Michael Dell recognised that the pinch point in the market – where there was greatest dissatisfaction and the maximum scope for saving – was between the producer and the end-user. Retailers were making 'tons of money' but failing to deliver any of the traditional benefits of middlemen.

Starting first as a customer, then as a new entrant, Dell spotted the weaknesses in the system faster than established firms with their retailer-focussed sales forces and established business systems. Many of these market weaknesses grew out of a lack of fit between the aspirations of the end-users and the policies of the major producers, notably IBM. The PC market is almost unique among consumer markets in being driven by consumers with clear and well articulated demands. In most consumer markets, the suppliers study consumer needs and offer buyers a complete offering to match their requirements.

The PC market was – and to some extent still is – very different. Many potential buyers have a clear picture of the potential of the technologies on offer. Purchasers actively search a large and highly accessible literature. The development of new components – especially silicon chips from firms like Intel – are studied by potential buyers in ways that are unknown in industries like cars, consumer durables or white goods. Purchases might be delayed until a new chip is available and buyers are loath to buy equipment with anything less than the latest technology.

In the early years of the PC market, IBM was slow to adapt its products to the latest available technology. A host of companies emerged to create a 'grey market' in IBM-based and compatible machines, with faster chips or other features of superior technologies. Dell was among the first companies in Texas to build its computers around Intel's 286 computer chip. Although keeping ahead of technology was important, the key to Dell's early success lay in staying close to its customers and focusing efforts on using this proximity for competitive advantage. This explains why even today 'Dell's plants are a remarkable balance between the cost-saving efficiencies of mass production and the value-added process of customisation.'

The perfect closed shop

Dell achieved its business breakthrough by designing organisation, delivery systems and approach to the market, to fully exploit the potential of modern communications. Fax, phone and the Internet provide effective links between the company and its buyers. These technologies allow the company to establish one-to-one relationships that are seldom possible when intermediaries are used or product is made for stock. The proximity of the relationship, however, puts immense pressures on information, production and distribution systems. Errors can accumulate quickly unless each element in the flow of information, production and delivery is in perfect harmony.

Dell is generally discussed in terms of its direct-to-customer distribution system, not least because Michael Dell often talks about 'direct selling – not using a reseller or the retail channel.' During the mid-1990s there was a great deal of discussion in the popular literature along the lines that 'the big story this year is that almost everybody's going to try to meet the direct model.' Major competitors like Compaq restructured their distribution operation to duplicate some of Dell's strengths. This emphasis was misleading where it understated the importance of production control and customer responsiveness.

At Dell's factories, 'an order form follows each PC across the factory floor, starting from when the machine is nothing more than a metal chassis. Drives, chips, and boards are added according to the customer's request. At one spot, partly assembled PCs roll up to an operator standing before a tall steel rack with drawers full of components. (Like an automat, it's restocked from the other side). Little red and green lights flash next to the drawers containing parts the worker must install. When he's done, the machine glides on down the line.' This type of production system relies heavily on effective lines of communication with the end-user. In the USA, Dell was especially effective at using 0800 freephone numbers to ensure that customers could deal directly with those controlling production.

Control over information, production and distribution allowed Dell to break free of the traditional leads and lags in markets. The leads occur when producers make for inventory based on knowledge or assumptions about demand. The lags exist when the firm (or the customer) adjusts to changes in markets or technologies. Dell's breakthrough is to create a real-time company built around real-time links with its markets. Michael Dell describes how the company uses the 1400 telephone calls its gets every day to ensure 'real time input from its customers regarding their product and service requirements, their views on various products in the market, and their response to company advertising.' The rapid collapse in the cost of electronic communication and the 'death of distance' described by Frances Cairncross provided the opportunity for a smart producer to establish this type of link with smart customers. Dell grew from a $1000 start-up company in 1984, to a firm with a market capitalisation of $85 million in 1988, to a firm with a turnover of $2 billion by 1992.

Under-promise and over-deliver

Much of Dell's early growth was driven by the company's focus on reducing the physical, technological and information 'distance' between the firm and its markets. Research engineers were encouraged to visit customers, sales staff were encouraged to be specialists with knowledge that could add value to their clients. The focus on rapid market response drove the company to introduce novel technologies before customer demand was fully articulated. Dell was, for example, quick to recognise the seemingly insatiable demand among PC buyers for faster machines. Their technological edge was reinforced by a determination to deliver better service and after-sales support than middleman suppliers. The core sales maxim was 'under-promise and over-deliver.'

These strategies served Dell very well during the high market growth years of the 1980s but created difficulties during the early 1990s when demand slowed. In many ways the difficulties reflected a failure to remain focussed on the company's core strengths. These strengths were epitomised in the close links to customers that permitted them to build to order and keep inventory low. Like many technology-based and new companies, Dell had become preoccupied with the technologies themselves, especially its Olympic development programme. Alongside this, the move to a public listing had shifted attention away from consumer markets to financial markets. These problems had an immediate impact on Dell's standing in the market as the company's stock price plummeted from $49 in January 1993 to $16 by July. In the words of one commentator 'the company seemed to be unravelling.' Another described Dell as 'a gangly, dysfunctional mess.'

Dell survived by recognising the nature of its breakthroughs and by making a series of decisions that took the company back to its core strengths. The immediate challenge was to improve information flows to enable the company to distinguish between loss-making activities, profitable lines, core activities and peripheral pursuits. Control over the company's future became synonymous with control over information about the company's present (and future). Directors like Tom Meredith talk about the phrase 'facts are your friend' as part of the renewed emphasis on market and business information. Lines were scrapped, developments aborted, as the company reasserted control.

Part of the change process was the decision to bring into the company new senior managers, with experience in firms like Sun Microsystems, Apple and Motorola. There was a complementary decision to use the new recruits to underpin the existing leadership group. There was sufficient confidence in the core strategy to stick with its architects, but awareness that change was necessary to provide the resources to sustain the company's ambitions. The focus on growth through real-time management was linked to a new emphasis on liquidity and profitability. The benefits of the new approach came quickly. In 1994 Dell delivered its investors a massive 81.4 per cent return, the highest total return to investors in the Fortune 500. Within two years sales soared by over 50 per cent. More important for the new approach, profits grew at over twice that rate, with a surge in sales to premium business and government customers. The value of Dell's shares rebounded to almost $75 a share.

A very nice idea

Most of Dell's strength at this time lay in the US market. This market seemed especially suitable to a growing company, which depended on close relations with its end-users. US demand was buoyant, there was a strong tradition of direct selling and features of the market such as the use of 0800 numbers seemed to make the American market uniquely suited to Dell's approach. There were many observers who questioned the company's ability to break out into international markets. Forbes summarised the view that 'Dell doubters offered a standard line that went like this: selling directly was a very nice idea for the US. But Dell could never become a global power. Dell could never sell PCs directly to customers overseas. There were no 0800 numbers abroad. Resellers were too strong in those markets. The cultural barriers would be too great.'

The challenge for Dell lay in using its control over real-time marketing and focus on mass customisation for direct buyers to gain maximum leverage in international markets. Some features of the international market in personal computers helped Dell gain the leverage it needed from its core strengths. Middlemen in Europe, Asia and Latin America suffered from the same weaknesses as US retailers and wholesalers. Intermediaries imposed the same high charges but delivered few tangible returns to customers in either holding stock, providing pre-sales support or after-sales assistance. Consumers worldwide read the same technical magazines, which gave Dell some level of recognition from its US advertising. There were, however, significant technical problems in providing the mixture of on-line technical support and direct selling that was important in North America.

Dell committed itself to ensuring the same levels of support to international customers that were available to its US clients. The company 'even has a customs department that sorts out all the logistical headaches and taxes of transnational shipping, allowing the client, be it in Bangkok or Brussels, to just to sit back and wait for its self-designed system to arrive.' This preoccupation with solving customer problems rather than presenting producer solutions provided the leverage for Dell's growth. In *Direct from Dell*, Michael Dell describes how he worked with BP in London to devise a method to pre-install software to their specifications and install the systems in place. This meant that BP no longer needed 'a whole floor of their headquarters building ... devoted to configuring PCs.'

The Internet

In the middle of the 1990s sales grew quickly in the US and internationally. By 1995 sales were almost $5 billion, and were increasing at three times the rate of the market. Offices existed in over 30 countries. The company was also in a position to take the next important step in real-time, direct relations with its market by using the Internet. The decision to focus on this route to the market delivers a range of benefits that build on Dell's core strengths. Among the most important of these assets is the link between the strategic use of information by the company and the low cost of information transmission on the Internet. 'Dell is a company with lots of transactions; order status, configurations, price. Each of these transactions costs money. On the Internet, there is almost no cost whatsoever for those transactions.' By the end of 1996, Dell was earning almost $1 million dollars per day through Internet sales.

Internet sales continue to grow alongside overall sales. In 1998 total company sales were over $18 billion, with the Internet accounting for around ten per cent. The breakthrough into international markets has been reinforced by the use of new technology. This allows Jan Gesmar-Larsen, who runs Dell Europe, to dismiss early reservations about the ability of real-time relations and the direct approach to succeed internationally as 'totally wrong [and] ... the proof is in the numbers.' Around a third of sales now come from outside the US, with market share growth in Europe and Asia compensating for some loss of share in the US. As a company using the new technologies to sell new technologies, Dell seems to be well placed to exploit its breakthroughs in customer relations and international markets to grow even larger.

Further reading

Dell, M. (1996) *Direct from Dell*, HarperCollins, New York.

Notes

1   Dell, M. (1999) *Direct From Dell*, HarperCollins, New York.

Chapter 19

The Great Experiment

Building and Redefining The Body Shop

Restlessness

T|he elements that come together to create a business break-through vary enormously. Sometimes it is hunger; more often it is the hunger for success. Seldom, however, have the elements come together in such a distinctive form as in the creation, development and success of The Body Shop. Some features of the company's development are shared with others. There was a family background in migration and small business. Anita Roddick's mother was Italian and her father was a first-generation New Yorker. Her parents ran a small café in Littlehampton, England.

There was a restlessness that could not be accommodated within a conventional enterprise. The now famous story of Gordon Roddick's horseback journey from Buenos Aires to New York with 'nothing but an Ordnance Survey map to find his way'[1] vividly illustrates the restlessness that pushed the company forward. The partners – Anita and Gordon – who came together complemented each other in ways that even they did not expect and they constantly adapted to new circumstances. When they ran a restaurant, 'Gordon ran the kitchen.' This surprised them both as Anita could cook but after a few days of Anita the kitchen 'looked like a bomb had hit it.'

An ancient trade

Together, the Roddicks created a business breakthrough that eventually redefined not only the specifics of their trade but key aspects of business itself. The core business of The Body Shop lies in cosmetics, soaps and perfumes. This is a trade that dates back millennia. Peter James and Nick Thorpe in their book *Ancient Inventions*[2] describe how 'the ancient Egyptians were great believers in cosmetics ... men as well as women commonly used black kohl and green lapis lazuli or malachite (a copper ore) as eye shadow.'

Many of the common features of the cosmetic industry – expensive packaging and extreme images – were as familiar to the ancient world as they are today. The extreme objectives and dangers from side effects were equally common. The people of the Indus Valley in the third millennium BC used a face cream of white lead to lighten their complexions. Soaps have a similarly long pedigree with the earliest identified in ancient Babylon. By the twelfth century, there was a well-established trade in heavily scented soaps in most major European cities. Perfumes have, if anything, an even longer history. Rich Egyptians were often buried with jars of perfume oil while Romans often sprinkled dinner guests with perfumes. The basic pattern of the industry was well established long before the modern industry was created at the end of the last century.

We sell dreams

This basic pattern centred on the effect being far more important than the means. Egyptian women, for example, perfumed their bodies by placing a solid lump of perfumed fat into a cone on the top of their head. During the course of the day or evening the fat would melt – covering the person with highly scented grease. The means of achieving this effect were not a matter of concern to the wearer. The Egyptians fought wars over frankincense. Venetian explorers and traders were equally ruthless in their search for the commodities that made up the popular cosmetics, soaps and perfumes of their day.

It is unusual to look at the mission and vision of a successful company and find that instead of return on capital, increased market share, profits growth or the host of other hard measures of business success, the company talks about wider social and environmental goals. At Body Shop the goals are to pursue social and environmental change, campaign to protect the environment while balancing the company's financial and human needs in a world where protection of the environment and ecolocial sustainability lie at the heart of the business. This total integration of the commercial goals of the enterprises with its social and environmental goals marked a fundamental shift in business thinking. Previous entrepreneurs like Rockefeller, Ford and Carnegie used their commercial success to support their philanthropy but generally saw these worlds as separate and self contained. Gordon and Anita Roddick broke this mold and used their new vision to drive the Body Shop forward.

They also turned their insights into retail branding, franchising and internationalism; to grow from a local base in Brighton, England, to an international business with 1663 shops across the world, turning over £600 million per annum, selling a product every 0.4 seconds, with over 86 million customers visiting stores worldwide to sample the current range of over 400 products and over 400 accessories. Body Shop's success is measured not only in sales and profits. The Company has spawned a host of imitators – with virtually every soaps and cosmetics retailer of substance in the world offering a Body Shop lookalike range – and local, national and international governments adopting parts of the company's social, ecological or environmental agenda.

In the nineteenth century, soap factories were common in major industrial cities. Their products were generally viewed as far more important than their environmental impact. Increased wealth and prosperity during the twentieth century stimulated demand

and transformed the economics of the industry. Giant international corporations like Colgate-Palmolive (1806), Procter & Gamble (1837) and Unilever (1886) were established and succeeded, in part, because of their ability to satisfy these new markets. Alongside these giants with their products, which ranged from chemicals to cosmetics, there were specialist companies that tapped these markets. Coco Chanel, Charles Revlon and Estée Lauder created enterprises that linked cosmetics, perfumes and soaps with image in ways that permeated most aspects of industrial society.

Distribution and advertising systems grew up alongside their producers to reinforce and help shape the nature of the industry. Giant department stories like Bloomindales in New York and Selfridges in London give up whole floors while specialist outlets like Boots in the UK place a high premium on the space devoted to soaps, cosmetics and perfumes. Major media rely equally on the sector with magazines like *Elle*, *Vanity Fair*, *Cosmopolitan* and *Vogue* generating half their advertising revenues from promotions that would 'Illuminate Your Skin', create an 'Individualist,' or 'Transform Your Dreams'. The sector seemed to confound economic principles with demand increasing as prices went up.

The cycle of retailing

Until the middle of the 1970s no one challenged the fundamentally hedonistic nature of the industry. Critics had pointed out the high price of the products. Criticism of the indulgent nature of the products and their promotion was not unusual. There was even growing concern about some the research practices employed in the cosmetics industry, especially the scale of animal experimentation. There was, however, no indication that the industry was about to be challenged, its values questioned and the balance of its activity changed by two people who originally 'were much more interested in taking a look at Haight-Ashbury, then the heart of the flower children's dream community.'

The origins of the breakthrough achieved by The Body Shop are a mixture of the application of classical business thinking, individual enterprise and a fundamental challenge to established thinking. Part of the company's success lay in the application, for example, of the classic wheel of retailing theory. This theory asserts that retailing goes in cycles. A successful retailer usually starts as a no-frills, low-price challenge to established outlets. In the UK, for example, the early success of supermarkets lay in challenging two groups of established retailers. These were traditional grocers and the co-operatives. These were relatively high priced and provided high levels of personal service through counter staff. Supermarkets challenged these by cutting back on staff and keeping prices low. Over time, however, the same retailers acquired large overheads and relatively expensive facilities. This meant that, during the 1980s, they were challenged by new, no-frills rivals in the UK like Kwik Save and Aldi.

The early Body Shop outlets were a direct challenge to established soap, perfume and cosmetics outlets. Their products were relatively cheap. Costs were kept down through the use of low-price packaging, which customers were encouraged to recycle. Anita Roddick makes clear that 'everything was done on a shoestring.' This contrasted sharply with the image and practice of established cosmetics retailers. Some decisions, however, were based on the strong sense of image and style that has characterised The Body Shop breakthrough. Bold, strong and clear images had played their part in the success of Chanel, Estee Lauder and others.

The Body Shop name might owe more to Anita's sense of irony than expensive market research but it carries a powerful aura. The logo retains its currency despite the passage of time. Anita's 'second world war mentality' might have persuaded her to use green paint to 'cover up all the damp patches' in her first shop, but the colour scheme continues to unify the company's image. The twin decisions – first, to establish this sense of coherence in design and, second, to extend it across every outlet – serve to unify the company. This was especially important, as the breakthrough from a small, local retailer to a major international business was rooted in The Body Shop's use of franchising.

Dressed in suits

The choice of franchising as a means of business growth partly reflected the severe resource constraints under which The Body Shop operated during its early years. Gordon and Anita Roddick did not bring massive financial resources into their new venture. They had started and learned from two earlier business start-ups. The first was a small hotel, while the second was a restaurant. The Roddicks had, however, learned the value (and limits) of hard work and resilience, the importance of flexibility and the value of preparation. The sharpest lesson in preparation and presentation probably occurred when Anita went to her bank seeking finance for her new Body Shop. The manager's initial refusal reinforced their belief in resilience when she and Gordon went back 'dressed in suits' and won backing.

The central business ideas behind The Body Shop are simple. On one level the aim was the classic wheel of retailing. Selling products in different sizes, in cheap containers that lots of people could afford. Alongside this, was the desire to raise awareness of the types of traditional materials and ingredients that people used across the world. The decision to invest in promoting awareness and use of these traditional materials was crucial to the long-term success of The Body Shop. This use of traditional materials was unique to The Body Shop in the early years.

This latter decision involved significant risks and costs. The risks lay in the unfamiliarity of customers with the products. The costs lay in tracking down the raw materials and finding partners who could produce sufficient qualities at acceptable prices. This problem of supply changed fundamentally in nature in the early years. Initially, the difficulty lay in finding someone to produce in small enough volumes – later the problem was find someone to produce enough. The decision to use materials from around the world also built on the strengths of the Roddicks as a team. Both were very cosmopolitan in their outlook. Gordon's horse trip across Latin America was matched by Anita's time working for the United Nations. This experience gave them a massive edge over traditional business people whose knowledge of international markets came from research reports or bulletins.

Once the basic business format was established, the challenge facing the Roddicks lay in choosing between a lifestyle enterprise and a global business. The first shops in Brighton and Chichester were successful. Many people in similar positions choose to keep the lifestyle of a small shopkeeper. The drive to grow and achieve a genuine business breakthrough was too strong for this to happen to the Body Shop. The initial difficulty lay in overcoming the shortage of capital that seemed certain to hamper their expansion. The Body Shop also faced the difficulty that the format could be copied relatively easily.

The decision to franchise their business idea solved two problems simultaneously. It allowed others to adopt the form while it gave The Body Shop control over the product range and its format. New outlets were supplied with product, advice, support and (in the early years, at least) personal help in preparing their shop. Growth using this formula was rapid, with sales exceeding £250,000 (£1 million at current prices) within three years of opening and approaching £1,000,000 (£2.1 million at current prices) within five years. The company faced the classic problem of franchise business – high volume but low margins – but their name and reputation in the market were secure.

The solution to the problem of building up margins came from two related aspects of the business. The wholesale operation – supplying product to outlets – lies at the heart of the company. It is the platform for product development besides linking the outlets with the company in very practical ways. Alongside the wholesale operation, The Body Shop's own stores have become increasingly important sources of growth, revenue and profit. The simultaneous development of a franchise business, a production capability and a wholesale business across the world highlights both the energy and ability of the founders.

The bottom line

It is, however, the wider campaigning role of The Body Shop and its founders that most clearly defines their business breakthrough. The notion that business can have a social purpose *from the start* is not new. Nor is it unusual today to find very large corporations placing environmental and social responsibility at the heart of their strategy. The Roddicks were, perhaps, the first significant international business of the post-World War II era to place a social purpose alongside their business goals from the start.

This view was relatively common in the last century. People like Robert Owen transformed thinking about the nature of economic activity in the first quarter of the nineteenth century because of the enterprises he built at New Lanark. The Co-operative Retail and Wholesale movement was created to use commerce to overcome social problems. Powerful entrepreneurial families like the Cadburys, Rowntrees and Levers in Britain, shared with the Carnegies, Mellons and Pews in the USA and the Duponts, Cavours and Seimens in Europe a belief that the economic power of business could be used to tackle social problems. This view had lost ground during the twentieth century under the pressures of apparent failure in the face of great social crises, such as the Depression, and the increased confidence of the state.

Friedmanite economics seemed to putting the last nails in the coffin of this wider role for business when a new generation of entrepreneurs and business people led by the Roddicks emerged to revive this role for business. The link between business and social goals poses problems for people across the political spectrum. The independent entrepreneur with a clear agenda cannot easily be accommodated within a modern statist view of the world. This approach sees social goods as the sole preserve of an all-wise, all-knowing state. Entrepreneurs with social goals do not fit into the statist worldview – nor can they be easily cajoled or bribed to comply. Free marketers have similar problems. Entrepreneurs who want to move into areas outside their normal commercial activities did not fit easily with either economic man or the profit-maximising enterprise. Even those in the middle and activists on social issues face problems because they are so conditioned by different aspects of either the statist or free market view.

The difficulty facing successful entrepreneurs like the Roddicks is made greater by the links between their social, environmental and commercial goals. Their long-term business breakthrough may lie in redefining these relationships. The Body Shop became actively involved in environmental and social campaigning within a year of starting the company. On the most basic level, the decision to display posters featuring Greenpeace's anti-whaling campaign was very simple. Like many independent retailers, they displayed posters for something the owners supported. The breakthrough for the Roddicks came in the decision to wed these issues, programmes and campaigns to the growth and strategic development of the company.

The campaigns seem to serve three distinct purposes. First, they tackle issues about which the company and its leadership group feel strongly. These can range from the overtly political, such as political repression in West Africa, to campaigns like Greenpeace's anti-whaling programme. Second, The Body Shop can internalise issues and address them through its operations. The clearest example of this is the search for and use of products and materials developed in disadvantaged parts of the world. This Trade Not Aid programme means buying materials and goods from indigenous people. The benefits for both are clear – sales for the locals and goods for The Body Shop. The process itself is, however, developmental for both. The local people learn about trade in a non-intrusive way while the underlying vision of The Body Shop absorbs this greater diversity. Finally, the campaigns and programmes work to bind The Body Shop, its employees, its franchisees, suppliers, customers and other 'stakeholders'.

There is a sense in which The Body Shop is emerging as one of a growing number of trust-based enterprises in which a powerful shared vision integrates the enterprise while building the wider business. The power of the vision has allowed the company to absorb a wide range of new and very diverse partners. Initial recruitment of franchisees was not systematic. Empathy and shared vision seemed to matter more than formal business qualifications. This was the right decision as it reinforced the core business strengths and sustaining control over the vision and strategy for the business. This approach enabled the company to focus more tightly on achieving growth, establishing presence and reinforcing The Body Shop brand in markets. The costs of failure when franchisees were unsuccessful were probably outweighed by the savings in process costs and image dilution.

The sincerest form of flattery

This high degree of personal control of the vision and the operations through the Roddicks themselves allowed the company to gain considerable leverage for growth. This growth was spectacular – the company grew to over 400 outlets in just over a decade. A decade further on, the rate of growth has slowed but there were almost 700 outlets around the world. Part of the slow-down can be attributed to increased competition. In the USA, The Limited uses a broadly similar format in its 500-plus outlets, while in Asia Red Dust has established a powerful market presence.

The real breakthrough, however, lies in the deep-rooted changes in the cosmetics industry. Virtually every major manufacturer and retailer of soaps and cosmetics has adapted their product range to incorporate aspects of The Body Shop message. At its most basic, this change can be seen in packaging and presentation. Simple, low cost containers stand alongside the more complex ones on retailers' shelves. Major campaigns have succeeded. The most dramatic recent success was the introduction in the UK of a ban on animal testing for soaps and cosmetics. It is, however, in the redefinition of business relations with the community that the greatest breakthrough may exist. The decision by The Body Shop to integrate social and environmental responsibility with an entrepreneurial business vision has shown that these can co-exist and gain from each other. The Body Shop shows that competitiveness and responsibility can live together.

Notes

1   Roddick, A. (1991) *Body and Soul*, Body Shop, Littlehampton.
2   James, P. And Thorpe, N. (1995) *Ancient Inventions*, Michael O'Mara Books, London.

Chapter 20

Not Quite a Paperback Writer

*The Story of Allan Lane
and the Paperback Revolution*

Ruddy Penguins

O nce a breakthrough has been achieved it is rare for people, especially rivals to admit their doubts as candidly as Jonathan Cape did in a conversation with Allan Lane. Cape was very important in the early years of Penguin Books. His company, Jonathon Cape, was the only mainstream publisher to sell Lane the rights to publish in paperback a list of modern authors. Jonathan Cape's was 'the list of the nineteen-twenties [with] Hemingway, Sinclair Lewis, Beverley Nichols, Mary Webb.'[1] Lane had been turned down by most of the major publishing houses so 'years later,' Lane recalled, 'when trade was not very good, I was talking to Jonathan and he said, "You're the B ... that has ruined the trade with your ruddy Penguins." I replied, "Well, I wouldn't have got off to such a good start if you hadn't helped me." He said, "I knew damn well you wouldn't, but like everyone else in the trade I thought you were bound to go bust, and I thought I'd take four hundred quid off you before you did."'[2]

Attitudes to Lane's proposal for a 'new sixpenny book' ranged from the hostile (in his own firm, the Bodley Head), through the indifferent (at Gollancz, who never replied to his letters) to the opportunistic (like Jonathan Cape). These reactions were understandable. There had been 'paperback' and cheap issues of books before. They had not prospered, generally existing at the margins of publishing. *The New Shell Book of Firsts*[3] claims that 'the first paperback book series was the "Collection of British Authors" published by Christian Bernhard Tauchnitz in Leipzig in 1841.'

Other claimants for the title of the first paperback publishers include several French publishing houses, notably Reclam's Universal Bibliothek who could put in a prior claim to the physical form of the paperback, while 'in the United States, the first series of paperback editions appeared in 1831. They became extremely successful after 1870. Many publishing houses began printing paperbacks and competing with each other for sales. By 1885, a third of the books published were a type of popular paperback called dime novels because they originally cost 10 cents. The mass production of books, however, led to a decline in the quality. Publishers printed many books on cheap paper that quickly turned brown and brittle with age. Bindings were often poorly glued, and they broke ... Paperback books declined in popularity in the early 1900s but made a comeback in the 1930s.'

The same source,[4] however, acknowledges that 'Penguin Books, founded in England in 1935, became a world leader in paperback publishing. Pocket Books, now one of the largest American paperback publishers, appeared in 1939. Today, almost two-thirds of all books sold in the United States are paperbacks.' The physical form of the paperback was only one aspect of the breakthrough achieved by Allan Lane. Equally important was his decision to sell them at 'the same price as ten cigarettes.' Other publishers had produced low-price editions. Routledge had its *Universal Library*, Cassell a *National Library* and Nelson a *New Century Library*. All sold at prices that compared with the 6d[5] that Lane wanted for his new paperbacks. These companies, however, concentrated on publishing established classics such as Jane Austen, Dickens or Shakespeare. These were attractive because there was a ready market for their work and they were out of copyright. Lane wanted his paperbacks to include contemporary authors whose work was still in copyright.

Allan Lane achieved his business breakthrough with Penguin books by taking a relatively well established idea, giving it a new form and presenting it creatively. The first paperback books had appeared in the middle of the nineteenh century but they had occupied a backwater in the induastry until Allan Lane launched Penguin. His skill lay in using the low price, paperback format to bring contemporary fiction to a new audience. He faced fierce opposition from established publsihers but cleverly used the pull of the market and the push of authors to overcome their resistance. His eye for style, marketing intuition and powerful branding created a new mainstream form of publishing that now dominates the book market worldwide.

Clean and bright as a new pin

Finally, he decided that the books must have a contemporary feel; 'clean and bright as a new pin, modern enough not to offend the sophisticated buyer, and yet straightforward and unpretentious.' The two bands of bright colour and the white band carrying the book title established a basic design that lasted almost half a century. The simple colour coding – orange for novels, green for crime – lasted even longer. The name and logo emerged from a process that draws on the confidence, exuberance and hint of amateurishness that marked the early days of the company.

Edward Young, the 21-year-old artist and office junior who set many of these standards, describes[6] how 'we spent nearly two hours searching the bird and animal kingdom, until we had narrowed the possibilities down to a short list of about half a dozen. Yet somehow none of these seemed right. We were in despair. Then suddenly [Joan Coles] the secretary's voice piped up … what about Penguins?' Edward was then dispatched to London Zoo to produce the drawing that is still used today.

Allan Lane had taken a long time to arrive at the point at which he was making decisions about layouts and designs. He was to face other obstacles as he sought to break out of the constraints of traditional publishing to create 'the paperback phenomenon.' Allan Lane had worked in publishing for just less than sixteen years after joining his uncle's firm, The Bodley Head, aged 16 in 1919. He had succeeded his uncle (John Lane) as Managing Director in 1925. The Bodley Head was established by John Lane in the late 1880s and published several notable authors, such as Anatole France, and had gained some notoriety at the end of the nineteenth century for its involvement in the *Yellow Book* scandal.[7]

There was relatively little in Allan Lane's early stewardship of The Bodley Head to indicate the direction he would take. He showed a flair for publicity but courted disaster, especially when he published the controversial *Whispering Sands*. He courted (as a publisher) Agatha Christie but lost her to Collins. He started building links with North America. He beat his rivals to gain the British publishing rights to *Ulysses*. Although his brothers Dick and John joined the company, his position was weakened by The Bodley Head's poor commercial performance. He was forced to bring new investors into the company – their investments diluted his holding but did little to stop the company's decline.

Lane had long been convinced that there was a mass market for books, if the price could be reduced sufficiently to be affordable. Returning from his first US trip, he wanted to publish a series of children's books at 2 shillings[8] each. It is said that the idea for his new paperback imprint came to him after a long wait on Exeter Station. None of the expensive offerings on the station bookstall appealed and he spent a long, boring, bookless journey back to London. He projected himself into the shoes of the tens of thousands of other railway travellers and decided there was a mass market for books provided the price was right, the titles were modern and the books were carried by a vast array of new outlets. He quickly won the support of his brothers but met with a wall of indifference – even hostility – from the rest of The Bodley Head board. They were against this type of distraction. They wanted their managing

Fig 20.1 The Penguin logo.

director to concentrate on the main business and stop its seemingly inexorable decline into bankruptcy.

What is a consignment order from Woolworth's?

Reluctantly, they agreed that the brothers could progress the idea 'providing always that there was no interruption of normal Bodley Head business'. The objections of the Board were minor compared to the practical difficulties posed by the economics of his new venture. There were three seemingly insuperable obstacles to success. First, he needed massive (in contemporary terms) sales just to break even. An initial print run of 15–20,000 books was the minimum required to keep the costs below 6d while still allowing a fee or royalty to authors and a margin for retailers. Second, building these volumes needed the backing of the book trade but retailers saw no value in products that replaced a high-margin item with a low-margin one. Third, he needed publishers and authors who would assign their rights for relatively small sums of money.

It took luck, energy and a series of key decisions by Lane to overcome these problems. The luck lay in the decision of publishers like Jonathan Cape to assign their rights. Others were not so helpful. Lane sent a self-addressed and stamped postcard to one with the following message:

> I shall be happy to negotiate/I am sorry but I cannot consider leasing to Penguins the following titles ...
> Please delete whichever phrase is inappropriate

And received the reply

> I shall be happy to negotiate/I am sorry but I cannot consider leasing to Penguins the following titles ...
> ~~Please delete whichever phrase is inappropriate~~

His key decisions lay in sticking with his original vision. He refused to compromise on any of the three key elements: the nature and quality of the authors; the quality of design and production; or the effort to move beyond traditional outlets. The initial breakthrough came out of the non-traditional retail sector. Woolworth's, then at the peak of its power and influence, agreed to take a 'consignment order' for the new Penguins. Lane accepted but had no idea of the size of such an order until a friend at Collins told him it was 'not less than 50,000 and could be 100,000.' The original ten titles are listed below:

The Mysterious Affair at Styles	Agatha Christie
Ariel	Andre Maurois
A Farewell to Arms	Ernest Hemmingway
Poet's Pub	Eric Linklater
Madame Claire	Susan Ertz
Twenty Five	Beverly Nichols
William	E.H. Young
Gone to Earth	Mary Webb
The Unpleasantness at the Bellona Club	Dorothy L. Sayers
Carnival	Compton MacKenzie

Lane expected some resistance from authors, especially as the initial royalty was only £25 against royalties of £1 for every thousand books sold, but he made clear that 'there is no fortune in this series for anyone concerned but if my premise is correct ... the Penguins are a means of converting book-borrowers into book-buyers.'

The authors, who met most of Allan's requirements, showed little of the expected resistance and the general response to the new imprint was immediate and positive. This initial success was achieved without significant support from either the traditional book trade or the media. Allan Lane had spotted a shift in the interests of a large new population of book buyers – some were book borrowers – but many were part of a newly literate and mobile class of potential book buyers. Allan was clear that 'Penguins will succeed,' but he knew that he had to innovate constantly to build up his franchise.

A postcard from Mr Shaw

The next stage in his breakthrough came from an unexpected source. Most publishers remained reluctant to release the rights to their stronger current titles and authors. The initial response of authors like George Orwell was, at best, mixed. 'As a reader I applaud Penguin Books,' Orwell commented, 'as a writer I pronounce them anathema.' Salvation of type came from George Bernard Shaw. He was generally feared by publishers, who found him one of the toughest negotiators for fees, advances and royalties. Shaw bought all the early Penguins, saw their popularity and wanted to get access to the new audience. Shaw wrote to Allan asking for his books to be included. Lane showed the opportunism that is the key to so many successes. He immediately agreed to purchase the rights to one of Shaw's novels but took the chance to extend the Penguin range into non-fiction. He asked Shaw for the right to publish his *Intelligent Woman's Guide to Socialism, Capitalism and Sovietism* with new sections on Bolshevism and Fascism. Shaw agreed.

These decisions added a new dimension to the business whilst securing his core business base. The fiction section grew as increasing numbers of authors wanted access to this new market and established publishers found it hard to refuse their writers. In 1937 the list included 100 titles. Traditional booksellers found that they were forced by customer demand to stock the list while new outlets worked to get included in the distribution system. Lane's determination to hold onto control of his idea was reinforced by his clear focus on quality texts for a mass market. This gave him increasing leverage in the trade – from writers, through publishers, to booksellers. This leverage allowed him to take two further decisions that simultaneously increased the strength of his balance sheet and his brand.

The first decision was largely forced on him. His existing offices and storage facilities could not cope with the scale of his business. Lane made the radical decision for a publisher at that time to move out of London. His margins did not permit him to acquire a large enough site in the city so he purchased a 3½-acre site in Harmondsworth, Middlesex. The site was found by his brother Dick and cost £2200 (including £200 for the crop of cabbages growing there). Allan's reasoning was simple. Most publishers needed to be in London for their authors but he dealt mainly with other publishers about rights, so a central London site was not needed. This decision allowed Penguin to break out from the high-cost confines of London.

Building the franchise

The next decision took the company beyond the confines of publishing fiction. He added H.G. Wells' *A Short History of the World*, G.D.H. Cole's *Practical Economics*, Olaf Stapleton's *Last and First Men* and G.E. Mainwaring's *The Floating Republic* to the new non-fiction imprint called Pelican. There are many tales about the choice of this name. Allan Lane's favourite tells how he 'went to a railway bookstall at St Pancras to see the manager and try to flog a few books and I had to wait and a woman went up to the book stall and said "Have you got any Pelican Books?" I know that there wasn't such a series – she really meant Penguins. But I knew that if someone else started the word Pelican they'd be stealing some of my thunder.'

He recognised the value of his franchise and was determined to protect it. Pelican gave the company the chance to publish original works of non-fiction. The series was launched in the middle of an international ferment of ideas and ideologies. The 1930s were characterised by intense debate about politics, economics, religion and social change. This turmoil would eventually lead to World War II but Pelican made the major ideas accessible to the mass of the British population.

The success of this latest innovation prompted further new products. These ranged from imprints like Puffin, Ptarmigan, King Penguin and Peregrine to series like Penguin Specials that operated on the boundaries between books and news. Allan Lane had established an enterprise that showed immense potential for adaptation and development. He took his new publishing idea to New York where Robert de Graff was establishing a powerful imitator in Pocket Books. By the start of the War in 1939, there were almost 150 Penguins in print, alongside 50 Pelicans. The US business was established but never became a serious threat to US-based imitators. The War slowed down the publishing revolution that Allan Lane started, but his success in breaking out from the confines of traditional publishing was never reversed.

Further reading

Flower, D. (1959) *The Paperback; Its Past, Present and Future*, Arborfield, London.

Hare, S. (ed.) (1995) *Allan Lane and the Penguin Editors 1935–1970*, Penguin, Harmondsworth.

Morpurgo, J.E. (1979) *Allan Lane: King Penguin*, Hutchinson, London.

Williams, W.E. (1956) *The Penguin Story*, Penguin, Harmondsworth.

1   Quoted by Allan Lane on his retirement.
2   Hare, S. (ed.) (1995) *Allan Lane and the Penguin Editors 1935–1970*, Penguin, Harmondsworth.

3   Robertson, P. (1995) *The New Shell Book of Firsts*, Headline, London.

4   IBM (1998) *The World Book: Multimedia Encyclopaedia*, IBM, New York.

5   6d is around 2.5p but in contemporary terms the price is around £3.00.

6   Young, E., 'The Early Days of Penguins', *The Book Collector*, Winter 1952.

7   The *Yellow Book* scandal centred on the publication of a series of 'scandalous' and 'decadent' journals in the 1890s. The journals became closely identified with Oscar Wilde when he was arrested with 'Yellow Book Under His Arm' according to one headline.

8   2 shillings is around 10p but in contemporary terms the price is around £10.00.

Conclusion

Common themes

A series of common themes emerge from the analysis of the business breakthroughs. The most successful enterprises are built around a recognition of the aspects of a technology, a market or an industry that need to be controlled to achieve competitive advantage. Outstanding businesses understand the 'pinch points' in their market or industry. These are the points in the market, industry or technology that make the most difference. This can be because the customer is least happy with the current offering. Walt Disney understood that customers were increasingly dissatisfied with the current offerings in amusement parks. Ray Kroc knew that increasingly affluent and mobile customers were dissatisfied with the poor and inconsistent quality offered by existing fast food outputs. Henry Food recognised that productions systems would need to change fundamentally to realised the potential of automobile.

Understanding the key point of control is only part of the picture. Focus is essential if that control is to lead to a sustainable business breakthrough. Walt Disney focused his attention on constantly enhancing the quality of the visitor experience. Rockefeller was determined to cut costs and improve efficiency. There was no detail too small to escape Rockefeller's attention. It could be the number of weld points on a barrel or the opportunity to open up a market.

Nike transformed the sports footwear market because it focused on the needs of athletes and sought to innovate constantly to improve their products and the performance of its clients.

The use of this focus to lever further opportunities and greater competitive advantage is a common theme. Bill Gates achieved this by creating and sustaining an industry standard for personal computers. Boeing produced the same effect by linking developments in one area, often its defence contracts, with projects elsewhere. This created such strength that when the link was broken Boeing continued to succeed. This type of virtuous circle recurs in the greatest business breakthroughs. The Body Shop's commitments to the environment and social justice create a bond with its customers that goes beyond buying its products. The Rochdale Pioneers used the 'Divi' to produce the same effect.

Thinking long and acting short

This type of virtuous circle relies on the type of ability to think long and act short that Cubbi Broccoli showed when he abandoned his existing film projects to concentrate on the Bond films. The tangible benefits where shown when he stuck with Sean Connery and refused to 'dump the Limey truck driver.' Walt Disney's ability to think long and act short was identified by Roy O Disney, and was vividly illustrated by the complex deals he constructed to finance the creation of Disneyworld. For Mayer Rothschild, thinking long and acting short sometimes involved making a loss on individual transactions as he courted the Elector of Hesse. If the legend is to be believed, it also meant losing his entire fortune.

Simple risk-taking is not enough. John D Rockefeller took risks when he thought long about the future of the oil industry, and acted short in buying up competitors or creating projects like the South Improvement Company. Rockefeller, however, had his fall back position so well organised that the collapse of the South Improvement Company had no effect on his plans.

Special features

In some breakthroughs particular features emerge as especially important. Edison, Boeing, Intel, Aspirin and Sony rooted their success on decisions about their core strengths, and invested heavily in these assets. It was harder for Ford, Rockefeller, Microsoft, Nike and Littlewoods to link their strengths with the needs of their industries as they were creating new industries. As their organisations grew and the industry developed they sustained their leadership by investing in and sustaining their core strengths. Using their skills, enterprise and capability as a platform Rothschild, Coca-Cola, McDonald's, Gillette and Broccoli grabbed a moment of opportunity and turned it into a strategy for long term success. Fear is seldom part of a business breakthrough. This is especially true when the company is forced to defy convention to realise its ambitions.

The intensity of the effort involved to carve out these opportunities is often understated in the analysis of business breakthroughs. Sometimes the effort is focussed on the specific development. Walt Disney lived for months in the little apartment over the fire station. Many breakthroughs rely as much on lessons from earlier ventures as the specific development. The link is especially clear with Ray Kroc. The decline of his mixer business prompted him to seek out the restaurant buying lots of mixers – against the market trend. Gordon and Anita Roddick tried several business ventures before creating The Body Shop.

These earlier experiences seem to produce both a greater determination to succeed and a reluctance to accept the compromises that can undermine the venture. This reluctance to compromise is especially clear in the approach to quality and innovation. Part of Ray Kroc's motivation in buying out the McDonald brothers was their willingness to compromise on quality. Microsoft drives forward by constant innovation. Intel share this focus on innovation – using the company's research strength to underpin their marketing and branding.

The power of a strong brand is clear in all these breakthroughs. Mayer Rothschild and the Rochdale Pioneers might find it hard to relate to the term, but they created powerful brands that became watchwords for quality. These brands made it easier for customers and clients to relate to the businesses and the underlying decisions. The companies were, in effect, making it easier for their clients. The KISS principle – Keep It Simple, Stupid – is a recurrent theme. This is not only true for links with customers but throughout the enterprise built around these breakthroughs.

Index